'A complete original.' *Saturday Review*

'An artist in both line and words . . . with talents of gold.' *Observer*

'The singularity of Bemelmans, whether he draws or writes, is his double capacity to see freshly like a child and comment shrewdly like a grown-up. The product is an awry wisdom, the wisdom of a reflective innocent who is surprised at nothing and delighted with everything.' Clifton Fadiman

'Witty, festive and picturesque . . . Ludwig Bemelmans' gifts are brilliant, visual simile and an eye for the rascality of his onetime trade.' V. S. Pritchett

'Mr Bemelmans is always pricking bubbles, discreetly, appreciatively, out of a sense of duty rather than a desire to shock, and the process is delightful.' *The Times*

'A note of expensive cosmopolitan is brilliantly sustained. There are stories here that could hardly be done better.' *New Statesman*

'Very entertaining . . . an excellent story-teller.' *Sunday Times*

'I know of no other writing that pleases the mental palate as pungently, swiftly and freshly as does Mr Bemelmans.' Elizabeth Bowen

'One reads Bemelmans not as one reads a serious novelist but for the sheer momentary pleasure given by his evocation of atmosphere and mood.' *Punch*

About the Author

Ludwig Bemelmans – author and illustrator of over 40 books – was born in the Austrian Tirol in 1898. A rebellious child, Bemelmans never finished his formal education and was apprenticed out to his Uncle Hans, a prosperous hotelier. After being dismissed from a series of hotels, he shot a headwaiter after a dispute and was given a choice between reform school and emigration to America. The 16-year-old Bemelmans left for New York in 1914 sporting two pistols with which to fend off hostile Indians. He had letters of introduction to managers of several large hotels and began working as a waiter. He enlisted in the US Army in 1917 and became naturalized in 1918. After the war he continued to work in the New York hotel and restaurant trade and honed his skills as an artist. He didn't turn to writing until 1934, when a friend in publishing saw his paintings and suggested he write a children's book. His first effort, *Hansi*, was followed by 15 other children's books including his greatest success *Madeline*. His adult writings began with *My War with the United States*, about his army experiences, in 1937. Other writings include several humorous volumes on hotel life: *Life Class* (1938), *Small Beer* (1939), *Hotel Splendide* (1941) and *I Love You, I Love You, I Love You* (1942). Bemelmans married in 1935 and settled down to life as a bon viveur. He contributed to the *New Yorker* and a host of other magazines. He designed sets for Broadway, wrote for Hollywood and kept his hand in in the restaurant business. He died in New York on 1 October, 1962. Bemelmans always claimed to have no imagination and that all his books were a product of his own life experience. Yet his writings always inhabited a uniquely enchanted world somewhere between fiction and autobiography.

WHEN YOU LUNCH WITH THE EMPEROR

LUDWIG BEMELMANS

EBURY
PRESS

3 5 7 9 10 8 6 4 2

First published 2004 by Ebury Press,
An imprint of Random House,
20 Vauxhall Bridge Road, London SW1V 2SA

Random House Australia (Pty) Limited
20 Alfred Street, Milsons Point, Sydney,
New South Wales 2061, Australia

Random House New Zealand Limited
18 Poland Road, Glenfield, Auckland 10, New Zealand

Random House South Africa (Pty) Limited
Endulini, 5a Jubilee Road, Parktown 2193, South Africa

The Random House Group Limited Reg. No. 954009

www.randomhouse.co.uk

A CIP catalogue record for this book is available from the British Library

Cover designed by Keenan

Typeset by SX Composing DTP, Rayleigh, Essex
Printed and bound in Great Britain by Bookmarque Ltd, Croydon

ISBN 0 091 89535 9

Contents

Introduction   vii

Childhood
Swan Country   3
Lausbub   13
Arrival in America   33

Work
My First Actress   37
The Splendide   45
Herr Otto Brauhaus   48
Mr. Sigsag   58
Art at the Hotel Splendide   75
The Homesick Bus Boy   85
Affair   94
Improved Jewish Wedding   108
Postmaster from Przemysl   116
Dinner Out   122
SS Zuider Zee   128
Good Son   141
The Old Ritz   153

A story: *Theodore and 'The Blue Danube'*   160

Play

Dear General What a Surprise 171
Dog Story 186
Bride of Berchtesgaden 200
I Love You, I Love You, I Love You 213
Star of Hope 222
Little Bit and the *America* 231
Cher Ami 255
The Morale of the Natives 264
Benitin and Eneas 273
Prison Visit 284
The Dog of the World 292
Sawmill in Tirol 298

A story: *The Elephant Cutlet* 307

Introduction

Ask around about Ludwig Bemelmans. Try dropping his name at a dinner party or your local reading group. If you *do* happen to encounter someone who recognises the name, a rare enough feat in itself, they will undoubtedly be recent parents or childhood devotees of his much-loved *Madeline* children's books which follow the adventures of a wayward, copper-haired convent school girl. Yet Bemelmans' prolific and enigmatic writing reached far beyond children's books. His varied output included novels, short stories, travel books and journalism. All of his adult writing was infused with a personal hybrid of autobiographical storytelling that, while by no means strictly fictional, was neither traditional memoir. The style seemed spontaneously self-invented with all the artless, robust attributes of the timeless forms of storytelling – the campfire, bar-room and bedtime tale. This is not to say that Bemelmans was not a showman with his own undoubted sophistication, but it is a showmanship combined with an honesty and immediacy that harks back to something long before modern storytelling developed its formal rules.

Born in 1898, Ludwig lived an idyllic childhood in the mountains of the Austrian Tirol where his father Lampert, a Belgian with bohemian tastes and a passion for painting, ran a hotel. He was largely raised by a beautiful French governess whom he called Gazelle because he was unable to pronounce Mademoiselle.

Ludwig was rudely awakened from this idyll at the age of six when his father ran away with a married woman from the town. It transpired too that Gazelle was pregnant with his father's child. Devastated, she committed suicide. Ludwig and his mother, who was also pregnant with his younger brother Oscar, left for her family home in Regensburg in Germany. Ludwig loathed his new life in Germany – the language, the dress, the expected discipline. A square peg in a round hole, he became wilful and disobedient and after several unsuccessful attempts at schooling him, he was returned age 14 to the Tirol in the hope he could at least learn the hotel business from his Uncle Hans. This too was an unmitigated disaster and after several 'episodes' – including, Bemelmans claimed, his attempting to shoot a headwaiter – his family threatened him with a correctional institution for boys. Finally, when conscription as a private in the German army loomed for Ludwig on the eve of the First World War, he took up his family's offer of emigration and a new start in America.

Young Ludwig arrived in New York on 24 December 1914. When his father, who had fled to America, failed to collect him as planned, Ludwig spent Christmas Eve alone on Ellis Island. Armed with a handful of letters of introduction from his Uncle Hans to some of the big New York hotels, he was soon ensconced at the Ritz-Carlton – the grandest hotel in Manhattan and symbol of an era of rich excess that was slowly fading. Other than for a two-year break serving in US Army and an unsuccessful attempt to become a cartoonist just prior to the Big Crash in 1929, the Ritz-Carlton would be his home for the next fifteen years, working his way up from bus boy to assistant manager. The hotel years would be a period that he wrote about more extensively than any other in his life. The hotel was a huge operation, a self-contained world with intricate rules and a law unto itself. The eccentric European staff and stream of colourful guests made Ludwig's fictionalised Ritz-Carlton the only backdrop he needed.

Eventually his writing saved him from the hotel trade and he could live the life he loved: that of the peripatetic bon vivant roaming the places he loved – Paris, London, the Tirol, the Mediterranean, the Caribbean, South America. Penning exotic stories and travel pieces for the likes of the *New Yorker*, *Vogue*, *Holiday* and *Town and Country* allowed him to keep travelling, stay in the finest hotels and dine where he chose. After a brief and troubled marriage to an English ballet dancer, Bemelmans met Madeleine Freud, a young model who had almost become a nun. He called her Mimi. They fell in love and married in 1935 and had a daughter Barbara a year and a half later. Both frequently accompanied him on his lively travels filled with eating, drinking, smoking, writing and painting.

Bemelmans was rarely still. He designed sets for Broadway, painted murals and frescos for apartments and hotels (most notably the bar at the Carlyle Hotel in New York), illustrated the covers of magazines, bought into restaurants and spent time screenwriting out in Hollywood until his antics at MGM forced Louis B. Mayer to utter the immortal words: 'Never let this son of a bitch back in the studio unless we need him.'

Ludwig's education had been erratic and informal to say the least, with a long list of expulsions from strict German schools where his different accent made it hard for him to fit in. So he learned the art of storytelling not from the classics, but as a child eavesdropping quietly on locals warm with beer in his uncle's restaurants and taverns, at his father's extraordinary dinner table and from the stories whispered over his crib. Later, as a young man, he would listen just as well behind the scenes in busy kitchens and amid the banter of the army barracks. He honed his skills on the page by writing letters to his mother, initially from the Tirol and then America.

The fact that English was not Bemelmans' original language gave him, like others before him, the ability to choose his words carefully and compose with greater exactitude. His phrasing continually gathers from all three languages and since he'd never had a single dominating mother tongue, he wasn't constrained in any way by the rules of one language. His first book for adults, *My War with the United States,* had been transcribed by Ludwig from his letters sent to his mother and his old friend Willy during his time in the US Army (he was based at a small fort on Lake Ontario – his German accent deemed him unsuitable for frontline action in France). Originally written in German, they offer a wonderfully stumbling poetry that direct English could not have fully rendered.

Bemelmans only told tales about what he knew and had experienced. The tales were composed for pleasure, to sate his readers' immediate appetite. Bemelmans always claimed he was without imagination and relied entirely on real life for his inspiration. Yet what he took from life he loved to mythologise and embellish; his showmanship turning the everyday – whether a New York hotel or a small South American town – into a grand stage on which he, and the larger-than-life characters he carved, could perform for our pleasure.

Bemelmans was a gifted artist. He illustrated as well as wrote the *Madeline* stories, and all of his books, including this one, are littered with his raw sketches. He actually thought of himself as an artist more than a writer. Indeed his work as an artist provides clues to the nature of his writing. As with his naïve style of illustration, Bemelmans' stories sometimes give the false sense that they care little for formal style and simply lay as they fell. But as with his pictures, so with his words: what interested him was sketching the details of a myriad of characters – to hold them forever, still fresh and vibrant. Plot and drama were of as little concern to him as perspective and traditional composition in his sketches. What Bemelmans brings to the page is a relish for simply painting scenes from life. One of the great pleasures of Bemelmans is the pure immediacy of his writing. You rejoice in the good food he lays before you and enjoy his sunsets simply as things in themselves and ask no more of them.

If Bemelmans had a fear it was the ties of humdrum normality. He felt that life should always be extraordinary – as he tried to recapture the love and freedom of his earliest years. He despised the quiet desperation and static rectitude of the middle classes. He loved reckless impulsiveness and romanticised the rootless low-life, the happy peasant, the freewheeling rich and blue-blood aristocrat. His heroes usually fell into two categories – charming, wealthy eccentrics, and comic downtrodden underlings. Both, of course, reflect different sides of Bemelmans. The early Ludwig put upon by teachers, family, commanding officers, unsympathetic work colleagues, and Ludwig the multi-talented entrepreneur, writer, artist and bon viveur whose conversational charm made him the envy of 1940s New York high society. Of course Ludwig's father was a great eccentric too. To live life to the full, by your own rules, was always Bemelmans' mantra.

Not even the harsh realities of life could stem the Bemelmans spirit. Ludwig had endured his fair share of suffering and disappointment – school brutality, loneliness, early professional failure, poverty, bouts of depression – but he never shied away from the darker side of life. Having said that, he only wrote about his most personal tragedies elliptically. His early divorce is rarely mentioned and the death of his younger brother Oscar (for which Ludwig felt responsible), falling into a lift shaft while working at the Ritz, is turned on the page into the death of Mr Sigsag. Yet Bemelmans was a kind of ringmaster who could imbue the movements of life with magic – make everything all right. He looked the world clearly in the eye and came back with the response Tell Them It Was Wonderful (as he wanted it to read on his gravestone). Perhaps his greatest gift was to retain the wondrous perception of a child. Even when writing for adults he was in a way still writing children's stories. As the *New Yorker* critic Clifton Fadiman put it: 'The singularity of Bemelmans, whether he draws or writes, is his double capacity to see freshly like a child and comment shrewdly like a grown-up. The product is an awry wisdom, the wisdom of a reflective innocent who is surprised at nothing and delighted with everything.'

When You Lunch with the Emperor is a brand new selection of tales arranged to offer an autobiographical glimpse of Bemelmans and his many adventures. It is divided into three main sections: Childhood, Work and Play. Work covers the hotel era, and Play covers the years of increasing leisure and travel (though the sections do occasionally overlap chronologically). Travel includes both pre- and post-war trips to Europe – Atlantic crossings, Paris (which would become his second home), Regensburg, Austria, Haiti and Ecuador. Within these pages lie enchanted tales of wild dogs, wayward daughters, charming criminals, happy prisoners, faithful manservants, comic Nazis, aristocrats, priests, chefs, waiters and at the centre of it all – the indomitable rascal himself – Ludwig.

Andrew Goodfellow

Childhood

Swan Country

AS IT is now, so it was then, only more so – a setting like the scenery for a Viennese operetta. A place in which, a plot in which nothing violent would happen. The décor was in pastel colors, gay and simple and immediately understood. In it people walked about in lovely costumes.

There was music everywhere. Men in uniforms, women who were elegant. Peasant women in beautifully embroidered silks. The emperor had a villa close by and a joke was told about Franz Josef, who was a serious man.

He had invited the Danny Kaye of those days, a comedian named Giradi, to cheer him up. They sat opposite each other and there was silence and then the emperor said: 'Why don't you say something funny?'

Giradi replied: 'What could you say that's funny when you lunch with the emperor?'

There was no radio, no television, nothing but music and conversation, and life was comfortable. Like the pages of a children's book, the days were turned and looked at, and the most important objects in this book were the sun, the moon and the stars; people, flowers and trees. Large trees, whose leaves throbbed with color and which reached up to the sky – black tree trunks, sometimes brownish black and shining in the rain, young in spring, and yellow in the autumn, when each leaf in the light of afternoon was like a lamp lit up. Pink and violet clouds, and flowers very clear and close, for when one is small one can put one's face close. Does one ever see things clearer than as a child? The sky is blue, the gardener's apron is greener than spinach. The eyes of Gazelle are large and brown and kind. A whistle is heard; a ship approaches. Suddenly it is close and big as a house, live and floating, snow-white and gold among the lavished wealth of color of garden, field and mountains. The ship's name is *Elisabet*. She turns and in a dead slowdown comes to the dock. The reflection wobbles for a while in the broad waves the ship made when the arrested paddle wheel dragged along. Now the captain waves, and I wave back, and then after a little while the captain pulls a cord. One sees this and a puff of white steam flowing upward, and then the sound of the steamer whistle is heard again. The steamer ripples the water, the floating deck makes a gurgling sound. The 'phlop, phlop, phlop' of the paddle wheel has stopped.

When the ship approaches, the swans go this way and that on the water, and when they hear its whistle they leave to make room for the *Elisabet*, and one of them, our swan, stretches, rises out of the water, beats his wings, and then awkwardly runs on the soles of his feet with much splashing, half running, half flying on the water. He finally takes off, with labored flight; he stretches his neck, making a straight long line; he sails overhead and then comes down; he lands with a swishing beat of wings, with his webbed feet stretched out in front of him – bracing himself against the water. He has his wings outstretched still and then folds them, and from a high, standing position he becomes suddenly the beautiful swan in the lake. He comes to our dock and climbs out. He is the most enterprising of the swans.

We eat in summer in what was once a hothouse and is now a

dining-room. My Papa is an impatient perfectionist, which makes life difficult for him. He has to have everything beautiful at once, and because it takes all summer for the grapes to ripe he has placed glass grapes among the foliage, and put electric lights in them. They hang among the thick foliage in what is called the *vignoble*, for we speak only French in this garden. The vines are dark green at the ceiling and light green along the sides. The swan waits to be fed, making sounds of impatience with his beak, as if he were a goose, sometimes even hissing when he has to wait too long.

The little city of Gmunden, on the Traunsee, in the Austrian province of Salzkammergut, is very cosmopolitan. The Duke of Cumberland has a vast estate there. The Queen of Greece was born there, and in 1953, when I went back to paint Schloss Ort, there was a car ahead of me with number 21 on a blue license plate, and it was she, who had come back to look at the beautiful lake and the scenes of childhood.

My father was a Belgian and a painter who had inherited property in Gmunden. Besides the mansion which, with its trees and park, stood surrounded by water, he owned a hotel called 'The Golden Ship.'

Its clientele was remarkable for variety and character. There came every year a Russian grand duke who occupied two floors. There were Parisians, Americans, Germans, Greeks – every nationality. I saw Papa rarely, and my mother I don't remember at all in those days. I lived with my governess in the garden on the lake. She was young and French. I could not say 'Mademoiselle' then, and addressed her as 'Gazelle.'

Papa, when he came to the place where I lived with Mademoiselle, was always busy arranging *plaisanteries*. He built me a complete little carpenter shop where I could work and paint alone and in which he never, as normal fathers would, puttered himself. He had his own workshop where he busied himself with modelling in clay, making frames, designing machinery and inventing. He was never without a project. He created the first Pedalo, a water-going bicycle, which he tried out on the lake. It was elaborate and in the shape of a swan. He had a very beautiful, small motorcar made for me and he presented me with these toys very formally and with an air of apology that made it difficult for me to thank him, or show my enthusiasm in full. I have inherited this and am very embarrassed when anyone thanks me for anything.

Papa sometimes came and sketched Gazelle wearing a helmet or a cuirass. He was fond of armor and collected it. He played the guitar and had a very good voice. The song he liked most to sing was *'Ouvre tes yeux bleus, ma mignonne.'* He dressed unlike other people, in velvet jackets, corduroy suits, large black hats, and flowing ties. He wore a mustache and a beard. He had very small feet, a whipping walk and small, nervous hands.

Papa sometimes would paint in the garden. He brought a small easel and a large palette and put on a blue smock. But he never painted me; he always looked at me with the curiosity of a stranger meeting someone for the first time. I bowed to him, he bowed to me.

I was presented to him, always carefully washed and dressed. He approved to the extent that he decided to make use of me as an angel during Christmas when I was four years old. Papa gave a Christmas party for the employees of the hotel and for the fishermen, boatmen, and peasants. A large table was in the center of the ballroom of the hotel, with gifts for the children. My golden curls were especially curled and brushed and they had made white wings for me and attached them to my shoulders. Overhead on the ceiling was a pulley, and a hook was attached to some white satin which had been wrapped around my middle, and I was pulled upward on a rope and suspended above the Christmas tree. I disappointed him badly, for the smell of burning wax candles, the pipe smoke, the heat and the fear of falling made me ill. I was taken down and abruptly dismissed. I cried, and Gazelle cried – and we went back to the security of our little park.

Papa surrounded himself with friends who, like himself, were determined to be outstandingly different from the provincial citizenry and the staid aristocrats who lived in Gmunden. Their worries were about the next day's happiness, which they made like the baker his rolls, and always while whistling, singing, or reeling in their fish. They found caves to illuminate at night and gave parties in them. They covered wooden floats with flowers and sailed them on the lake. They sent off rockets that awoke the town and exploded high in the sky and filled the night with a rain of phosphorescent stars that were all reflected in the lake. They gave concerts, sang operas and acted in their own plays, and Papa was the president of a society which was called 'Schlaraffia.'

The hotel existed merely to cater to these celebrations. The *maître d'hôtel*, Monsieur Zobal, a very distinguished-looking, quiet, small man who invariably wore snow-white linen and tailcoat, was busy blowing up balloons, helping Papa gild plaster statues, setting off fireworks and stringing up lampions.

Above all I admired his skill with napkins. After deft and precise folding of the snow-white linen, he turned the napkins with a last twist into the shapes of fans, ships, plants and swans. He also chiseled swans and castles out of blocks of ice. Whenever there was something especially good for dessert over in the hotel, Monsieur Zobal saved some of it for us and brought it across the next day.

In the hothouse where we ate, the meals were gay. We sat facing the lake; there were Papa's dogs who came and the swan. There was conversation and, in two carafes, red and white wine. Gazelle drank out of a glass on a thin stem; I had a little golden mug with my name written on it. Monsieur Zobal brought gifts and the chef sometimes came himself. The swan was sometimes rough in his affection for me and once knocked me off balance and into the lake. Gazelle jumped in and saved me.

We left the house at nine on our daily walk, hand in hand, along the promenade. I was always neatly dressed, my curls combed, my shoelaces properly tied and always with white gloves. I was her little blue fish, her little treasure, her small green duckling, her dear sweet cabbage, her amour.

Summer, winter, autumn, spring – there was every day a long promenade with Gazelle, and we always came to a place with thistly bushes, where quinces grew, and then to a garden and a field, rose-colored with the blossoms of heather, and after that to a small inn, where cakes and chocolate were served.

All is still there – quinces, heather, the small inn, all unchanged. The daughter now runs the inn but she has the same smile, the same voice, the same ease and air of comfort and of peace that her mother had.

This intimate life in the small park and the old house on the lake – being bathed, dressed, fed, cared for – was only clouded by such tragedies as having toenails cut or getting soap into my eyes, when the big, clear tears of childhood rolled down my cheeks.

The other person who cried frequently was God. The God of that time and garden in Gmunden was 'le Bon Dieu' who worried only about making this life beautiful, and from whom all good things came. He was a beautiful old grandfather, and when it rained it was because people were bad; He had to cry and the tears ran over His cheeks and down His beard and over the lake. Mademoiselle said that the Bon Dieu was everywhere in every flower, animal, and cloud. And therefore one did not need to go to church.

I never was visited by other children. These long years of childhood were spent in the seclusion of the park and the vast house alone with Gazelle.

Monsieur Zobal came over to supervise the cooking, which was French. Papa came also when he needed the hothouse to celebrate in or to rehearse musicians, or when he tied his sailboat to the dock.

One time, when I was six, he wanted to take me on a drive around the country.

Among the few German words I knew was *Pferd*, which means horse; the coachman's name was Ferdinand, and because he had to do with horses I called him Pferdinand.

The coach, like everything Papa had, was an extraordinary vehicle, a shiny black landau, the body suspended on heavy straps of red Russian leather with gilt buckles. Pferdinand in top hat and livery and a bear rug over his legs waited. Two white Borzoi dogs also waited to run after us.

This was to be a family outing and Mama came and sat down in the carriage. I was handed over, with my golden curls squeezed down by a hat held in place with a stinging rubber band. Whenever I was taken from the side and hand of Gazelle, there were tears. I sat and cried as we waited. At last Papa came, looked at me seated in the coach and, lifting his hat, said to Mama that he was sorry but he couldn't come, because it would bore him. 'I'll talk to him, later – when he understands – when he is seventeen,' he said, and turned on his heel. As on that Christmas night when I had been an angel, I was happy again to be handed back to Gazelle, who cried also, and then le Bon Dieu started to cry – it rained. It rained almost every day in Gmunden – rain that sounded like the water of a shower falling full force on bathwater in the tub. It rained especially when one thought that it would be a lovely day, and when there was a patch of pale blue sky overhead in the morning.

It still rained the last time I was there. I painted the castle in rain. On this voyage I became aware that my palette is still of that landscape in rain.

The colors of houses and landscapes mostly in rain sank into my eyes in early childhood. This time, spent in a restricted place and in solitude, impressed on me the objects in nature which I still see in the shape and colors in which they were.

There was often fog on the lake. The fog was green, blue, violet, gray; it floated into the garden like gauze. It stood sometimes in shapes under trees, then disappeared as it had come. It determined the coloration of water, of the swans, of the eyes of Gazelle and of her hair. And sometimes it was like an immense white shroud, covering all. When the wind tore into it, it moved, and there suddenly appeared again the lake, the *Elisabet*, a swan, the bridge. On my recent visit the old steamer was still paddling 'Phlop, phlop, phlop' around the lake.

The seasons passed slowly in my childhood. There were the many phases of spring, with snow melting and running off the roofs, and icicles falling, and the birds drinking in the puddles made by the dripping water, and the sun reflecting in them. One of the many miracles I beheld then was the reflection of the sun in every puddle, even the smallest and dirtiest ones. My favorite season was autumn, the rich autumn of the russet and of all the dark reds and umber, the yellow autumn when all the chestnut trees were lit up with sun, and another phase when the leaves had fallen and the ground was a tapestry of ochre leaves with the trunks of trees turned several shades darker. I remember the smells of autumn, of ripening fruit along the espalier trees, especially of apricots, which were harvested and taken to the chef. He made from them my favorite dessert – dumplings of light dough with an apricot inside and breadcrumbs and sugar outside. This dessert is called *Marillenknoedel* – and I was able to eat a dozen of them at one sitting.

Then the last stage of autumn, the park cleared of the ochre leaves, the promenades swept, the trees now bare and the leaves sunk down to the bottom of the lake, shining upward and gilding the water. And, finally, the *Elisabet* was put to bed for the winter on the other side of the lake, tied to a dock next to a tavern. And one day she was covered and went to sleep under a coverlet of snow.

Long hours now were spent indoors with the collection of postal cards of Paris, the Album of Paris, the children's stories of France, the songs written for French children.

And then one autumn the leaves in the park were not raked, the swan stood there forlorn and it was all over – all had come to an end. Papa was gone and so was my governess, and I wished so much that he had run away with Mama and left me Gazelle.

I found myself in the arms of a strange woman, my mother, who was twenty-four years old then and very beautiful. She held me close and wept almost the entire journey from Gmunden to Regensburg.

We arrived with a night train. My mother was expecting a

child. The arrival was so planned that no one would see. A closed coach took us to the Arnulfsplatz. My grandfather wept and repeated, '*Armes Weiberl, armes Weiberl*,' meaning 'poor little woman, poor little woman.' My grandmother held me in her arms and looked stone-faced, for she had made the path even and promoted the match. It was also said that among her many lovers had been my father.

For a long time, my mother locked herself into her rooms and never went out. That was because she was the first divorced woman in Regensburg. Except for the scandal with King Ludwig I and Lola Montez, no one had ever heard of a case like this. People were married – men had illegal children with servant girls and provided for them, and all that was accepted, but marriage was a sacred institution. They did not bother to ask who was the guilty party. The woman was marked. My grandfather, who had been very much against the marriage, insisted on the divorce.

In the beginning Mama tried to replace Gazelle; mostly in tears, she dressed me and undressed me. There were no children's books, and she would tell me stories about her own childhood – of how alone she had been as a little girl and how she was shipped off to a convent school in Altötting, which was run by the kind nuns of an order known as the '*Englische Fraülein*.' She described the life there – how the girls slept in little beds that stood in two rows and how they went walking in two straight lines, all dressed alike. She was much happier there than at home, for her parents had never had any time for her. This made me very sad. She cried, and I cried. She lifted me up; I looked at her closely, and a dreadful fear came over me. I saw how beautiful she was, and I thought how terrible it would be if ever she got old and ugly.

Lausbub

REGENSBURG IS a Bavarian city on the banks of the Danube, and it possesses one of the finest Gothic cathedrals. When I was little it had about sixty thousand inhabitants, first among whom was the Duke of Thurn und Taxis. He lived in a castle which it took fifteen minutes to pass; it stood in a park that encircled the city. The Duke retained the Spanish etiquette at his court; his servants wore livery and powdered wigs; he rode about in a gilded coach cradled in saffron leather and drawn by white horses. He supported several jewelers, the city's theater, a private orchestra, and the race track.

Grandfather's brewery stood on a square facing the Duke's theater, in the oldest part of town. His daughter, my mother, was born in Regensburg. Grandfather loved the city.

My father, who lived there for a time, did not. He called it the cloaca of the world, but with a broader, more Bavarian word, which in Regensburg is used frequently as a term of rough endearment among friends. And so he went to Munich whenever he could escape from Regensburg; and when he could not, he walked out to the railroad station at least one evening a week. When all the other people went to the breweries, he would walk up and down the station platform until the signal bell announced the approach of the fast train from Paris. This train stopped for three minutes in Regensburg, and in that time my father would

lean over the iron barrier and look into the bright windows of the dining-car over which brass letters spelled out the elegant phrase, *Compagnie des Wagons-Lits et Express Européens*, and under which were a coat of arms and the word *Mitropa*, in carved wood. There he hung, drinking in the perfume, looking at the furs, at the few fortunate people who were walking up and down and climbing into the carmine-upholstered compartments. He would wait until the red signal lamp at the end of the train had slid down over the narrowing rails and disappeared around a curve on its way to Vienna. When he came back, he would complain of Regensburg's houses, its people, its way of life.

He was not altogether wrong, for it was a small provincial town, slow and gossipy. Regensburg went to sleep at nine in the evening, its surrounding country was without much excitement or good scenery, and I disliked it chiefly because I had to attend the Gymnasium there and all my professors came to eat in the restaurant of Grandfather's brewery, so that he was always informed that I would not pass the examinations, that I was unruly, impertinent, never serious, always late, and kept bad company.

At the end of my first year at the Gymnasium I had to repeat, and when this first year came to its second ending, and it had to be repeated once more, it was decided to send me away to a quiet little academy in Rothenburg, privately managed, for backward boys, where even an idiot could slowly be advanced. But even there I failed again to pass. The Rector, a very thorough and patient man, wrote home and asked to have me taken away.

Mother came to Rothenburg. We sat in the Rector's living room under an eyeless plaster bust of Pericles. The Rector, in a shabby green coat, felt his way around; almost blind, he looked through spectacles as thick as the bottom of a beer glass, and in the frames of which his eyes swam somewhere outside of his face, immense and unreal. After he had said 'Amen' to my future, Mother started to weep, and we left his room.

I said good-by to my friends. My linen and my stockings and clothes, all neatly marked '51' with the numbers in red on a white tape, were packed by the Rector's wife. We ate at the inn, called the Iron Hat, before we went to the station.

It was a silent trip. I could not find my voice. I wanted to kiss my mother and ask her forgiveness and somehow promise that she should not be sorry, that I would start a new and good life. But at that age one cannot say anything and after a while I played with the long leather strap that hung down from the window of the compartment. Embossed on it was 'Royal Bavarian Railway,' and I thought how I would like to take my pocket knife and cut it off. It was such a nice strong leather strap and would be useful for many purposes.

There was a stop in Nürnberg, and a buffet on the station platform. 'You don't deserve this,' said Mother, but she bought me a pair of the lovely little sausages, which are nowhere else better, and a small beer, and then she put her hand on my head and said: '*Es wird schon werden, Ludwig*' – 'Everything will come out all right in the end.'

The hope and prayer of every German mother at that time was that her boy would at least finish the six years of Gymnasium, which made of him a better-grade soldier when the time came for his military service. He would not be an officer; for that he had to enter the cadet corps. But he was allowed to sleep at home, he did not have to wear the formless baggy uniform issued by the service, the clumsy boots, the cap without a visor. He was marked off, besides having his own well-tailored uniform and a stiff cap with visor, by two little shoulder straps, with a narrow blue and white border. He did not have to stand at attention when an officer passed, hold that position and follow the officer with his eyes until he had passed. He simply saluted. His term of service was only one year instead of three.

It was a disgrace to be a common soldier, mingling in the barracks with the louts that came from the potato-growing country around Regensburg, commanded to do every kind of stable duty, to shine officers' boots, and to be addressed as '*Gemeiner*' – 'common one'. But this awaited me. Mother had said over and over in the train from Rothenburg: 'Disgrace, disgrace, disgrace.'

When we came back to Regensburg, to the brewery, I found Grandfather not at all upset. He was happy about not having another 'studied one' in the family wasting money. He felt my arms and saw that I was strong.

In his living-room, in the old house next to the brewery, he outlined a career for me that included one year's apprenticeship with a butcher, to learn how to judge meat and cut it and make sausages, then a year with a plumber and electrician, and then going into the brewery and starting there the way his own father and grandfather had done and the way he had learned to make beer himself.

Mother held me all the while and said: 'No, Papa, not to the butcher, not to the electrician, and not into the brewery.'

Attached to the brewery by mortgages were thirty-seven inns, all over the countryside, in which Grandfather's beer was sold. He had two kinds of beer: one a bitter-sweet, thick, black soupy brew; the other a blond beer, light-bodied, with much snowy foam, and bitter. Every spring Grandfather went on a round of visits to his inns, and my picture of happiness will always be one of him and his hunting wagon.

First the sound of the slim wheels on the gravel in the inner garden; then, the deep liquid 'clop clop clop' of the horse's hoofs as the wagon came out of the brewery through the tunnel, over creosote-soaked wooden blocks; and finally the clatter of the hoofs on the cobblestones in front of the house. Grandfather slowly climbing up in front, on to the reed basket seat of the delicate little wagon, almost turning it over on its red wheels, as he puts his great weight on its side.

He wore a loose green coat, with buttons cut from antlers, a brush on his mountain hat, a whip for decoration in his big hands.

He made a sound with his tongue, and the trotter lifted its knees up to its chest, and, weaving back and forth, its neck arched in a coy, young pose, it sailed out. From the back seat waved Grandfather's servant Alois, who always went with him. They stopped and drank and ate in all the inns, and bought calves for the butchery, which was part of the brewery. After years of experience Grandfather could drink thirty-six big stone mugs of beer in one evening. He ate heavy meals besides, hardly any vegetables, only dumplings and potatoes, potatoes and dumplings, and much meat.

In consequence of this diet, Grandfather had several times a year attacks of very painful gout, which in Bavaria is called *Zipperl*. Much of the time, one or the other of his legs was wrapped in cotton and elephantine bandages. If people came near it, even Mother, he chased them away with his stick, saying: 'Ah, ah, ah' in an ecstasy of pain and widening his eyes as if he saw something very beautiful far away. Then he would rise up in his seat, while his voice changed to a whimpering 'Jesus, Jesus, Jesus.' He said he could feel the change in weather in his toes, through the thick bandages. But he did not stop eating or drinking.

He had a wheelchair at such times, and Alois had to push him on his visits to the other breweries or restaurants in Regensburg. A kind of track was built for this chair in the backyard of the house; it swung over the roof of the shack where the barrels were kept and came down to the ground in a wide serpentine. Then there were little wooden inclines, to make it possible to wheel Grandfather painlessly over the doorsteps, in front and in back of the house and out into the square.

On the ground floor of the house was a baker, and the stairway and all the rooms in the house smelled of freshly baked bread, nicest on cold winter days. The baker, white of face and clothes, could see Grandfather being wheeled out, and he would say: 'The *Zipperl*! Aha! It's got you again, Herr Fischer!' and so said the policeman outside, while he made the streetcar wait, and so did all the other people. Everybody in the city knew Grandfather, and since life was without any other excitement, they had time to say: 'Have you seen Herr Fischer? The *Zipperl* has him again!' And Grandfather said nothing but 'Jesus, Jesus, God Almighty, ah ah ah, be careful, be careful, Alois. The *Zipperl*!'

I had a small room in Grandfather's house almost up under the gable of the house. It was most beautiful at night; from my window I could see the whole square at once without turning head or eyes, and when it was dark and the theater was lit, after the Duke had arrived, his carriages were driven slowly, just to keep the horses warm, around the circle of plants and trees and the small statue which stood in the center of the square within an iron fence. The rich harness, the liveries of the coachmen and footmen, the lamps, made a magical, lit-up, jeweled merry-go-round.

On the driver's seat of the finest coach, the Duke's, sat a bearded man in pale blue livery, a bearskin cape over his shoulders and a plume on his hat, a hat such as admirals wear, worn sideways with the wide part to the front. I watched this for hours until the play ended, until the circle became a line and the carriages drove under the portico of the small theater and away to the castle.

In the morning Grandfather had coffee at his window, with a canary bird sitting on the backrest of his chair. There was the smell of cigar smoke, of snuff, of coffee and fresh bread. He dipped four crescent rolls into his coffee and looked out over the square, to observe the people and the business of the city. He had a mirror on the outside of the house so he could see who came to visit us. Around him hung more cages with canaries; he fed them in the morning, and trimmed their claws and changed their diet for them, experimenting how to make them lay more eggs or sing better. He marked the results down in a little book, of which he had two; in the other he kept the business of his brewery. So easy and secure was his life.

On the table in front of him was paper, paste, and a pair of big shears. He made helmets with them, out of stacks of large sheets of durable packing paper, which he bought especially for this purpose. They were simple triangular paper hats, with a bush of blue and white crepe paper stuck on at the end, and they were given away. Any child in Regensburg who came and asked could have one. He made these helmets in great quantities, for the orphanage of Regensburg and the surrounding villages. The children of the orphanage and of the dumb and blind institute waved up whenever they passed the house. So that they could fight properly in two armies, he made, for the children who could see, two kinds of helmets, one with a blue bush and one with red. The blue and white were the Bavarian colors; the red, the French.

This work took up a few hours. Afterwards he looked up

orders and was very conscientious about filling them, and then, when the rheumatism did not bother him, he took a walk around the park with the brewmaster and listened to his report and told him what to do about the beer.

The brewery also had its own fire department, which always arrived ahead of the city firemen. It consisted of an old beer wagon, painted red and yellow, fixed up with a bell, hose, ladders, hooks, and buckets. It thundered out of the tunnel of the brewery, pulled by the best horses, the skin of their haunches stretched into folds as they pushed the ground away from under them, sparks raining from under their hoofs as they struck the cobblestones. The wagon had to run around the square twice, before it could slow down enough to head into the street that led to the fire.

Next to Mother and myself, Grandfather's greatest trouble was my Uncle Veri; Veri is short for Xavier. He was my favorite uncle; he had the strong dispassionate face of a sportsman; he was so big that the funeral wagon of Regensburg was made to his measure; he was as strong as he was big. When someone had to be thrown out of the brewery – and the men in Regensburg are big and heavy, and can fight – Uncle Veri did it. He would drag the man to the door, go out a little, measure his distance, take a good hold on trousers and coat collar, and throw the man over the iron fence into the bushes that stood around the small statue.

Uncle Veri loved betting. He once made a wager with a city official that he could make a million dots in eight hours. Two brewery hands had to sharpen pencils, and Uncle Veri stuck them between his fingers, four to each hand. The city official wanted to back out, he said it was cheating, he meant it should be done with one or at most two pencils, but finally he gave in. Uncle Veri hammered with both hands at the sheets of paper, while the waitresses, the brewmaster and his crew, the city official and his friends, all counted dots and crossed them off. It was a typical Regensburg form of amusement, for it could all have been calculated in a few minutes, especially since the city official happened to be in the Department of Taxation, who won, of course. But meanwhile they drank and ate and sat there and it helped to pass an evening, and at the end everyone was tired and certain that even Uncle Veri could not do it.

But he could lift the stone in the beergarden that had an iron ring hammered into it, and that with one finger. He did that often and for anyone who asked him; the next strongest man in Regensburg needed two hands to do it. To keep in trim, Uncle Veri carried a cast-iron walking-stick, and an umbrella with a heavy iron bar down its center. He pushed the big brewery horses around as if they were flies; and if he saw a brewery man, anywhere in the middle of the city, groan while lifting barrels, Uncle Veri would say to him: 'You make me sick to look at,' especially if it was a man from another brewery, and he would hand him his iron walking-stick to hold, and then himself load or unload the wagon, bouncing the heavy barrels on the big leather cushion which is put down to protect the cobblestones. He even slept strongly, sometimes going to bed on Monday night and waking up fresh and rested on Wednesday morning. Everyone had respect for him.

He was bad only with women. All of Grandfather's serious troubles came from that; Grandfather had to pay for the children. When someone looked up from the square, and saw Grandfather busy with stacks of paper hats, and then turned his head and said something to a friend, and both of them smiled, then Grandfather knew that the joke had been told again, that he was busy making paper hats for Uncle Veri's children. Few people, however, laughed up any more, only strangers, because in Regensburg it was an old joke.

Grandfather said that I should start to learn from Uncle Veri how to wash barrels.

Mother cried and said no, she would rather have me dead than be a butcher's apprentice and wash barrels and then be a common soldier and stand at attention while people like the sons of the girls who had gone to the convent with her, and who had studied enough to be officers, passed by. Mother's name was Franziska, and Grandfather called her Fannerl. 'You're crazy, Fannerl,' he said. Mother took me by the hand and we went out to visit Uncle Wallner.

This uncle was thin, little, and, for Regensburg, a gentleman. He lived in the best, new part of the town, in a villa with a small park. He was a city father, wore a top hat on Sunday and black clothes and gloves and a golden pince-nez – but even with the golden pince-nez he could not see very well. He was very polite to the proper people in Regensburg; he said it was very important to show reverence and respect to important personages. When I walked with him, very slowly because he took little steps, and we met someone he knew and thought worthy, he would swing his hat almost down to the ground and pronounce the name carefully in greeting.

Sometimes when I was with him and we passed one of Grandfather's waitresses on the other side of the street, too far away for Uncle Wallner to recognize her, or the lady who took care of the public washroom at the railway station, or one of the rough girls that Uncle Veri liked, I would get Uncle Wallner's attention and tell him that was the Frau Direktor across the way, or the Frau Inspektor, or the French Consul's wife. Uncle

Wallner would stop immediately and turn and whisper the name across the street and sweep his hat through the air, making a respectful compliment, and he would tell me what a worthy, fine, and gentle lady the washroom woman was. He owned a wholesale grocery business, which was why he was so polite, and, after all, that was a little fun in this stupid city.

Uncle Wallner always advised Mother. He liked to put French phrases into his conversation and speak of a journey he had made to the Paris Exposition in 1889, and to London. '*Mais ça ne va pas, ma chère*,' he said to Mother when she told him about the brewery plans. 'A butcher, a plumber, and with Veri as a teacher he would soon turn into a nice little ruffian. No, *ma chère*,' he said, and drummed on the windowpane, and then he sent me out to get him some cigars, so that he could talk alone with Mother.

When I came back, he smiled. He was just showing Mother his new visiting-cards; he had become a Herr Kommerzienrat, a Commercial Councillor of the King in Munich, and had had new cards printed with this title on them, and his housekeeper for two days had already been addressing him continually as Herr Kommerzienrat. 'Will the Herr Kommerzienrat have tea now?' she asked, and Uncle said yes. She brought tea and cake, and after this was cleared away, Uncle Wallner drummed on the top of a very beautiful cherrywood table, inlaid with cigar bands under glass. He asked me to sit close to him and Mother and then he started as one does a letter: 'Dear Ludwig,' and he said that I should think about going to Uncle Hans in Tirol, to Father's brother. Uncle Wallner looked very happy when he said that; he added that Uncle Hans was a very wise man, rich and respected and good.

'He is a good man,' Uncle Wallner repeated several times, because up to now I had been told that Uncle Hans was not so good, that Uncle Hans Bemelmans in Tirol was full of 'amerikanische Tricks'.

Uncle Hans Bemelmans, said Uncle Wallner, had many hotels, and hotels are a very fine business. One always has interesting people around, the great of the world; one can travel, see much of life; one eats better than anyone else. In a few years a boy as bright as I was would no doubt be the manager, or even the proprietor, of such a hotel as Uncle Hans had in Tirol. Right there, with Uncle Bemelmans, was the great opportunity. He had not one hotel, he had a chain of them.

There was the Hotel Maximilian in Igls, near Innsbruck, the Grand Hotel des Alpes on the Dolomite Road in San Martino di Castrozza, the Hotel Scholastika on the Achen See, the Hotel Alte Post in Klobenstein, where Uncle Bemelmans had his headquarters, and the Mountain Castle in Meran. In the Mountain Castle even Royalty stopped.

This was wonderful and surprising to me. When Grandfather spoke of Uncle Hans Bemelmans, he called him the 'other *Lump*,' the first *Lump* being my father, the painter. The 'amerikanische Tricks', Grandfather said, Uncle Hans had learned during several years spent in the United States. The trick which he had brought back from there and which Grandfather told most often was the 'Sanatorium Trick'; it went like this:

For speculative purposes, Uncle Hans had bought a piece of ground in Meran, in Tirol. He found out later that he had made one of his rare mistakes. But overlooking his land was the façade of a very fine private dwelling belonging to a Leipzig builder of funiculars. When he realized he had made a bad buy, Uncle Hans offered his land to this man from Leipzig to enlarge his park, but the man said that his park was big enough. Uncle Hans said nothing and went home. The view from the man's balconies was the best in Meran; it overlooked all the mountains as well as Uncle's ground. So Uncle Hans arrived one day with engineers and measuring instruments and a workman who stuck red and white poles into the ground, close to the fence of the rich man, who watched all this from his balcony. A few days later more men came and unloaded sand and bricks and started to dig while others unrolled blueprints on a table under a corrugated shed. When the rich man could not stand it any longer, he came to the fence and asked Uncle Hans: 'What's going on here, Herr Bemelmans? What are you doing here?'

Uncle Hans smiled and said: 'I'm building a hotel here, the Grand Hotel Tirol. The kitchen and pantry will be right here where we are standing, and the hotel will be eight stories high and look out on that beautiful panorama.'

'Oh, a hotel!' said the man.

'Well, not exactly a hotel,' said Uncle Hans, 'more a sanatorium.' He took a deep breath. 'The air here,' he said, and hit himself on the chest, 'the air here is very beneficial for certain afflictions,' and he cleared his throat and coughed loudly.

'I see,' said the rich man, and he bought the property a few days later. Now he had to pay much more for it, because there were in addition the charges for bricks and sand and surveying and the shack and the labor. He even paid for having it all taken away again. Uncle Hans took care of that too. He had the sand and bricks delivered to the Mountain Castle, his hotel, where he made a terrace out of them for afternoon dancing and tea.

'That,' Grandfather said, 'was an American trick, well done and complete.'

Uncle Bemelmans, Grandfather said, was in possession of the

knowledge of every such device, and that was why he had so many hotels. But though he was rich, Grandfather thought of him as another *Lump*, chiefly because he was a Bemelmans.

'They,' said Grandfather, 'are washed with every kind of soap and water, and rubbed in with slick oil, and they are therefore hard to catch and slippery.'

Mother came back with Uncle Wallner, but it was hard to change Grandfather's mind, for he too had friends who advised him, three of them, and they had all agreed that the brewery was the right thing for me.

These friends were the Bartel brothers, people to whose wives Uncle Wallner did not raise his hat. One was called 'Cider' Bartel, because he had a cider factory; another was called 'Pitch' Bartel, because he made pitch and creosote blocks and the beer barrels for the brewery; and the third was called 'Dreck' Bartel. This last had a string of evil-smelling wagons with long tubular barrels on them, and a pumping-machine; attached to the last wagon rolled a low cart, in which lay thick, solid, round pieces of hose that fitted together, and out of these an awful juice dripped on to the pavement of the city. One could tell with closed eyes at what house Dreck Bartel and his two sons were pumping clean a cesspool.

Dreck Bartel did not like me very much. I had written a poem about him in the Bavarian dialect, and was caught with it in class, and had to sit 'in arrest' for six hours, and a letter went to Mother about it, and I told Uncle Veri about it, and Uncle Veri knew a tune that went well with it, and in a little while it was known all over the city, and Uncle Veri one night had to throw Dreck Bartel into the park because he became too loud and said he would drown me in a cesspool if he ever caught me.

But finally Mother and Uncle Wallner won.

The old seamstress, who worked in the house all year fixing napkins and torn tablecloths, took the number '51' off all my linen, clothes, and stockings; and with a new traveling bag, Mother took me to the train for Munich, Mittenwald, Innsbruck, Meran.

I was surprised at the first conductor I saw on the Austrian railway and at the stationmaster and switchmen, at their manners and dress. I had learned that only the German is reliable and orderly, and here was proof of it. These men were careless, their coat collars open; they played bowls in a shed next to the station while the customs examination took place. It seemed a remote, disorderly, un-German land, beautiful though it was. When the train started, even the signal sounded strange; the sharp policeman's whistle was replaced by a brass trumpet, its sound was the bleat of a young sheep; and the conductor and the train were in no hurry to start.

I crossed the Brenner and came to Bozen, never leaving the window of the train; from Bozen the cogwheel railway goes up the Ritten, to Klobenstein, to Uncle Hans's hotel, the Alte Post. Klobenstein was beautiful; it stood in a ring of distant mountains. The hotel was a lovely, flower-covered, wide, solid mountain house with thick walls and low ceilings. Uncle Hans and Aunt Marie met me at the station.

From the very beginning Uncle Hans called me 'Lausbub.' Lausbub literally means 'lousy boy,' but in South Germany and Austria it is almost a tender word and means something like 'rascal.' Uncle Bemelmans was comfortably built, but not fat; he wore a beard like the English King Edward's, but on the little finger of his right hand was an immense solitaire diamond, so big that it looked false, like circus jewelry.

He had received letters from Uncle Wallner. It was through

Uncle Wallner, because he had traveled and was elegant, that all the Fischer-Bemelmans affairs were arranged. Uncle Bemelmans explained at length why I had come and how I was going to be dealt with. He read me long lectures in his little office, a low, warm, paneled room, decorated with many antiques and heated by a painted white porcelain stove.

In this office there was a carpet on the floor and I could soon draw from memory all the plants, animals, and symbols in its pattern, because I looked at it for such long stretches while Uncle Hans walked up and down over it, back and forth for hours, his hands folded under the seat of his trousers, and over them hanging the square-cut tails of his cutaway.

In the back of the hotel, along with the iceboxes and the pantries, in a stone-floored room, was an old-fashioned ice machine that pounded away in a steady rhythm. Uncle Hans was always listening to that rhythm. He noticed the moment it became irregular and he would let no one else touch the machine. The instant it changed tempo, he would leave whatever he was doing to fix it. During a lecture he would stop suddenly, reach for his hat, and run to the machine, telling me to wait till he came back. He looked very funny then, because he was in a hurry, and hurry did not go well with the dignity of his face and clothes.

He always quoted America, telling me often that in America *Lausbuben* like me sometimes turned out to be very rich men. But in Tirol too, he said, there was bigger opportunity for a *Lausbub* than for a good boy who did as he was told and would perhaps make a good employee but never be rich.

Here in the hotel I found evidence of a lighter kind of life: the cooking was French, without kraut and heavy dumplings; the conversation had more variety, was not so much of buildings, horses, the Bartels, beer, and the *pot de chambre* humor of Regensburg. I was disturbed by a sense of disloyalty to my Grandfather, because I felt I should not like anything else but his house and his person.

I had brought some drawings and watercolors and given them to Aunt Marie. When Uncle Hans saw them and heard Aunt Marie suggest that I study painting, he got very angry. Painters, he said, were hunger candidates, nothing in front and nothing in back of them; besides, if I liked painting, I could always hire an artist, when I became rich by following his teachings. He said I must bury the past and start a new life and be a joy and pride to my poor mother and for God's sake not to become an artist like my father. I would have to start all the way at the bottom of the ladder, he said, like Rockefeller and Edison, and work up from there. There was no reason, he said, why I should not in a few years be a hôtelier like himself, or at least manager of a hotel.

Aunt Marie would come into the little office when the lectures lasted too long, and say: 'I think that's enough for today, Hans, let him go.'

The first day, when she showed me the lovely room that overlooked the Dolomites and told me the names of the mountains, and looked at my pictures, she asked me what I liked most to eat. I told her 'apricot dumplings.' We had them for supper, and Uncle Hans complained that the *Lausbub* was being spoiled right from the beginning.

My birthday came soon after my arrival, and Aunt Marie bought me a box of the best watercolors and a drawing pad. I had a week of wonderful vacation and was given a horse on which I rode all over the beautiful mountains. Then one day it was decided that from eight in the morning until three in the afternoon I would be an employee and do all the work that was required of me, and for the rest of the time, before and after, and during the night, I would be Uncle's nephew and eat at the family table, and could have the horse.

The mornings at Tirol are the most beautiful time in all the world. I got up at five, saddled my horse, and rode to the sawmill. It stood on a turbulent brook, flanked by high, straight walls of dolomite granite, among tall trees. Nearby, under the two tallest and oldest trees, stood a little inn, with a garden, a curved wooden bench, and two round redstone tables. There I stopped at seven every morning and drank a pint of red wine, dipping the hard peasant bread in it. I stayed as long as I could and then rode in a gallop back to the hotel to be on time for duty.

The first morning I did this, Aunt Marie was up, and Uncle Hans out on his morning walk. He had said: 'At least he gets up early, the *Lausbub*; that's something; some of them you can't get out of bed.'

Aunt Marie always looked at me and felt my head and said it must be the change in altitude. 'He has a fever every morning, and look how his eyes shine.' But then they found out about the wine and several other things, and Uncle said that this half-nephew, half-employee arrangement was at an end. He said it would be better to send me to one of the other hotels where Aunt Marie could not help me out of every scrape.

And so I was sent first to the Mountain Castle in Meran, and then in the space of a year I ran through all of Uncle Hans's hotels. Every manager was tried out on me; they all failed and sent me back. The last time was after a very serious offence. Uncle walked up and down again; Aunt Marie cried and said to me while Uncle was with his ice machine: 'Ludwig, Ludwig, what is going to become of you? We love you so much and you are so bad. How will it end? What will become of you?' She embraced me and wiped her tears and mine from our eyes.

When Uncle Hans came back he said there were two places for me to choose between. The first was a correctional institution, a kind of reform school, German, on board a ship, where unruly boys were trained for the merchant marine and disciplined with the ends of ropes soaked in tar.

The second was America.

I decided to go to America.

Uncle Hans was very happy. He said that in the United States they would shear my pelt and clip my horns.

He wrote some letters to hotel people he knew, he gave me much advice, and he said that if I ever became a great hotel man, I would only become so by looking upon all employees as paid enemies; there is an exception here and there, but it takes too long to find out and is too risky to take a chance. Then he said: 'Dear Ludwig,' like Uncle Wallner, 'now we'll forget all about what has happened. I'll find out when a boat sails. Now you have a vacation, ride all you want, and we'll all be happy together.' I cried then because I was sorry I was so rotten and always in trouble when they were so kind to me.

Then I went back to Mother, and there it was also difficult, when I saw how she took money for my passage out of envelopes that were marked for other purposes for her own use. We got up early one morning to meet the express to Rotterdam. I was the only passenger from Regensburg on the lonely platform, and Mother said, with her hand on my head, for the second time: 'Everything will come out all right in the end, Ludwig.'

And that is how I left for America.

Arrival in America

When I arrived in New York in December 1914, I was sixteen years old.

The quality of my mind and its information at that time was such that, on sailing for America from the port of Rotterdam, I bought two pistols and much ammunition. With these I intended to protect myself against the Indians.

I had read of them in the books of Karl May and Fenimore Cooper, and intently hope for their presence without number on the outskirts of New York City.

My second idea was that the elevated railroad of New York ran over the housetops, adapting itself to the height of the buildings in the manner of a roller coaster.

Before sailing, the captain of the steamer *Ryndam* persuaded me to return the guns. The shopkeeper in Rotterdam, however, would only exchange them for other hardware, and I traded them for twelve pairs of finely chiseled Solingen scissors and three complicated pocket knives.

On this steamer, the S.S. *Ryndam* of the Holland America Line, was a smoking room. The benches and restful chairs in this saloon were upholstered with very durable gun-colored material with much horsehair in it.

My plan at the time was to have one strong suit made of this material. I reasoned that such a garment would last me for ten years, and in this time I could put by enough money to go back to Tirol and buy a sawmill that stands in a pine forest on the top of a mountain in the Dolomites.

Work

My First Actress

MY FIRST job in New York, at the Hotel Astor, did not last long. I filled water bottles and carried out trays with dishes, until I broke too many. So with my uncle's second letter I went to the Hotel McAlpin, where I got a job that lasted a year, at the end of which I spoke passable English, though I was still little better than a bus boy.

Here I wore for breakfast a white suit, yellow shoes, and, suspended in front of me on a thick leather strap, a silver machine, hot and the size of a baby's coffin. For three hours every morning I walked around the men's café, dreaming of Monday and my Actress, with the heavy silver coffin hanging before me. It contained in a lower compartment two heated bricks, and above on a wire net an assortment of hot cross buns, muffins, biscuits, croissants, and every other kind of rolls, soft and hard.

This work ceased at half-past ten, and then I sat for half an hour on the red tile floor in the grillroom and polished an elaborate fence of stout brass pipes which kept apart the waiters rushing in and those rushing out. I could, from where I sat, see the nice knees of a young lady cashier seated on a platform, but I never did, because I was in love with my Actress.

In the evening my hands were as cold as my stomach was warm in the morning, for at dinner, in another white suit and with white gloves and white shoes, I walked around the main dining-room with a silver tray. On the tray rested a thick layer of ice, and bedded in the ice, frosted with coldness, were silver butterchips. I exchanged full butterchips for empty ones.

A small orchestra played – selections from *La Bohème* and *Madame Butterfly*, the 'Dance of the Hours,' and a Dixie piece that ended in an almost audible 'Hooray, hooray!' I wrote requests on little cards and passed them up to the orchestra leader. I asked for tunes from the Merry Widow, music that was allied to my Actress. I would forget then to change the butterchips and would walk around the dining-room, softly whistling and thinking about Monday and the Irving Place Theater, and several times the headwaiter warned me, 'Hey, you, wake up!'

I lived on Thirty-second Street in a brownstone house that belonged to a detective, who also owned two parrots, and who sat in the evening with his feet in a tub of hot water while he read the papers aloud to his wife. From her, this Irishman had taken on a German accent. They lived on a diet of sauerbraten and cabbage, and the house smelled of it. They drank containers of beer with their meals.

I had at the time two hundred and fifty dollars. Two hundred were in the bank; fifty I carried in my pocket.

On a bedside table in my room, in a frame, stood the picture of my Actress. It was not her picture, strictly speaking. It was cut out of an advertisement for a railroad, but it looked exactly like her. My Actress had no pictures in the paper. That is why I thought that fifty dollars would be enough.

I had written several letters to her, but I always tore them up. I knew that for an actress one had to send flowers, a little card, an invitation to supper, a *chambre séparée*, a bottle of wine. And at the end of this routine, I reasoned, since it was a simple theater, since she was not well known, being a German actress, I might be able to tell her with fifty dollars.

The rest of my life was very orderly. I kept a small notebook; on the first page was written:

With God, New York, 1916.

On the following pages appeared a strict account of my finances: on one side, income from the hotel and from home; opposite, the outgo. The expenses varied but were about:

Rent	$3.00
Laundry	.68
Fruit	.30
Postage	.06
Shines	.20

Only on Mondays did the page become wild and exciting. Then I wiped away the hotel with a luncheon in a nice place, where they said: 'Good day, sir,' pulled out my chair, and said: 'Good-by, sir.' I wore my new suit, smoked a cigar, drank a glass of beer, and in the afternoon walked to the theater to enjoy the buying of the ticket. Perhaps to see her come or go from a rehearsal, to walk up and down awhile and wait for her. Perhaps to speak to her.

There was an additional pleasure at the ticket window: the man knew me by name, he gave me the same seat every Monday, second row on the aisle. '*Grüss Gott*, Herr Bemelmans,' he said in Bavarian German.

Over a circle of several blocks around this theater lay, like a vapor, a melancholy, bitter-sweet mood. I walked into it at Sixteenth Street, my heart beating faster, and at Irving Place my hands were moist.

The last Monday I ever saw her, the company was presenting

a musical comedy entitled *Her Highness Dances a Waltz*. She was Her Highness.

There was a small orchestra of simple German musicians who looked somehow like their instruments. The flutist was most so, as most flute-players are, thin, long, with all the lines of his face drawn down to the small apron of his upper lip which rested on the wet end of his flute.

The conductor swam over the notes. With the tempo of the music, his rear collar button came out over and disappeared under the edge of his coat collar. He caressed and scolded the music out of his men. His hair fell in his eyes at the *fortissimi*, and he completely disarranged himself with three mounting rages amidst his instruments when they blew, fiddled, and drummed, crash, boom boom boom, the overture to its one, two, three time ending.

With contempt still on his red face, he turned to the audience and thanked them for the applause. An immense handkerchief waited in his hand to wipe under his chin, over his face, around the back of the neck, inside his collar, while he bowed his thanks to the orchestra, the balconies, into all the corners.

It was fine, honest theater, played in a small house and to a good audience. No one came late. They were plain people, not rich, not poor, and not bored. They wanted to believe, their eyes moistened easily, and they laughed loud and long, and applauded with generous hands. They pointed at things they liked, and at favorite passages they nudged each other in the side.

They left slowly, waiting until some of the lights went out, until the last musician bent down, pushed his instrument case ahead of him and disappeared through the low door under the stage. They hung around the lobby, hummed the melodies, and said: '*Das war wieder schön*,' '*Schön wars*,' and '*Schön iss gwesn*.'

On that last Monday, after the overture, the lights went dim, the ramp lit up, the bottom of the curtain swayed and rose on the first act of *Hoheit tanzt Walzer*. The program said that the scene was an inn on the outskirts of Vienna, the garden of the inn.

The walls of the inn bulged with backstage drafts, the tree swayed; its foliage was a collection of tired, faded green handkerchiefs tied to torn netting. On the backdrop, patched, scraped, and worn with years of service, as was the outdoors in every play of this theater, hung a terrible garden.

To make marble of it, laborious blue worms had been painted into the wide stairway that came down the center of the garden. The stairway was flanked by two nudes, executed with such modesty that it was impossible to decide whether these German ladies stood with their ample fronts or backsides toward the audience. The towers of a castle rose out of the trees, and two fountains with swans in them played to the left and right of the nudes.

An Austrian Archduke, young and sad, had come to the inn to live incognito, to forget his princess who was to marry someone else for reasons of state.

There was one lovely detail in this scene. The Archduke sat at a table in the garden under a tree, and Franzl, the piccolo of the hotel, brought him his coffee, a demi-tasse. The Archduke put one lump of sugar into the coffee, the second he broke in half. One half he dropped into the cup, the other half he threw in the air over his shoulder into the open mouth of the piccolo, who stood behind him waiting for it, like a dog. This had to be repeated three times, so much did the audience love this good piece of nonsense.

After the Archduke had stirred his coffee, the waiter came out of the hotel, and, being an Austrian, the Archduke put his arm around the waiter and told him why he was here. They sang a duet while the piccolo cleared the coffee away. They sang that love for prince and waiter is alike, hopeless and sad.

Then the waiter heard something; he cupped his ear and listened into the back garden, and he said that he heard an elegant carriage with rubber wheels and two horses coming from Vienna. The Archduke disappeared into the hotel.

My Actress walked on. She did not walk, she was there with the grace of a young animal. She stood between the modest nudes; theater and music sank away. She pointed at the tree, lifted a fine white arm, a slim gloved hand, to the leaves, tilted back her lovely head, widened her nostrils, half closed her eyes, drank in the air, said it was spring, and began to sing.

I don't know what she sang, or what the Archduke said to her when he returned and discovered that she was the princess. I just saw throat, eyes, hair.

They sat on a bench and sang of how they loved each other, of how they had loved each other all their lives, ever since, as children five years old, they had first met in the park of Archduke Leopold's castle in Ischl, twenty years ago.

First the flowers, I decided, while he kissed her, and I got up and went out of the theater. A little man in the lobby called a taxi. We drove uptown in a U around Gramercy Park and up Lexington, to Madison, to Fifth, but all the florist shops were closed – light shone only in Thorley's.

There was little left in the way of flowers, shabby pots with single tulips, a few geraniums, hortensias – all flowers for housewives, no single, determined elegant plant. The man finally thought of a rose tree he had in another room. Trained into the shape of a basket, four feet high, decorated with a giant butterfly of a carmine bow, it was very heavy, and worth the twenty-five dollars he asked for it.

I wrote a card, and asked for a large envelope to put it into; we attached it with wire, where it could easily be seen. Back to the theater we drove, so fast that going around corners I had to hold the plant with both feet, and the upper part, with the white roses, with both hands.

The taximan was strong, he carried the rose tree into the lobby alone. From there the two girl ushers would carry it down, after the princess's next song came to its end, and hand it to her. I went down to my seat in the second row on the aisle.

The second act was half played. The stairway with the nudes was now a ducal park; there was a little mat of artificial grass, the same tree, a bench on the left side of the stage. On the bench sat two small children, arm in arm, a boy and a girl.

The little girl had on ruffled pantalettes and a mauve crinoline; the boy was in white silk breeches, an apricot-colored velvet Biedermeir frock-coat, and lace at throat and wrists. They sang and danced a minuet.

The conductor, with raised eyebrows, pointed lips, kept the music fragile. Carefully, as if holding a fine Dresden teacup in his hand, with his little finger stuck out, he leaned over the flute and counted time for the frail notes. Through the quiet melody, the careful opening of a door in the rear of the theater was loud and disturbing. Then a few voices way in the back whispered '*Ah, wie schön,*' and soon the '*Ah*' was running down the middle of the audience.

The minuet was over; the audience shook the theater with applause and demanded an encore. Tears were in the eyes of all the women. The conductor tapped on his desk and the children started to dance once more. I turned around. My rose tree was wobbling down over the heads of the audience, over in the far aisle; it shone in the darkness.

I unrolled my program. There, under 'Second Act,' was printed:

SCENE: The Park of Archduke Leopold's Castle in Ischl.
           Time has rolled back twenty years.
PRINCE   . . . . .Hansi Pschoor, aged 5
PRINCESS   . . . . .Lisl Stolz, aged 6

It was too late to do anything. The 'Ahh' was all over the theater now. The rose tree was in the light of the stage, it was tilted past the bass fiddle and the kettledrums, the 'cellist stood up to let it pass and, together with the two ushers and the conductor, to help lift it over the ramp and stand it in the middle of the park in Ischl, twenty years ago.

The waiter came from the wings, and pushed the little girl to the rose tree, and pointed to the card. The little princess hopped from one foot to the other. She looked back at her mama, whose face came out between one of the modest nudes and the tree.

The little princess twisted the envelope from the basket and cramped it tightly in her hand. She made small curtsies, awkward, unrehearsed motions, and threw kisses into the orchestra, the balcony, and back to her mama.

The waiter took the note to open it, to let the little princess read its contents to the audience, to thank whatever kind uncle had sent it. I got up. Leaving the theater, I stumbled and almost knocked over a worried little bearded man who stood in the lobby and with a small silver shovel filled paper bags with little German peppermints. I left just in time.

The waiter had raised his hand. The audience was quiet. The little girl was about to read:

'Will you have supper with me at Luchow's after the performance? I think I love you. Ludwig.'

The Splendide

THE NEXT day I was fired. But not for whistling, as I had been warned I would be. I was standing miserably, with my tray of butterchips behind a terra cotta column, waiting for the orchestra to play a piece I had just requested – 'Nur wer die Sehnsucht kennt' ('None But the Lonely Heart'). One of the musicians had gone to get the music for it from an upstairs closet.

The headwaiter came, looking for me, and noticed that I was wearing one white and one yellow shoe. He took me roughly by the arm to push me with my butterchips out among the guests, and I told him to go to the devil. I waited until the orchestra had finished my piece and then went home.

For a week I was unhappy. I visited the Aquarium, the Zoo, and the Metropolitan Museum of Art; I made sketches of the scenery of the Irving Place Theater; and then I looked in my trunk for another letter. The last one was to Mr. Otto Brauhaus, manager of the Hotel Splendide.

The Splendide, from the outside, was a plain building, but its interior was like that of a great private house. It completely lacked the anonymous feeling of the usual hotel, in which one might fall asleep in the lobby, be carried to another hotel, wake up, and never know it was another.

A page in silken breeches, a livery as rich as that of the Duke of Thurn und Taxis and of the same blue, showed me to the office. Under a sign that read: 'Don't worry, it won't last long, nothing does,' sat Mr. Otto Brauhaus. He spoke to me in German, wrote something on a little card, and then gave it and the letter from Uncle Hans to the page.

The page took me to the dining-room of the hotel, to a thin, foreign-looking man who looked like a high-placed Jesuit. His face in a frame of closely shaven violet beard-stubble, he spoke with controlled, eloquent motions of his head and long thin hands. He never looked at me but kept his eyes downcast as if hearing a confession. His altogether appropriate name was Serafini. He was from Siena and was the assistant headwaiter of the Hotel Splendide. To me he looked like St. Francis in a tailcoat.

In a *hôtel de grand luxe*, such as the Splendide, which is a European island in New York, there is no headwaiter, no captain, no waiter. Everything is much more elegant. The manager of the hotel is *le patron*; and the head man in the restaurant, more important in such a hotel than the manager, or even the chef, is simply 'Monsieur Grégoire,' 'Monsieur Théodore,' 'Monsieur Victor,' or whatever his first name is, and no matter what his nationality. His lieutenants, the captains, are called *maîtres d'hôtel*; and under them the waiters are not *garçons* (that is more the term for a café waiter), but *chefs de rang*, because each one has for his station a rank of several tables. The chef de rang never leaves his tables or the dining-room; he has a young man who runs out to the kitchen for him, and this quick young waiter is a commis de rang. Even the bus boys are called *débarrasseurs*.

Mr. Serafini said very considerately that there was no

position for me at the Splendide, since all the employees in the dining-room were obliged to speak French. When I told him I spoke French, he changed the conversation to that language and then asked me to wait.

I waited in the high, oval dining-room for a long time, happily observing the well-designed salt cellars and pepper mills, the fine clean pattern on the plates, the stucco ceiling, and the carpets. Waiters came to set up the room, and they were distinguished-looking men, of better appearance than the guests in the other hotels I had worked in, carefully dressed, quick, capable. Most of them, however, wore spats and pretty shirts. I waited until these had gone and an orchestra arrived and tuned its instruments. Finally, the headwaiter-in-chief, that is, Monsieur Victor, appeared.

Serafini looked down at my hands and whispered to me to come. He placed Mr. Brauhaus's cards and Uncle Hans's letter before Monsieur Victor. On Uncle Hans's letterhead were not only the names but also the pictures of every one of his hotels, and Monsieur Serafini said in French: 'A young man of good family, he is recommended by the *patron*.'

Without looking at me longer than was necessary to see that I was there, Monsieur Victor said:

'Engage him, put him to work as a commis, see what he can do.'

Herr Otto Brauhaus

THE SPLENDIDE had four hundred rooms, a great number for a luxurious hotel. Hotels larger than this become like railroad stations, eating and sleeping institutions. They have to take in anyone who comes along. The staff changes too frequently to give perfect service, to become acquainted with the guests. In the bigger hotels, the manager is usually a financial person, a one-time accountant who leaves actual contact with the guests to a platoon of day and night assistants, a kind of floorwalker with a small desk in the middle of the lobby and no authority except to say good-morning and good-night, a man whose business it is to shake hands and watch the bellboys and be in charge in case of fire.

In a hotel like the Splendide, however, it must be assumed, for the purposes of good management, that every guest is a distinguished and elegant person who, of course, has a great deal of money. The prices are high and must be high; the cost of provisions is probably the smallest item. The charges are for marble columns, uniforms, thick carpets, fine linen, thin glasses, many servants, and a good orchestra. And the management of such a hotel is a difficult, delicate business. It produces in most cases a type of man whose face is like a towel on which everyone has wiped his hands, a smooth, smiling, bowing man, in ever freshly pressed clothes, a flower in his lapel, *précieux* and well fed.

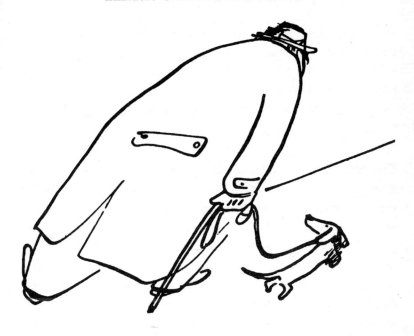

Rarely does one find in America a hotel manager who has survived the winds of complaint, the climate of worry, and the floods of people, and of whom one can still say that, besides being short or tall, thin or fat, he has this or that kind of personality. Such a one, a real person, honest always himself with a unique character, was Otto Brauhaus, manager of the Hotel Splendide.

Otto Brauhaus was an immense stout man; he had to bend down to pass under the tall doorways of his hotel. Big as his feet, which gave him much trouble, telegraphing their sorrows to his ever-worried face, was his heart. For despite his conception of himself as a stern executive, and strict disciplinarian, he could not conceal his kindness. He liked to laugh with guests and employees alike, and the result was that his countenance was the scene of an unending emotional conflict.

He was a German, from the soft-speaking Palatinate. For all his years in America, he had somehow never been able to improve his accent. Too genuine a person to learn the affected English of Monsieur Victor, who was a fellow-countryman, Brauhaus spoke a thick dialect that sometimes sounded like a vaudeville comedian trying for effect. He was, in any case, inarticulate, and hated to talk. Two expressions recurred in his speech like commas; without them he seemed hardly able to speak: 'Cheeses Greisd!' and 'Gotdemn it!'

His friends were all solid men like himself. Most of them seemed to be brewers, and they would have occasional dinners together, small beer-fests, up in the top-floor suite. There they drank enormous quantities of beer and ate canvasback ducks with wild rice. They held little speeches afterwards and ate again at midnight. They spoke mostly about how proud they were of being brewers. Almost weeping with sentiment and pounding on the table with his fist, one of them would always get up and say: 'My father was a brewer. So was my grandfather, and his father was a brewer before him. I feel beer flowing in my veins.'

Then Herr Brauhaus usually summed up their feelings by rising to say: 'My friends, we are all here together around this table because we are friends. I am demn glad to see all my friends here.' They would all nod and applaud and drink again.

But things had not been going too well with Brauhaus's friends, these elderly men who ate and drank too well. In one week Mr. Brauhaus went to two funerals. He came back very gloomy from the second, saying: 'Gotdemn it, Cheeses Greisd, every time I see a friend of mine, he's dead.'

Beautiful was it also when he described his art gallery. Of the Rubens sketch he owned, he often said: 'If something happens to me, Anna still has the Rubens,' and of his primitives he said: 'Sometimes when I'm alone, I look at them, and they look at me, so brimidif, like this,' and he would look sideways out of his face, just like his primitives.

He was not given to false conceptions of personal dignity though he insisted on his hotel's being treated with proper respect. Once when he had hung up outside his office, one hour after he had bought it, a beautiful expensive heavy coat lined with mink, and it was stolen, Mr. Brauhaus ran out into the luncheon crowd which filled the lobby and howled: 'Where is my furgoat, Cheeses Greisd!' But it was gone and never came back.

On the other hand one day when Mr. Brauhaus happened to be walking through the Jade Lounge, he saw an elderly lady sitting there alone at a small glasstop table, on which were tea and crumpets. She was knitting. Turning to me he said: 'What do they think this is? Go over there and tell that women to stop knitting.' He pronounced the 'k' in the last word. 'Tell her that this is a first-class hotel and we don't want any knitting here in our Jade Lounges.' He disappeared into his office.

I was a little afraid to follow orders, for the elderly lady was severely dressed and looked quite able to taking care of herself. I therefore passed the patron's instructions on to Monsieur Serafini, who looked at the lady, went 'Tsk, tsk, tsk' with his tongue, and called a waiter. Fortunately, before the waiter could reach her, the old lady packed her knitting into an immense bag and smiled up at a tall man who had come in the door. She was his mother, and he was the new British Ambassador.

*

Brauhaus's goodness of heart, his reliance on the decency of his people, his unwillingness to face them when they had caused trouble, meant that he was always being taken advantage of by the smooth, tricky, much-traveled people who were his employees. 'Why doesn't everybody do his duty, why do I have to bawl them out all the time?' he pleaded with them.

But when someone went too far, then Otto Brauhaus exploded. His big face turned red, his voice keeled over, he yelled and threatened murder. The culprit's head somewhere on a level with Brauhaus's watch chain, the storm and thunder of the big man's wrath would tower and sweep over him. Brauhaus's fists would be raised up at the ceiling, pounding the air; the crystals on the chandelier would dance at the sound of his voice: 'I'll drown you oud, I'll kill you, gotdemn it, Cheeses Greisd, ged oud of here!'

Fifteen minutes later, he enters his office and finds waiting for him the man he has been shouting at. Brauhaus looks miserable, stares at the floor like a little boy. He puts his hand on the man's shoulder and squeezes out a few embarrassed sentences. First he says: 'Ah, ah – ah,' then comes a small prayer: 'You know I am a very pusy man. I have a lot of worries. I get excited and then I say things I don't mean. You have been here a long time with me, and I know you work very hard, and that you are a nice feller.' Finally a few more 'Ah – ah – ah's' and then he turns away. To any man with a spark of decency, all this hurts; almost there are tears in one's eyes and one's loyalty to Otto Brauhaus is sewn doubly strong with the big stitches of affection.

Since he could not fire anyone, someone else had to get rid of the altogether impossible people, and then an elaborate guard had to be thrown around Brauhaus to keep the discharged employees from reaching him in person or by telephone. Once a man got by this guard, all the firing was for nothing.

One night it was announced that Mr. Brauhaus was leaving on his vacation. Such information seeps through the hotel immediately, as in a prison. The trunks were sent on ahead, and late that night Mr. Brauhaus took a cab to the station. But he missed his train, and, since the hotel was not far from the station, he decided to walk back. With his little Tirolese hat, his heavy cane, and his dachshund, which he took with him on trips, he came marching into his hotel. Outside he found no carriage man, no doorman, inside no one to turn the revolving door, no night clerk, also no bellboy and no elevator man. The lobby was quite deserted; only from the cashier's cage came happy voices and much laughter.

Mr. Brauhaus stormed back there and exploded: 'What is diss? Gotdemn it! Cheeses Greisd! You have a birdtay zelepration here?'

They made themselves scarce and rushed for their posts. Only the bottles of beer were left, as the revolving door was turned, without guests in it, the elevator starter slipped on his gloves, and the night clerk vaulted behind the counter and began to write. 'You are fired, all fired everyone here is fired, gotdemn it!' screamed Herr Brauhaus. 'Everyone here is fired, you hear, raus, everyone, you and you and you.' He growled on: '*Lumpenpack, Tagediebe, Schweinebande!*' He had never heard or seen anything like this.

The men very slowly started to leave. 'No, not now, come back, tomorrow you are fired,' Brauhaus shouted at them.

He was so angry he could not think of going to sleep, and as always on the occasions when he was upset, he walked all the way around the hotel and back to the main entrance. There the doorman got hold of him. With sad eyes, he intercepted Mr. Brauhaus, mumbled something about the twelve years he had been with the hotel, that only tonight, for the first time, had he failed in his duty, that he had a sick child and a little house in Flatbush and that his life would be ruined.

'All right,' said Brauhaus. 'You stay, John. All the others gotdemn it, are fired.'

But there was no one to protect him that night. Inside he heard the same story, with changes as to the particular family misfortunes and the location of the little houses. They had all been with the Splendide since the hotel was built; the bellboy had gray hair and was fifty-six years old. Mr. Brauhaus walked out again and around the block. When he came back, he called them all together. He delivered them what was for him a long lecture on discipline, banging the floor with his stick, while the dachshund smelled the doorman's pants.

'I am a zdrikt disziblinarian,' he said. They would all have to work together; this hotel was not a gotdemn joke, Cheeses Greisd. It was hard enough to manage it when everyone did his duty, gotdemn it. 'And now get back to work.'

A late guest arrived. He swung through the door, saluted, wished a good-night, expressed up to his room with a morning paper and a passkey in the hands of the gray-haired bellboy. No guest had ever been so well and quickly served. 'That's good, that's how it should be all the time,' said Otto Brauhaus. 'Why isn't it like this all the time?' Then he went to bed.

Besides all of Mr. Brauhaus's other troubles, there was the World War, and his hotel was filled in front with guests, and staffed in the rear with employees, of every warring nation. Whenever this problem arose, he always shouted: 'We are all neudral here, gotdemn it, and friendts!'

One Thursday afternoon, about five-thirty, I had been sent to the kitchen to get some small sandwiches for some tea guests. The man who makes these sandwiches is called the *garde-manger*. Instead of ovens, this cook has only large iceboxes, in which he keeps caviar, pâté de foie gras, herrings, pickles, salmon, sturgeon, all the various hams, cold turkeys, partridges, tongues, the cold sauces, mayonnaise. Next to him is the oyster-man, so that all the cold things are together.

In spite of being in a cool place instead of, as most cooks are all day, in front of a hot stove, this man was as nervous and excitable as any cook. Also I came at the worst possible time to ask anything of a cook, that is, while he was eating. He sat all the way in the back of his department, and before him were a plate of warm soup on a marble-topped table and a copy of the *Courrier des Etats Unis*, which announced in thick headlines a big French victory on the western front.

To order the sandwiches, the commis had first to write out a little slip, announce the order aloud, go to the coffee-man at the other end of the kitchen for the bread, and finally bring the bread to the garde-manger to be spread with butter, covered, and cut into little squares.

The garde-manger was still eating, but since the guest was in a hurry, I repeated the order to him. 'Go away,' the cook said angrily. 'Can't you see I'm eating? Come back later.'

I insisted he make the sandwiches now. 'Go away!' he repeated. '*Sale Boche!*'

I called him a French pig. Near him was a box of little iceflakes to put under cold dishes; he reached into this box, came forward, and threw a handful of ice into my face. On the stone counter next to me stood a tower of heavy silver platters, oval, thick, and each large enough to hold six lobsters on ice; I took one of these platters, swung, and let it fly. It wobbled through the air, struck him at the side of the head between the eye and ear, and then fell on the tiled floor with a loud clatter. A woman who was scrubbing a table close by screamed.

Her scream brought the cooks from all the departments as well as the cooks who were eating and the first chef. Four of them carried the garde-manger to the open space in front of the ranges. There he kicked and turned up his eyes; blood ran from the side of his face, and skin hung down under a wide gash. They poured water on him, shouted for the police, and everybody ran around in circles.

It was then I put into practice the Splendide maxim I had already learned: Get to Mr. Brauhaus first. I ran up the stairs and found him as usual worrying in his office under the sign: 'Don't worry, it won't last, nothing does.' I told him my story as quickly as I could. 'What did he call you?' said Mr. Brauhaus, getting up. 'A *Boche*, a *sale Boche*? Come with me.' He took me by the hand and we went down to the kitchen.

On one side of the garde-manger stood all the cooks; on the other, the waiters, most of whom were Germans. But the French and the Italian waiters were also with them, for all waiters hate all cooks and all cooks hate all waiters. In the forefront of the waiters was Monsieur Victor; in the van of the cooks stood the first chef.

One side was dressed in white, the other in black. The cooks fiddled around in the air with knives and big ladles, and the waiters with napkins. They insulted each other and each other's countries; even the calm first chef was red in the face. The garde-manger lay on the floor, no longer kicking; sometimes he gulped and his lips fluttered. I thought he was going to die while we waited for an ambulance.

Everyone made room for Mr. Brauhaus. He waved them all back to work and went into the office with the first chef and me. 'You hear me, Chef,' he said, 'I don't want no gotdemn badriodism in this gotdemn hotel, only good cooking and good service is what I want, Cheeses Greisd!' If the cook had done his work, he said, and not called me a '*sale Boche*,' he would not have had his head knocked in; he got what he deserved and he, Brauhaus, wasn't sorry for him. 'This little poy is not to blame, it's your gotdemn dumm cooks,' he shouted.

When the garde-manger came out of the hospital after some days, he waited for me on the service stairs of the hotel. 'Hsst!' he said, and pointed to his head turbaned in bandages. 'You know,' he went on, 'perhaps I should not have insulted you. I am sorry and here is my hand.' I shook his hand. 'But,' he said, pointing again to his head, 'it would be very dear for you, my friend, if I should make you pay for the pain. But let us forget that, I will ask you to pay only for the doctor and the hospital. Here is the bill, it is seventy-five dollars.'

I did not have that much money, of course, but Monsieur Serafini lent it to me out of his pocket after I had signed a note promising to pay it back in weekly installments of five dollars.

Mr. Sigsag

ONE MORNING I slipped and upset a tray full of breakfasts that were wanted in a hurry. It was on a day when the German Ambassador, Count von Bernstorff, and his attaché von Papen were in a hurry to get to Washington. They complained about missing the train, or going without breakfast, and they complained outside at the front office, which was bad, because it came back from there directly to Monsieur Victor and could not be hushed up by Monsieur Serafini. And when Serafini tried to dissuade Victor from firing me, he was reminded of the Affair of the Garde-Manger. I was discharged.

But because Monsieur Serafini was my friend and I still owed him money, he got me a job in the Grill Room behind the restaurant. The Grill was also under the charge of a man named Victor, but whereas Victor of the restaurant was corpulent, Victor of the Grill was thin. Fat Victor was German, but thin Victor was Hungarian, and therefore more elegant. They hated each other, never spoke, and thin Victor undoubtedly engaged me because it would annoy the restaurant's Monsieur Victor.

Thin Victor was never arrogant to his guests; the bad ones he would keep waiting with promises, and then hide them behind pillars. He had a sense of humor, but also theatrical attacks of temper. When something went wrong, he would wring his hands in front of his guests and call the waiters 'criminals'; he would stamp his feet at an omelet that was not fluffy enough, but he was good to work for; unlike the other Monsieur Victor, who fired someone every day, he discharged no one if he could possibly help it.

All the *maître d'hôtel* and all the chefs de rang in front looked down upon the staff of the Grill Room. These men were shorter and fatter, as the room was also lower and the columns at its sides thicker and shorter. The waiters here were mostly Italians, with a few Armenians and Bohemians and a Greek. They spoke bad French and waited on a lower class of people. Pushed away to one side of the Grill Room, which was always full, was a three-piece orchestra whose only function was to drown out the noise of the service, the clatter of dishes, glasses, and silver.

The great Society went in front; back here came musical comedy stars, and millionaires in search of a quiet corner behind a pillar, where they could not be seen while they squeezed the hands of their young women. Here came film presidents, who ate in a hurry and chattered and haggled over the table with knives or forks in their hands; stockbrokers, owners of fur businesses, people who ran fast, risky undertakings, who talked of nothing but money. They spent it freely too, and made few demands except for hurried service. In the lobby, one could separate them: the sheep going to the restaurant, the wolves to the Grill.

My job was to stand in a white apron and help fix up a buffet, to wheel around curries and learn to slice ham and to cut up ducks, chickens, and turkeys. I thus became acquainted with a little Bohemian waiter stationed way in the back of this room. His name was Wladimir Slezack, but since no one could pronounce it, it had gradually become Mr. Sigsag. He was the smallest man in the restaurant, and because he worked very hard and was very fast on his feet, he was a favorite of thin Victor.

WORK

Every waiter in a hotel has a 'side job.' A side job is extra work, other than serving, that he must perform before or after meals; most of it is done in the morning. One man is in charge of filling and collecting all the salt and pepper and paprika shakers and seeing that they are kept clean. Others must get the clean linen from the linen room every morning and check it at night; others collect the dirty linens. Two who write a good hand get out of unpleasant work by writing little menus for special parties and keeping various accounts. Another has to keep the stock of sauces and pickles, make the French and Russian salad dressing, keep clean the oil and vinegar bottles and the mustard pots. This side job is called the 'drug store,' and it was assigned to Mr. Sigsag.

Mr. Sigsag lived in a little room on the East Side, where he read the works, in many volumes bound in limp green leather with gold stamping, of a man who called himself the 'Sage of East Aurora.' These concerned trips to the homes of great men, but the biggest book was one entitled *Elbert Hubbard's Scrapbook* (that was the name of the Sage). With these books and included in their total price had come candlesticks, jars of honey, maple sugar candies, and other souvenirs, all in the one package with the volumes. When I visited him he was expecting some new volumes from East Aurora, this time with bookends included to hold his little library together.

Mr. Sigsag studied these books earnestly and drew the lessons from them that he should. They filled him with respect for a life of work and success. He was also a student by correspondence of the La Salle University and had subscribed to several courses, but he told me that what was most important in life was not knowledge, or hard work, but the right connections, also the ability to 'sell' oneself, to call guests by their correct names and to remember their faces.

From his library, now lying one volume on top of another, he took a book of which he was very fond, a waiter's bible. After his working hours at the Bristol in Vienna, he had attended a school which the hôteliers of Vienna maintained for the training of new waiters. He graduated from it with high honors. A diploma, a colored lithograph, decorated like a menu with pheasants, geese, wine bottles, and grapes, surrounded his name printed in the center. It was signed by the dean of the school and the president of the Society of Hôteliers, Restaurateurs, Cafetiers, and Innkeepers of Vienna and by the city's burgomaster, and hung in a frame over Mr. Sigsag's desk. So well had he been liked at the school, that the *maître d'hôtel* principal had had him pose for the photographs that illustrated the manual of the waiter's art, which was learnedly entitled: *Ein Leitfaden der Servierkunde mit besonderer Berücksichtigung des Küchenwesens* ('An Introduction to the Science of Serving, with Special Reference to Culinary Matters').

The photographs showed Mr. Sigsag, a little waiter in a tailcoat, standing in the proper positions for receiving a guest and for recommending dishes from the menu, and also standing incorrectly while doing this. They showed him handing a newspaper to a guest, carrying a tray, lighting a diner's cigar, and demonstrating how to carry the sidetowel, as well as various ways of how not to carry it. There was a list of books at the end of the book, for further study, among them the *Almanach de Gotha* and various cookbooks, and there were color charts of sleeve stripes and collar stars showing the various grades of army and naval officers. One whole chapter was given over to the art of folding napkins in the shapes of swans, windmills, boats, and fans.

Mr. Sigsag spent his free time puttering on a second-hand motorboat which he kept up near Dyckman Street; he asked me to visit him there sometimes. Two weeks from the day I first visited him, he told me that thin Victor was giving a party at a small place outside of the city, along the ocean, in Bath Beach. Several of the *maîtres d'hôtel*, the head cashier Madame Dombasle, and even the room clerk were invited to it, and so was he, Sigsag, because of his motorboat, in which he was to take Madame Dombasle and her two beautiful daughters out there. After the luncheon he would take all the guests for a little fishing trip, and Monsieur Victor would pay for the oil and the gasoline. A little more work had to be done on the boat and Mr. Sigsag invited me to help him and to come along to the party.

He seemed to have influence. We got days off, with mysterious ease, to work on the boat. These were lovely days. Arriving at Dyckman Street by subway, we put on old pants and undershirts and washed and scraped the little boat as it stood high and dry on the land while Mr. Sigsag talked of the importance of having friends and of working hard, and also of Madame Dombasle's two beautiful daughters.

Mr. Sigsag, who always played as seriously as a little boy, had ordered two uniforms for us: for himself a double-breasted, gold-buttoned blue coat and a white cap with the name of his ship, the *Wahabee*, in gold lettering on it; and another with a little less gold for me. The boat was finally burned off, scraped, and painted and the one hard job after calking it was to get the red paint at the bottom to end in a straight line in spite of the curve of the wide belly of the boat.

Mr. Sigsag

Later we went to a little lunch-wagon where we got wonderful ham and eggs, and some beer to take back with us to the boat. Then we lit a lamp, and if one did not look at the big electric powerhouse across the river, this was a scene of peace. The niceness of people could be seen here in their desire to flee from the city; all about us were other little grounded boats, on which men had labored after working hours, quiet, simple men with pipes and old clothes and without much money. The decks of their boats, high above the land and surrounded by grass, looked amusing; on them sat their wives and cooked on little oilburners or gasoline stoves. The boats were of comical design: impossible cabins were built on decks much too small for them and had to be broken up, with half a cabin in the stern and another piece of it stuck on in the bow. On some of them were little roof gardens with flowerboxes, hammocks, easy chairs, and even birdcages. They made up a little city of green, yellow, and blue houses that could swim away. It had none of that impersonal elegance or mass ugliness of manufactured things; everyone had done something with his own hands for his own pleasure. It was all so happy and sad and, above all, good; even the ground was nice, covered with coils of rope, old dinghies, rusted anchors, and green and red lanterns.

As the lights grew stronger in the little portholes and were reflected on the sides of the boats next to them, and the gramophones started to play, and the smell of food came out of imitation funnels, we stopped work and sat in the cabin while Mr. Sigsag told me of his youth.

Wladimir Slezack, the eleventh son of a Bohemian blacksmith, was born in a village two hours out of Przemysl. When he was old enough, though still a child, his father paid to have him apprenticed as a piccolo at the great Hotel King Wenzeslaus in Przemysl. Here he served part of his apprenticeship and then went on to Vienna, where, his recommendations being of the best, he got a job in a small hotel.

The child piccolo is an institution in all European restaurants. His head barely reaches above the table; his ears are red and stand out, because everybody pulls them. And when he is a man, he will still pull his head quickly to one side if anyone close to him suddenly moves, because he always did that to soften the blows that rained on him from the proprietor down to the last chambermaid; they hit him mostly out of habit.

For the rest the boy learned to wash glasses, to fold newspapers into the bamboo holders and hang them on the wall, to learn the grade of an officer by the stars on his collar, to bow, to chase flies from the tables without upsetting the glasses, to carry water and coffee without spilling, and to know the fifty-one varieties of coffee that are served in Viennese restaurants.

He studied how to make up and write the bill of fare, let the awnings up and down over the sidewalk in the summer, and scatter ashes out on the ice on winter mornings. He also cleaned ashtrays and matchstands, and one could still see his right thumb bent sideways from polishing two hundred of these every day; they were made of a light-colored, very sensitive brass, and the cigarettes burned deep stains into them that were hard to get out.

The boys started to work at six in the morning; they ate standing up, and got to bed at eleven at night. A free day was not provided for, since on Sundays and holidays the restaurant was busier than on other days, serving happy people. The piccolos slept in the restaurant, and Wladi, who was the smallest of them, slept in a kitchen drawer under the pastry cook's noodle board, where it was warm. The others had to sleep in the dining-room on cold benches under which their dirty pillows and covers were stowed away in a drawer during the day.

Little Waldi was fortunate not only in his sleeping quarters, in which he was at least warm, but also in his parentage. So many of the other boys were the chance sons of a chambermaid and a transient guest or waiter, or at best a soldier loved on a bench when the trees were in bloom and all was beautiful on the Prater.

A restaurant in the morning, before it is aired and swept, and the guests enter, is an unhappy place. The stale smells of tobacco smoke, of empty beer and wine glasses, and of spilled food and coffee stay and hang about the draperies and furniture. It is no place for a growing child; this life eventually draws on the faces of these little boys two lines from their nostrils to the corner of their young lips and it makes them pale and brings out the thin veins at their temples. They get to look tired and high-bred; in later years this pallor and nervousness will give them just the right touch of grand hotel elegance they will need for their parts. The boys also learn to repeat the smut they hear from the guests, and to smoke, and to drink themselves to sleep.

Nevertheless, the piccolo was looked upon with envy by the apprentices of plumbers and cobblers; they had the red ears, too, but not enough to eat, and no cigarettes, no drinks, no tips. The piccolo could at least save money. It was the custom in Austria for guests to leave three separate tips. The biggest was for the *Zahlkellner*, the captain to whom one paid the bill and who had taken the order; the next was for the *Speisenträger* or *Saalkellner*, the ordinary waiter who actually served one; and the third, a little stack of coppers, was for the piccolo. These three tips had to be left in clearly defined heaps and far enough apart from each other;

for the restaurant law was that all the coins that the first waiter could get within the reach of his outstretched thumb and index finger was his. That is why, in old Viennese restaurants the three tips were always left very far apart from one another, almost on the edges of the small marble tables.

Despite the big hands of the headwaiters, the piccolo was often able to earn and put aside a good sum of money; he had little chance to spend it. His dress coat, a child's garment, he had made by a cheap tailor, or bought it second-hand from another piccolo; his trousers could be dark blue or gray, for in the bad light of the restaurants no one could see below the levels of the tables; finally there was a waistcoat. Under the latter the piccolo need not wear a shirt; a celluloid plastron, like a bosom cut out of an evening shirt, was attached by a button to his celluloid collar, and a tie held the arrangement together. Save for his shoes and socks, the dickey and cuffs, which were stuck in his coat sleeves, the piccolo stood naked in his trousers and frock-coat. His hair was plastered down with brilliantine, and kept in order with a greasy comb that he carried in his waistcoat pocket.

He knew all about love and women, and had never played. He looked most unhappy when in the spring he brought ice cream out to the restaurant garden for some well-dressed child with its father and mother, who smiled at him when the music played and the large-grained sand was hard to walk on. And when one sees somewhere in a cheap restaurant, say in a beer hall in Coney Island, one of those old waiters who are known as 'hashers' leaning on a chair, with ugly, lightless eyes and a dead face that is filled with misery and meanness, one is seeing that little boy grown old, with flat crippled feet on which he has dragged almost to the end of his useless life his dead childhood.

But little Wladimir was made of stronger material, he survived, he went to school, he saved his money and paid his father back what had been spent to make him a piccolo, and he went to France and England and finally to America. Now he had a job as chef de rang in the best hotel in New York, in the Grill Room of the Splendide, and the *maître d'hôtel* was his friend. When looked at from Przemysl, this was as great and brave a success as any recorded in the high tales Mr. Sigsag read in the honey and candlestick books of Elbert Hubbard.

After he had ended his story, Mr. Sigsag looked in his little account book; he had set aside a certain sum for entertainment, another for the launching of the boat, for the uniforms and the beer, but we also needed some food to serve on the trip. He promised to show me something tomorrow: how to get a little food without paying for it.

The next day, after all the guests had left and the lights were turned out in the Grill Room and the cashier had added up her bills, closed the books, and gone away with the money, Mr. Sigsag led me to the little tiled closet where he prepared his salad dressings. He kept all his sauces, the mayonnaise, and the mustards in an icebox which had a small door, about three feet high and four wide, at the height of his head; he had to stand on a box to reach into it. This mustard closet was built into a huge refrigerator that opened out on the kitchen and had its back to the Grill Room, and it hung like a cage some feet above the level of the kitchen.

Mr. Sigsag made sure no one was around and then started to take everything out of the small icebox. He placed on a table the bottles of chili sauce, A-One sauce, sauce Escoffier, walnut and tarragon sauce, all the vinegar bottles, the chutneys, and the twenty-five French and twenty-five English mustard pots which were in daily use. Then he lifted out the grating on which the bottles had stood, and now I could see the big kitchen icebox filled with cheeses, tubs of rolled butter in ice water, and salads. He brought over a chair and asked me to hold his legs while he reached for a cheese.

'Shh,' said Mr. Sigsag, and I looked around once more; there was no one outside. He climbed in and reached down, but he was too short to reach the cheeses. I held his knees, then his ankles, and then his shoes; then I had his shoes in my hands and Mr. Sigsag was down with his face in some Camembert. Also there was a noise. I closed the icebox door. It was the night watchman; he looked in and I polished away at some bottles. The man sat down, lit a pipe, and started to talk; it was a long time before he left again on his rounds.

In the meantime, Mr. Sigsag had been trying to get up; kneeling and standing and sliding and then sitting down again in all kinds of cheese. He first handed out a Pont Lévêque, hard and solid. 'There will be trouble anyway,' he said, 'we might as well take it along.' Then he gave me his cold hands, but for some time I could not lift him out. They were smeared with cheese and slipped out of mine. I gave him a napkin, with which he cleaned his face and hands, and finally I could pull him out, his sleeves and trousers full of cheese. He took a shower downstairs, and washed his trousers, but he still smelled.

The next morning, Sunday, I met him very early at the boat, which was in the water now, looking new and beautiful. The sun had just risen and shone warmly on the planks. We put the beer on board, and the cheese, also knives and paper napkins, and then we dressed in the uniforms, scattered around cushions, bought oil and gasoline, and started off, past the electric light plant, and out into the Hudson, under the railroad bridge at Spuyten Duyvil.

The trouble started at about One Hundred and Sixty-eighth Street – pop, then pop, and poppoppop, and one more pop, and the motor stopped. The boat started to rock and turn around. Mr. Sigsag took a big piece of motor out of the one large cylinder, sandpapered the points, and poured some mixture he called 'dynamite' out of a little can into the cylinder. The motor almost flew out of the boat and tiny lightning flashes shot out all over the loose parts. This happened three more times before we reached the Battery, and Mr. Sigsag's uniform was soiled with fingermarks.

'There they are,' said Mr. Sigsag and pointed to three women, who were strolling up and down to the left of the Aquarium. Madame Dombasle and her two daughters were very French-looking and sweet in their airy batiste gowns that reached to the floor. Madame carried a fragile parasol and the young girls wore large satin sashes and bows around their waists and openwork gloves up to their elbows. We tooted the whistle three times and they waved their arms and the parasol.

The entrance to the little harbor at the Battery is hard to negotiate; there are strong currents and only a small opening between high sea walls. We almost made it, were swept away, and then turned and tried again; finally, by keeping the boat, which was almost as wide as it was long, away from the wall of one side with a hook and on the other with our feet, we made the calm square of water, filled with driftwood and a broken life preserver. Madame was helped on board, which was not easy, for she was stout and giggled and did not jump when Mr. Sigsag said 'jump.' She almost got one foot between the pier and the boat. The daughters, tall, lovely, dark, and young, were easier.

Madame admired the boat, the uniforms, *le petit commandant*. 'How many tons has your little liner?' she asked. Mr. Sigsag took them to the roof of the cabin from which they could enjoy the best view of the harbor; there they sat on cushions, under the parasol, and smiled back, a little afraid, jumping when we tooted the horn as a signal that we were off.

I steered the boat while Mr. Sigsag sat in front and explained New York to the ladies, who, having landed in Boston, had not seen much of it – the beautiful bridges, the Statue of Liberty, the ferryboats, the tall buildings. There is a powerful current here; the tide comes in through the Narrows, and it is besides a very much disturbed area of water. There is much driftwood that may get into the propeller, and ocean liners go in and out, fire and police boats, private yachts, the great Staten Island ferryboats making high waves, railroad tugs with strings of cars on long barges. Waves came in from all directions, so that one cannot bother to cut them at the proper angles, and the little boat was tossed high and to all sides.

I noticed that after half an hour we had not reached the

latitude of Governor's Island; in another half-hour the prison on that island moved slowly past and ten minutes later the motor coughed and stopped. Mr. Sigsag was just serving beer and cheese sandwiches. While Madame Dombasle and her daughters rose up and down in front, Mr. Sigsag disappeared inside to fix the motor. We lost much distance and were back again near the prison and close to the island; then came a ferryboat and the ladies were wetted to the knees. They shrieked but they were afraid to move, and looked around just as Mr. Sigsag came out of the cabin. The smell of oil and beer and the rocking had made him sick and he bent over the side of the boat. When I saw that, I also got sick. The boat turned again. Mr. Sigsag got up, took a deep breath, smiled at the ladies, and then went in to his motor again.

Then the ladies got sick and held onto each other. In the low cabin were two benches: Mr. Sigsag put the cushions on them and slowly pulled Madame Dombasle back on the narrow gangway, knocking her head as they went in. When she had lain down, Mr. Sigsag offered her some beer, but she whimpered: 'No, please, no.' The daughters got sicker and the younger one was taken down and laid on the other bench with her long slim legs folded back. The bottles rolled over the cabin top and jumped into the bay.

We crossed over away from the main current and made better speed along the Staten Island shoreline. Mr. Sigsag felt better and cracked jokes, but in the cabin the ladies were sick again, and seasick women are not attractive. One of the daughters came out for air, her dress wet and ruined; she sat up bravely and leaned into the wind and brushed her black hair from her cheeks where it was stuck in spittle. We forged slowly ahead, and it is a wonderful thing that a boat goes on even when everybody on board is feeling terrible.

We turned past the Arsenal at Fort Totten and went to the right and finally came to Bath Beach, where we tooted the horn again. Thin Victor and his wife, the *maîtres d'hôtel,* and Mr. Fassi, the chief room clerk, were at the dock to meet us. They all looked strange without their dress coats and stiff shirts, wearing instead gay suits with belts at the back and straw hats with colored bands; but when we arrived there was as much scraping and bowing as at the hotel. The color came back to our ladies' faces; they retired to a room and came down again in good order, with hardly a trace of damage in their clothes and hair. Frenchwomen know how to repair themselves very quickly after a disaster. The trip was soon forgotten and even laughed over.

Built of wood, with whitewashed stone urns around it, in which were planted palms, the old hotel gave one somehow a feeling of vacation and freedom. It stood near the shore in a large garden with children's swings in it. The Hungarian chief bus boy had decorated a corner of the dining-room, which was panelled with long strips of dark-varnished wood and contained a piano. There were flowers on the table, and one of the Splendide cooks had been brought out to prepare a very good meal. There was a printed menu and good wines; cigars and cigarettes were handed around; and the *maîtres d'hôtel* sat about in accented comfort, their legs spread wide apart, smoking with a careless air, and saying with face, hands, and feet: 'We are gentlemen today.' Also they summoned the old waiter by calling 'Psst,' something they themselves detested when the guests in the Splendide did it, but here it meant: 'See how thoroughly we can be guests.'

Madame Dombasle and her beautiful daughters were toasted; then the younger one, Céleste, sat down at the piano and played. The instrument needed tuning, many of the strings rattled in rust, and it sounded as if one were hearing an echo, but she played several salon pieces, '*Ouvre tes yeux bleus, ma mignonne,*' and '*Si j'avais des ailes.*' Then there was conversation, everyone sat down, and Monsieur Victor spoke.

As would an old colonel explain delicate tactical problems to his subalterns, so he went over many phases of his career. The talk covered the Continent; it was of glorious dinners, of places and people, of Monte Carlo and Ostende, of the Carlton in London, of encounters with difficult guests of the highest position, of Prince Bibesco, the Kaiser, and other trying cases, and of old King Leopold. Victor told of the time when His Majesty, Alfonso of Spain, came to the Carlton grill, and there was only one table left, reserved for Marie Tempest, the actress, who came in just as the King did. It was a breathless moment. 'I don't know how I did it, it came to me from somewhere, the inspiration,' said Victor, but he solved the terrible dilemma – simply with the phrase, 'The great king, the great actress,' and he sat them both down at the same table. A whispered 'Ah' went around our table, accompanied by French, Italian, Hungarian, and German gestures of appreciation of so brilliant a performance.

Thin Victor shrugged his shoulders at these expressions of grateful admiration from his *maîtres d'hôtel* and went on to the problems confronting him now, reviewing matters that had gone badly or very well. The *maîtres d'hôtel* furnished details, agreed or disputed as to dates or the number of people that had been at a certain table on a certain day or the dishes they had ordered. It slowed up the storytelling, but it brought them closer together. Their eyes hung on Victor's lips.

Next to me, all the way at the end of the table, sat Mr. Sigsag, and when I sometimes asked him a question, he said: 'Shh!' very angrily, and listened intently to the head of the table, and laughed at the jokes, and looked dark at serious passages. He let no detail escape him.

Only one man remained aloof. This was Fassi, the room clerk, who had observed a certain distance all evening long. He sat at the right of Victor; smoking his cigar and gazing at the ash, he carried to his table the disdain of the front office for restaurant and kitchen help. Only when Victor told what Mr. Joseph Widener had ordered for dinner yesterday did Fassi stir and say: 'Ah, yes, yes, yes, Joseph Widener,' leaving the Mr. off, 'Joseph Widener, I spoke to him only yesterday, no, Thursday, wasn't it?' and he made it clear therewith that, while Victor took the orders of Mr. Widener, he, Fassi, spoke to the great man about the weather, about horses, and about the general things men talk about.

Most of the time I spent looking at Madame Dombasle's beautiful daughters. Frenchwomen, I think, are rarely beautiful, but when they are they hurt with their perfection. There was dancing afterwards, and the room clerk danced with one of the daughters, Victor with the other, and Mr. Sigsag with the mother.

The party was not without some profit to me, for when I came to change my apron the next day, the Hungarian chief bus boy said loudly, so that all the others could hear: 'Guess how many glasses of Tokay I drank last night at Monsieur Victor's party. You saw me there, didn't you?' He had more respect for me from then on as did also the *maîtres d'hôtel*. Madame Dombasle corrected my French mistakes at her desk, and Victor let me carry his dress coat to his tailor to have a new lining put in. As for Mr. Sigsag, he was soon a *maître d'hôtel*, and we never heard anything about the cheese.

Art at the Hotel Splendide

'FROM NOW on,' lisped Monsieur Victor, as if he were pinning on me the Grand Cross of the Legion of Honor, 'you will be a waiter.'

It was about a year after I had gone to work at the Splendide as Mespoulets's bus boy, and only a month or two after I had been promoted to *commis*. A *commis* feels more self-satisfied than a bus boy and has a better life all around, but to become a waiter is to make a really worthwhile progress.

The cause of my promotion was a waiters' mutiny. On a rainy afternoon several of the waiters had suddenly thrown down their napkins and aprons and walked out. One had punched the chief bus boy in the nose and another had upset a tray filled with Spode demitasse cups. They wanted ten dollars a week instead of six; they wanted to do away with certain penalties that were imposed on them, such as a fine of fifty cents for using a serving napkin to clean an ashtray; and they wanted a full day off instead of having to come back on their free day to serve dinner, which was the custom at the Splendide, as at most other New York hotels. The good waiters did not go on strike. A few idealists spoke too loudly and got fired, and a lot of bad waiters, who had mediocre stations, left.

After my promotion I was stationed at the far end of the room, on the 'undesirables'' balcony, and my two tables were next to Mespoulets's.

It rained all that first day and all the next, and there were no guests on the bad balcony. With nothing to do, Mespoulets and I stood and looked at the ceiling, talked, or sat on overturned linen-baskets out in the pantry and yawned. I drew some pictures on my order-pad – small sketches of a pantryman, a row of glasses, a stack of silver trays, a bus boy counting napkins. Mespoulets had a rubber band, which, with two fingers of each hand, he stretched into various geometric shapes. He was impressed by my drawings.

The second night the dining-room was half full, but not a single guest sat at our tables. Mespoulets pulled at my serving napkin and whispered, 'If I were you, if I had your talent, that is what I would do,' and then he waved his napkin toward the center of the room.

There a small group of the best guests of the Splendide sat at dinner. He waved his napkin at Table No. 18, where a man was sitting with a very beautiful woman. Mespoulets explained to me that this gentleman was a famous cartoonist, that he drew pictures of a big and a little man. The big man always hit the little man on the head. In this simple fashion the creator of those two figures made a lot of money.

We left our tables to go down and look at him. While I stood off to one side, Mespoulets circled around the table and cleaned the cartoonist's ashtray so that he could see whether or not the lady's jewelry was genuine. 'Yes, that's what I would do if I had your talent. Why do you want to be an actor? It's almost as bad as being a waiter,' he said when we returned to our station. We walked down again later on. This time Mespoulets spoke to the waiter who served Table No. 18, a Frenchman named Herriot, and asked what kind of guest the cartoonist was. Was he liberal?

'Ah,' said Herriot, 'c'ui là? Ah, oui alors! C'est un très bon client, extrêmement généreux. C'est un gentleman par excellence.' And in English he added, 'He's A-1, that one. If only they were all like him! Never looks at the bill, never complains – and so full of jokes! It is a pleasure to serve him. C'est un chic type.'

After the famous cartoonist got his change, Herriot stood by waiting for the tip, and Mespoulets cruised around the table. Herriot quickly snatched up the tip; both waiters examined it, and then Mespoulets climbed back to the balcony. 'Magnifique,' he said to me. 'You are an idiot if you do not become a cartoonist. I am an old man – I have sixty years. All my children are dead, all except my daughter Mélanie, and for me it is too late for anything. I will always be a waiter. But you – you are young, you are a boy, you have talent. We shall see what can be done with it.'

Mespoulets investigated the famous cartoonist as if he were going to make him a loan or marry his daughter off to him. He interviewed chambermaids, telephone operators, and room waiters. 'I hear the same thing from the rest of the hotel,' he reported on the third rainy day. 'He lives here at the hotel, he has a suite, he is married to a countess, he owns a Rolls-Royce. He gives wonderful parties, eats grouse out of season, drinks vintage champagne at ten in the morning. He spends half the year in Paris and has a place in the south of France. When the accounting department is stuck with a charge they've forgotten to put on somebody's bill they just put it on his. He never looks at them.'

'Break it up, break it up. Sh-h-h. Quiet,' said Monsieur Maxim, the *maître d'hôtel* on our station.

Mespoulets and I retired into the pantry, where we could talk more freely.

'It's a very agreeable life, this cartoonist life,' Mespoulets continued, stretching his rubber band. 'I would never counsel you to be an actor or an artist-painter. But a cartoonist, that is different. Think what fun you can have. All you do is think of amusing things, make pictures with pen and ink, have a big man hit a little man on the head, and write a few words over it. And I know you can do this easily. You are made for it.'

That afternoon, between luncheon and dinner, we went out to find a place where cartooning was taught. As we marched along Madison Avenue, Mespoulets noticed a man walking in front of us. He had flat feet and he walked painfully, like a skier going uphill.

Mespoulets said 'Pst,' and the man turned around. They recognized each other and promptly said, '*Ah, bonjour.*'

'You see?' Mespoulets said to me when we had turned into a side street. 'A waiter. A dog. Call "Pst," click your tongue, snap your fingers, and they turn around even when they are out for a walk and say, "Yes sir, no sir, *bonjour Monsieurdame.*" Trained poodles! For God's sakes, don't stay a waiter! If you can't be a cartoonist, be a street-cleaner, a dish-washer, anything. But don't be an actor or a waiter. It's the most awful occupation in the world. The abuse I have taken, the long hours, the smoke and dust in my lungs and eyes, and the complaints – *ah, c'est la barbe, ce métier.* My boy, profit by my experience. Take it very seriously, this cartooning.'

For months one does not meet anybody on the street with his neck in an aluminium-and-leather collar such as is worn in cases of ambulatory cervical fractures, and then in a single day one sees three of them. Or one hears Mount Chimborazo mentioned five times. This day was a flat-foot day. Mespoulets, like the waiter we met on Madison Avenue, had flat feet. And so did the teacher in the Andrea del Sarto Art Academy. Before this man had finished interviewing me, Mespoulets whispered in my ear, 'Looks and talks like a waiter. Let's get out of here.'

On our way back to the hotel we bought a book on cartooning, a drawing-board, pens and a penholder, and several soft pencils. On the first page of the book we read that before one could cartoon or make caricatures, one must be able to draw a face – a man, a woman – from nature. That was very simple, said Mespoulets. We had lots of time and the Splendide was filled with models. Two days later he bought another book on art and we visited the Metropolitan Museum. We bought all the newspapers that had comic strips. And the next week Mespoulets looked around, and everywhere among the guests he saw funny people. He continued to read to me from the book on how to become a cartoonist.

WORK

The book said keep a number of sharpened, very soft pencils handy for your work. I did, and for a while I was almost the only waiter who had a pencil when a guest asked for one. 'And remember,' said the book, 'you can never be an expert in caricaturing people unless you shake off the fear of drawing people.' I tried to shake off the fear.

'Most people like to have their own pictures drawn,' Mespoulets read solemnly. 'Regular-featured people should be avoided, as they are too simple to draw. Your attention should be concentrated on the faces with unique features.'

The most 'unique' faces at the Splendide belonged to Monsieur and Madame Lawrance Potter Dreyspool. Madame Dreyspool was very rich; her husband was not. He traveled with her as a sort of companion-butler, pulling her chair, helping her to get up, carrying books, flasks, dog-leashes, small purchases, and opera-glasses. He was also like the attendant at a sideshow, for Madame was a monstrosity and everyone stared at her. They were both very fat, but she was enormous. It was said that she got her clothes from a couturier specializing in costumes for women who were *enceinte*, and that to pull everything in shape and get into her dresses she had to lie down on the floor. She was fond of light pastel-colored fabrics, and her ensembles had the colors of pigeons, hyacinths, and boudoir upholstery. Her coat covered her shoes and a wide fur piece her neck, and even in the middle of winter she wore immense garden hats that were as elaborate as wedding cakes.

Monsieur and Madame Dreyspool were the terror of *maîtres d'hôtel* all over the world. Wherever they stayed, they had the table nearest the entrance to the dining-room. This table was reserved for them at the Splendide in New York, at Claridge's in

London, at the Ritz in Paris, and in various restaurants on the luxurious boats on which they crossed. Like the first snow-flakes, Monsieur and Madame Dreyspool always appeared in the Splendide at the beginning of the season. They left for Palm Beach at the first sign of its end.

Their entrance into the dining-room was spectacular. First Madame waddled in, then Monsieur with a Pekingese, one of the few dogs allowed in the main dining-room. Madame answered with one painful nod Monsieur Victor's deep bow, climbed up the two steps to the balcony on the right, where their table was, and elaborately sat down. Everyone in society knew them and nodded, coming in and going out. Monsieur and Madame thanked them briefly from the throne. They never spoke to each other and they never smiled.

Monsieur Dreyspool had consoled himself with whiskey so many years that his face was purple. The gossip in the couriers' dining-room, where the valets and maids and chauffeurs ate, was that he also consoled himself with Susanne, Madame's personal maid. He did not seem so fat when he was alone, but when he and Madame were sitting together at their table on the good balcony, they looked like two old toads on a lily leaf.

The *maître d'hôtel* who took care of them was a Belgian and had come from the Hôtel de Londres in Antwerp. He never took his eyes off their table, and raced to it whenever Monsieur Dreyspool turned his head. Monsieur and Madame were waited upon by a patient old Italian waiter named Giuseppe. Because he never lost his temper and never made mistakes, he got all the terrible guests, most of whom paid him badly. Madame Dreyspool was not allowed any sugar. Her vegetables had to be cooked in a special fashion. A long letter of instruction about her various peculiarities hung in the offices of the chefs and *maîtres d'hôtel* of all the hotels she went to. It was mailed ahead to the various managers by Monsieur.

The exit of Monsieur and Madame Dreyspool was as festive as the entrance. When they were ready to leave, the *maître d'hôtel* pulled Monsieur's chair out. Monsieur pulled out Madame's chair. Madame produced the dog from her generous lap – it had slept there under a fold of the tablecloth while she ate – and gave the dog to Monsieur, who placed it on the carpet. Then the *maître d'hôtel*, taking steps as small as Madame's, escorted her out, walking on her left side and talking to her solicitously, his face close to hers. Monsieur followed about six feet behind, with a big Belinda Fancy Tales cigar between his teeth, his hands in his pockets, and the leash of the dog slipped over one wrist. From where Mespoulets and I stood on the bad balcony, she looked like several pieces of comfortable furniture piled together under a velvet cover and being slowly pushed along on little wheels.

Mespoulets was convinced that Madame Dreyspool was the very best possible model for me to begin drawing. The book said not to be afraid. 'Take a piece of paper,' it said, 'draw a line down the centre, divide this line, and draw another from left to right so that the paper is divided into four equal parts.' I took an old menu and stood on the good balcony between a screen and a marble column. It was possible there to observe and sketch Madame Dreyspool unnoticed. I divided the back of the menu into four equal parts. Once I started to draw, I saw that Madame's left half-face extended farther out from the nose than her right and that one eye was always half closed. When someone she knew came in, the eyelid went up over the rim of the pupil in greeting and the corners of the lips gave a short upward jump and then sank down again into a steady mask of disgust.

Monsieur and Madame were easy to draw, they hardly moved. They sat and stared – stared, ate, stared, stirred their coffee. Only their eyes moved, when Giuseppe brought the cheese or the pastry tray. Quickly, shiftily, they glanced over it, as one looks at something distasteful or dubious. Always the same sideways glance at the cheek, at Giuseppe when he took the tip, at the Belgian *maître d'hôtel*, and at Monsieur Victor as they left.

I took my sketches back to Mespoulets, who had been studying the book on art in the linen closet. 'It shows effort and talent,' he said. 'It is not very good, but it is not bad. It is too stiff – looks too much like pigs, and while there is much pig at that table, it is marvellously complicated pig.' He considered the book a moment and then slapped it shut. 'I think,' he said, 'I understand the gist of art without reading any more of this. Try and be free of the helping lines. Tomorrow, when they come again, think of the kidney trouble, of the thousand pâtés and sauces they have eaten. Imagine those knees, the knees of Madame under the table – they must be so fat that faces are on each knee – two faces, one on each knee, laughing and frowning as she walks along. All that must be in the portrait. And the ankles that spill over her shoes – this must be evident in your drawing of her face.'

Monsieur and Madame came again the next day, and I stood under a palm and drew them on the back of another menu. Mespoulets came and watched me, broke a roll in half, and kneaded the soft part of the bread into an eraser. 'Much better,' he said. 'Try and try again. Don't give up. Remember the thousand fat sauces, the ankles. The eyes already are wonderful. Go ahead.'

He went back to his station, and soon after I heard 'Tsk, tsk, tsk, tsk!' over my shoulder. It was the Belgian *maître d'hôtel* and he was terror-stricken. He took the menu out of my hand and disappeared with it.

When I came to work the next noon I was told to report to the office of Monsieur Victor. I went to Monsieur Victor's desk. Slowly, precisely, without looking up from his list of reservations, he said, 'Ah, the *Wunderkind*.' Then, in the manner in which he discharged people, he continued, 'You are a talented young man. If I were you, I would most certainly become an artist. I think you should give all your time to it.' He looked up, lifted the top of his desk, and took out the portrait of Monsieur and Madame Lawrance Potter Dreyspool. 'As your first client, I would like to order four of these from you,' he said. 'Nicely done, like this one, but on good paper. If possible with some color – green and blue and purple. And don't forget Monsieur's nose – the strawberry effect, the little blue veins – or the bags under the eyes. That will be very nice. A souvenir for my colleagues in London, Paris, Nice, and one for the *maître d'hôtel* on the *Mauretania*. You can have the rest of the day off to start on them.'

The Homesick Bus Boy

IN A corner of the main dining-room of the Splendide, behind an arrangement of screens and large palms that were bedded in antique Chinese vases, six ladies of uncertain age used to sit making out luncheon and dinner checks. When a guest at the Splendide called for the bill, it was brought to him in longhand – contrary to the practice in most other hotels in New York City – in purple ink, on fine paper decorated with the hotel crest. The six ladies, seated at a long desk near the exit to the kitchens, attended to that. And since there were periods when they had little to do, one of them, a Miss Tappin, found time to befriend the bus boy Fritzl, from Regensburg.

Fritzl was not much more than a child. He wore a white jacket and a long white apron, and he carried in his pocket a comb which he had brought all the way from Regensburg. A scene of the city was etched on the side of it. Fritzl's hair stood up straight, moist, and yellow, and he had the only red cheeks in the dining-room. When anyone spoke to him, his ears also turned red, and he looked as if he had just been slapped twice in the face.

Miss Tappin was very English. She had seen better days, and in her youth had travelled on the Continent. She detested the *maître d'hôtel*, the waiters, and the captains, but she was drawn to the lonesome bus boy, who seemed to be of nice family, had manners, and was shy. Fritzl did not like the *maître d'hôtel*, the waiters, or the captains either. Least of all he liked the waiter he worked for, a nervous wreck of a Frenchman who was constantly coming behind the screens and palms, saying 'Psst!' and dragging Fritzl out on to the floor of the restaurant to carry away some dirty dishes.

When Fritzl was thus called away, Miss Tappin would sigh and then look into the distance. She called Fritzl 'a dear,' and said that he was the living image of a nephew of hers who was at Sandhurst – the son, by a previous marriage, of her late sister's husband, a Major Graves. 'What a pity!' Miss Tappin would say whenever she thought of Fritzl. 'He's such a superior type, that boy. Such a dear. So unlike the bobtail, ragtag, and guttersnipes around him. I do hope he'll come through all right!' Then she would sigh again and go back to her bills. Every time Fritzl passed the long desk, whether with butter, water-bottles, or dirty dishes, a quick signal of sympathy passed between them.

The conversations with Fritzl afforded Miss Tappin an exquisite weapon with which to irritate the other five ladies who shared the desk – women who came from places like Perth Amboy, Pittsburgh, and Newark. With Fritzl leaning on her blotter, she could discuss such topics as the quaintness of Munich and its inhabitants and the charm and grandeur of the Bavarian Alps. These beautiful mountains neither Fritzl nor Miss Tappin had ever seen. Regensburg is not far away from the Alps, but Fritzl's parents were much too poor ever to have sent him there. Miss Tappin's stay in Munich had been limited to a half-hour wait between trains at the railroad station while she was on her way to visit her sister in Budapest.

Regensburg, however, she soon came to know thoroughly from Fritzl, who often spread a deck of pocket-worn postcards and calendar pictures on the desk in front of her. These views showed every worthwhile street corner and square of his beloved city. He acquainted her with Regensburg's history and described its people and the surrounding country. He read her all the letters he received from home, and gradually Miss Tappin came to know everybody in Regensburg.

'Dear boy,' she would say, touching his arm, 'I can see it all clearly. I can picture your dear mother sitting in front of her little house on the banks of the Danube – the little radish garden, the dog, the cathedral, and the wonderful stone bridge. What a lovely place it must be!'

Then her eyes would cloud, for Miss Tappin had the peculiar British addiction to scenes that are material for postcards. Into the middle of these flights always came the nervous 'Psst!' of the old French waiter. Then Fritzl would lift his apron, stow the postcards away in the back pocket of his trousers, and run. When he passed that way later with a tray of dirty dishes, he sent her his smile, and again when he came back with an armful of water-bottles or a basin of cracked ice and a basket of bread. They recognized each other as two nice people do, walking their dogs in the same street.

WORK

Fritzl's service table stood in another corner of the restaurant, and near it was another palm in another Chinese vase. When he was not at Miss Tappin's desk or in the kitchen or busy with his dirty dishes, Fritzl hid behind this palm. He was afraid of everyone, even the guests. He came out from behind his palm only when his waiter called him, or when the orchestra played Wagner, Weber, or Strauss music, or when I, his other friend in the hotel, passed by.

By this time I was assistant manager in the banquet department, but Fritzl was not afraid of me. I was his friend because I, too, came from Regensburg. Sometimes when I appeared in the restaurant, Fritzl would lean out from behind his palm and say in a hoarse whisper, '*Du*, Ludwig, have you a minute for me?' Once he put his arm around my neck and started to walk with me through the dining-room as if we were boys in Regensburg. When I told him that that was not done, he looked hurt, but later, in the pantry, he forgave me and told me all the latest and most important news of Regensburg.

Another time he showed me a little book he had made out of discarded menus. In this book he had written down what he earned and what he spent. His income was eight dollars a week, and his expenses, including an English lesson at one dollar, were seven. In three years, he calculated, he would have enough money to go back to Regensburg. I told him he could make much more money if he attended to his job and got to be a waiter, and he said he would try. But Fritzl was very bad dining-room material. He was slow, earnest, and awkward. A good waiter jumps, turns fast, and has his eyes everywhere. One can almost tell by watching a new man walk across the room whether he will be a good or an indifferent waiter. One can also tell, as a rule, if he will last.

We sometimes took a walk together, Fritzl and I, usually up or down Fifth Avenue, in the lull between luncheon and dinner. One day, in the upper window of a store building near Thirty-fourth Street, Fritzl saw an advertisement that showed a round face smoking a cigar. Under the face was written, 'E. Regensburg & Sons, Havana Cigars.' From that day on, Fritzl always wanted to walk downtown towards Thirty-fourth Street. He would point up at the window as we passed and say, 'Look, Ludwig – Regensburg.'

He also liked to stop in front of St Patrick's Cathedral, because it reminded him of the Dom in Regensburg. But St Patrick's was not half as big as the Dom, he said, and its outside looked as if it were made of fresh cement, and its bells were those of a village church. He was very disappointed by the interior as well.

Once I took him on an excursion boat up the Hudson. 'Fritzl, look,' I said to him, 'isn't this river more beautiful than the Danube?'

He was quiet for several miles. Opposite Tarrytown, he said, 'It's without castles. I have not seen a single castle, only smoke-stacks.' Up at Poughkeepsie, he pointed to the railroad bridge and said, 'Look at it, and think of the stone bridge across the Danube at Regensburg. And besides, where is Vienna on this river, or a city like Budapest?' For the rest, he said, it was all right.

I sometimes wondered why Fritzl should love Regensburg, for I knew that he had grown up there in misery. His parents lived on the outskirts of the city and worked as tenants on a few soggy acres planted with radishes and cabbages. The land lay along the river and was submerged whenever the water rose. The Danube rose very often. The place where they lived was called Reinhausen. One came to it by crossing an old stone bridge and walking through another city, which was to Regensburg what Brooklyn is to New York. The people who lived in this small Brooklyn always explained why they were living there – the air was better, the view nicer, it was better for their children, quieter – but they all excused themselves. The place resembled Brooklyn also in that one got lost there very easily and that no cab-driver in Regensburg could find his way there without asking a policeman for directions.

When I asked Fritzl why he loved Regensburg so much, his answer sounded like Heinrich Heine. 'Do you remember the seven stone steps,' he said, 'the worn stones that lead down from the Street of St. Pancraz to the small fish market? The old ivy-covered fountain whose water comes from the mouth of two green dolphins? The row of tall oaks with a bench between every other pair of trees? The sand-pit next to the fountain where children play, where young girls walk arm in arm, where the lamp-lighter arrives at seven, and where, sitting on a bench, I can see, between the leaning walls of two houses, a wide strip of moving water – the Danube – and beyond it my parents' house? There I grew up. There every stone is known to me. I know the sound of every bell, the name of every child, and everyone greets me.'

Like a child himself then, he would repeat over and over, 'Oh, let me go home. I want to go home to Regensburg. Oh, I don't like it here. What am I here? Nobody. When I told Herr Professor Hellsang I wanted to come to America, he said to me, "*Ja*, go to America, become a waiter – the formula for every good-for-nothing. But remember, America is the land where the flowers have no perfume, where the birds lack song, and where the women offer no love." And Herr Professor Hellsang was right. It is so. Oh, I want to go back to Regensburg!'

When we returned to the hotel for an afternoon walk, Fritzl always disappeared into the Splendide's basement, where the dressing-rooms for the bus boys were, and changed his clothes. The other bus boys' lockers were lined with clippings from *La Vie Parisienne* and with pictures of cyclists and boxers. The door of Fritzl's was covered with views of Regensburg.

One evening Fritzl came up from his locker to assist at a dinner-party given by Lord Rosslare, who had ordered a fairly good dinner, long and difficult to serve. He was a moody client, gay one day, unbearable the next. When he complained, his voice could be heard out on the street. Rosslare's table was in the centre of the room, and next to it was a smaller table on which to ladle out the soup, divide the fish into portions, and carve the rack of lamb. The *maître d'hôtel* and his assistant supervised all this. Fritzl's waiter was moist with nervousness and fear. Everything went well, however, until the rack of lamb was to be carved.

The lamb had arrived from the kitchen and stood on an electric heater on Fritzl's service table behind the palm. Next to Lord Rosslare stood the *maître d'hôtel*, who intended to carve. He had the knife in one hand and a large fork in the other. He looked along the edge of the knife and tested its sharpness. The old waiter polished the hot plates in which the lamb was to be served and then carried the stack of them and the sauce to the table. Because the *maître d'hôtel* was shouting at him to hurry up, he told Fritzl to follow with the rack of lamb. All Fritzl had to do was to take the copper casserole and follow him. To save time, they walked across the dance-floor instead of around it. Rosslare leaned back and complained about the slowness of the service. The *maître d'hôtel* stamped his feet and waved the carving-knife. With his mouth stretched, he signalled to the old waiter and Fritzl so they could read his lips: '*Dépêchez-vous, espèces de salauds.*'

All this made Fritzl nervous, and in the middle of the dance-floor he tripped and fell. The rack of lamb jumped out of the casserole. Then an even more terrible thing happened. Fritzl, on all fours, crept over to the lamb, picked it up calmly and put it back in the casserole, licked his slippery fingers, got to his feet, and, to everyone's horror, carried it over to the table to be served.

Rosslare laughed. The whole dining-room laughed. Only Monsieur Victor, the *maître d'hôtel*, was not amused. He retired to his office and bit into his fist. Next day the captain at that station got a severe reprimand. The old waiter was to be laid off for two weeks and Fritzl was to be discharged.

In a hotel that employed hundreds of people there were always changes in personnel. And fortunately an old Greek who had been attendant in the men's washroom in the banquet department left on that day for his homeland. His job was vacant, and Fritzl got it.

In the washroom, Fritzl was his own master. There were no *maîtres d'hôtel*, captains, and waiters to be afraid of. No one said 'Psst!' and 'Come here!' to him. He began to be more cheerful. One of his uncles, he told me, a veteran of the War of 1870, had, in recognition of his services, been given the washroom concession at the Walhalla, a national shrine built of marble, like the washroom in the banquet department of the Splendide, and situated not far from Regensburg.

Every morning Fritzl went down to the storeroom and got his supply of brushes, soap, ammonia, and disinfectants. Next he went to the linen-room and exchanged his dirty towels for clean ones. Then he put his washroom in order. He whistled while he polished the knobs and handles and water-faucets, and when everything was shining he conscientiously flushed all the toilets and pressed the golden buttons that released a spray of water into the porcelain basins, to see that they were working. If any of the plumbing was out of order, he telephoned down to the engineers. At noon he reported to the banquet office and was told whether any parties would take place during the afternoon or evening. If the banquet-rooms were not engaged, he was free the rest of the day.

When Fritzl worked, he made good money. He soon learned to brush the guests off and to hold them up at the narrow door so that none escaped without producing a dime or a quarter. In busy seasons he sometimes made as much as thirty dollars a week.

He became more tolerant of America and found that, contrary to the belief of Herr Professor Hellsang, birds do sing here and flowers do have a perfume. Late at night, after he had locked up the men's room, Fritzl arranged his coins in neat stacks and entered the total in his book. He often came into the banquet office, when everyone else was gone, and asked to use my typewriter. On this machine, using two fingers, he slowly composed glowing prospectuses of the hotel – letters that his mother would proudly show around. On the hotel's stationery he wrote that the Splendide was the most luxurious hotel in the world; that it was twenty-two stories high; that it had seven hundred apartments, any one of which was better furnished than the rooms in the castle of the Duke of Thurn und Taxis in Regensburg; that in these apartments lived the richest people in America; that he was employed at a lucrative income in the Department of Sanitation; and that he would probably come home for a short visit in the summer.

Affair

JEWISH WEDDINGS were an important and very remunerative part of the Splendide's banqueting business. They took place in the relatively quiet months, and much money was spent on them for food, wine, and floral decorations. The menus were never less than seven dollars and fifty cents per person, and went up as high as fifteen dollars. The floral decorations cost on an average a thousand dollars, and this did not include the bouquets for the bride and the bridesmaids. Wines came to about another thousand dollars, and an orchestra to play during the ceremony, the dinner, and the dancing was again almost that much.

There was in addition a rental charge for the rooms of about three hundred dollars, about which most of them complained:

'They don't charge that at Sherry's or any place else.' For that Mr. Sigsag had learned a very cool answer, the only stiff words he ever used: 'Madame, the Splendide competes with no one.'

For such weddings, the Orchid Salon, the large staircase, the foyer of the Ballroom, and the Ballroom proper were used, to which were also added a suite in which the bride and groom could stay overnight and which was connected with the Ballroom by a high-speed elevator, and a room for each set of parents.

The ceremony is staged in the Orchid Salon, and after the ceremony the upper landing of the staircase provides an excellent place to kiss the bride, the scene being reflected in the forty panels of high mirrored doors that lead to the oval restaurant. The Kissing of the Bride takes a long time, so long that for a while before the conversation of the upcoming guests drowns it, one thinks a baby is being smacked on the backside. Then they climb up another beautiful staircase that swings left and right, to the Ballroom level, where caviar and cocktails are served until everybody has come up and the music can start. The curtains are drawn back, revealing the high mirrored Ballroom. The glasses, linen, and china shine on the tables in the glow of the candles. The lights of the chandeliers are reflected in the many mirrors; there are no columns to spoil the spacious effect. Public rooms should always be built like these to include several levels broken up by stairways, where women can stop, turn, go back again, up and down, and show their dresses.

The people who wished to have their daughter's wedding here were usually brought to the Splendide by a friend who had already given such a party. They came to the restaurant for luncheon, long before the date of the wedding. Mr. Sigsag went down with his date book, the day was chosen and booked, a deposit of several hundred dollars was paid, and the rooms were looked at. Mr. Sigsag had learned two phrases for these interviews which he thought very highly of and used very often. One was 'the Affair,' a word loved by the Jewish matrons: 'We were to an Affair at the Plaza.' The other he had fished out of the rotogravure sections of the Sunday newspapers – 'the Bride Elect.' Therefore we had constantly recurring in these conversations: 'We don't compete with anyone, Madame,' 'the Affair,' and 'the Bride Elect.'

There were many other visits after the first: plans were made and changed, menus worked over, wines selected, dishes tasted, music engaged, prices arrived at, cigars ordered. All this went into contracts and estimates. Then there were several rehearsals, at which some man who had made millions running a big business could be seen in all his awkwardness: always starting off with the wrong foot, almost falling down the stairs, and becoming more helpless the more he was talked to. For these rehearsals Mr. Sigsag sang: 'La la la la!' to the wedding march of *Lohengrin*. He upset tradition, too, by having the mothers of the bride and the groom march down in front of the procession a little ahead of the parade. They loved this.

When finally everything is settled and written down, all the details are gone over once more. The menu is most important and is discussed at length. The soup has to have something swimming in it; if it is a cream of asparagus, there must be little pieces of asparagus in it; it has to be thick and golden, so the spoon can almost be stood up in it. The fish is for the most part trout in butter with almonds, but of most concern is the squab, an individual squab chicken. They always anxiously come back to this, although the reputation of former weddings is great: 'You won't forget, Mr. Wladi?'

They look deeply into his eyes, when they talk or listen to him; he belongs to the family almost, and the father has slapped Mr. Sigsag on the back and told him to come to the store and he'll put a piece of goods on his back, the best in the place. 'You won't forget, Mr. Wladi, the individual broilers, with lots of gravy, lots of gravy. An individual broiler for everybody. We want this Affair to be a big success.'

'Yes, lots of gravy, Madame.' It is underlined in our copy of the estimate, and the order that goes down to the chef reads:

'*Poussins individuels, avec beaucoup de jus.*'

The salad, covered with Russian dressing, is a mixture of endives, a slice of pineapple, and a little ball of cream cheese with chopped chives. 'Mmm – oh, that's wonderful, Mr. Wladi.' Mr. Wladi has some six such terrible combinations which he has cut out from an advertisement in a magazine, a double page in full colors with which the chef almost threw him out of the office.

After this, the dessert. With a silver pencil that writes in three colours – red, yellow, and blue – Mr. Sigsag shows that 'it's a dream, a little temple of ice cream, on a floating block of ice, in which is a little light. Inside the temple are a miniature bride and groom, and around the ice are crushed strawberries or nectarines in a cream sauce.' For this all the lights will be lowered, and the music will play 'Midsummer Night's Dream,' and the waiters will march with all the little lights in their ice cream temples in a long row all around the room. The march is shown on the plan; that again is 'wonderful.'

While coffee is being served outside, the entire Ballroom will be transformed in fifteen minutes; when the curtains are again drawn back, the musicians will have eaten, the tables and service will have been cleared away, and there will be a wide dance-floor, with, at one end of the room, a large buffet containing a silver bowl of orangeade, drinks, and cigars and cigarettes. Fauteuils will be distributed on strips of carpet all around the room, in which the older people can sit while the waiters pass them refreshments.

Another great moment follows this. The wedding cake is wheeled in. The bride, with a spotlight shining down on her from the balcony and to a roll of the drums, will make the first cut; the rest will be cut for her. Everybody will get a piece of wedding cake to eat and another piece to take home, wrapped in silver paper and put into a little box with gold initials and a silk ribbon.

The dancing starts; the bride will throw the bouquet from the balcony; and Mr. Sigsag will then take the newlyweds up to their apartment by way of a private passage and private elevator. As he explains this, their eyes hang on his face, like those of children on a Christmas tree; of all the people who come here, they are the only ones who are happy without being drunk.

'He's wonderful, that little Mr. Wladi,' they say. 'And this is the only place to have an Affair. They charge you for it, but it's worth it.'

When the last interview is ended, Mama gets up first, pushes herself in the stomach, adjusts her bosom, and then goes with the back of her hands down her backside. The Bride Elect, who has spoken very little, gets up and smiles, and the father shakes hands with Mr. Sigsag. They are great friends; the father admires the brevity, the business acumen, of Mr. Wladi. During

the interview, Mr. Sigsag has given several orders to assistants in bad French and German, and that has impressed them greatly; such a smart fellow, he has been called to the phone a dozen times, and spoken to various people, having his information always ready in his mind. Besides, he looks tired and worried and is nervous, which is always a great asset in the eyes of a fellow-businessman. They walk down the stairs, look into the Ballroom once more; point to the place where the bride will be kissed, 'and then we go up this way for the cocktails.'

Finally they leave. Mama looks over her bosom down at the steps below and feels for them with her tight shoes. Half-way down the stairs, she stops once more, and for the last time the phrase is sent up: 'And don't forget, Mr. Wladi, lots of gravy with the broilers.' If it happens that they meet, coming through the door of the restaurant, friends who have the next appointment, then they stop briefly and sing: 'Oh, you having an Affair here too?'

If then one wished to sell them something additional – a more elaborate menu, better wines, more musicians or flowers – it was necessary only to call them up and inform them during the conversation that their friends had ordered it. They would become angry that we hadn't suggested it in the first place. 'Sure we want it. Now you just go ahead, Mr. Wladi. We want to do things right. Thirty-five musicians? Sure, I know the room is big.'

On the day of the wedding the bride arrives about five o'clock and is immediately whisked upstairs. It is the first personal touch of the untiring Mr. Sigsag; he waits for her. But he has been here since nine o'clock in the morning, setting up and upsetting the room. He has, with the aid of the housemen, placed on the dais the table for the bride, the groom, and their families, measuring everything himself, and also carrying legs for the tables and helping move the platforms. Then in the middle of the room, in front of the bride's table, he has built the young people's table in three sections, in the shape of a heart, with its center open for dancing. He has seen to it that the old people's table is placed where they will be comfortable, out of the draft, and near the wedding families; the other tables are placed and replaced, and pushed back and forth, to get everybody seated. He has shown the florists where to place a fountain, and has arranged to cover up the lower edge of some old smilax from a previous party that has been sold over again, with a few fresh inches of greenery. When the tables are ready for setting with silver and glasses, and the bride is upstairs, Mr. Sigsag goes up to take a shower and dress.

Below, in the Ballroom kitchen, Kalakobé the Senegalese is dragging the huge casseroles up out of the elevator with an iron hook; they have come from the main kitchen, where they have been partly prepared, and they are lifted onto steamtables where the chefs arrange the food on silver platters, and stow them away in hot compartments – hundreds of trout, the individual broilers with the gravy separate. In the pantries stand long tables and shelves on which the caviar, the salads, the dressing for the salads, bread and butter, celery and olive services, and the services for dessert and coffee are being prepared, as well as the rolling table for the wedding cake. Nothing must be forgotten.

As Mr. Sigsag goes up to dress, I come down dressed, and all the waiters are assembled in the Ballroom. I have a list of them and give them their stations; each one gets eight people to wait on. The best, fastest, serve the bride's table and the family; slow, considerate, and elderly men get the old people. We have one man who is almost blind; he has been with us since the hotel opened; he sometimes spills things and goes with his nose close to the plates to see them and also passes cigars to the ladies. He is teamed up with a young, quick man to help him and he gets the table next to the kitchen, where he does not have to walk far. The youngest men get the tables far away; they can run faster.

Then the other employees have to be checked: there has to be a doorman outside, a man in gala livery to turn the revolving door; coatroom attendants, maids, washroom boys; a man to show the guests down to the Orchid Salon for the ceremony; a man down there at the electric controls of the lights; a man in the lobby with a counting machine so that we may know just how many guests have arrived. All the room decorations must be supervised, the décor of the Orchid Salon, which is that of a night club, is hidden with greenery, and in front of a fountain at its far end is placed the bower, filled with white roses, lilies, and rows of white candles. The engineers are called to adjust the temperature; wines have to be opened.

When all this is checked, the ceremony can begin. The chairs, which are arranged as in a chapel, slowly fill with the guests. The best man and the groom stand waiting behind the bower and the bride has been spirited upstairs. The Rabbi arrives, the family comes and is seated in the first rows reserved for them, musicians and a singer are hidden behind palms, the fountain is turned low, everything has been rehearsed, and the wedding starts now!

First the lights are lowered while the singer sings 'Oh, Promise Me.' The Rabbi goes to the post where he will stand during the ceremony. Mr. Sigsag lifts a little finger, and all the people turn around as a curtain is pulled back at the top of the stairs; the mothers of the bride and groom march down as, at a signal, the musicians play the Wedding March. Mr. Sigsag is upstairs counting one, two, three, four; they have started off on the wrong foot, but it doesn't matter. At the last moment, Mr. Sigsag kneels on the floor behind the bride to arrange her train as widely and beautifully as possible before she descends into the salon, which is again brightly lit by the sparkling oval chandelier, to face the Rabbi.

If Rabbi Stephen Wise is officiating, the service is brief. He comes in as if he were trying to step on two alternating cockroaches that run about a foot ahead of him; he faces the audience and rocks his tall form back and forth, looking up at the ceiling, with his hands folded in front of him. A heroic man with much dignity, his wide mouth is a straight line; sometimes he blows his nose loudly while waiting, and blinks his eyes impatiently up the stairway. When the procession is in front of him, he hammers a sermon down on them that sounds as if someone were cracking cigar boxes by walking over them, a sermon designed for Madison Square Garden. At the end he reaches up over them, blesses them beautifully, and then the great man lopes out, stooping, holding both lapels of his coat in his hands. He never stays for dinner and seems to be glad when his part is over.

But heaven help us when, with the fidelity with which Jewish people cling to their friends and the people who were with them in their beginnings, they bring along a little orthodox Rabbi, one from Far Rockaway or another such place, whose day of glory has come with such a wedding. He speaks a very precise English, as if he were in a school of elocution; also he behaves with great condescension. He wishes to run the entire wedding and has to be subdued. He brings with him most of his congregation, to look on; they are placed out of the way up on a balcony, but before the party is over, they are always invited to stay and join in. Since no provision has been made for them, this is upsetting; extra tables have to be carried in and a menu improvised.

Such a Rabbi always brings a little imaginary ship with him; it is the ship of marriage, and he starts it on endless voyages. Whenever his sermon runs low, the little ship appears again. On board this ship, the husband is the captain, the wife is the crew. The ship goes out into a storm and comes back again into the harbor; the captain cannot steer it alone, neither can the crew; both must steer it together. The little ship is new with fresh paint in youth, and old with mended sails in age, but there is a harbor, a beautiful harbor, waiting for it. This little ship travels about while the caviar gets warm and the soup thickens upstairs. We make signs to him, and turn the fountain on full force to drown out his words, but he is not to be stopped. Finally he has exhausted all the uses of the ship, the chandelier lights are lowered, the mothers weep in loud sobbing rhythm, the fathers' mouths lose shape, the orchestra has put mutes on the fiddles, and while they play softly, the Rockaway Rabbi says an endless blessing over them. Bride and groom drink out of a silver cup; the groom crushes a glass with his foot. The orchestra plays the Mendelssohn Wedding March, all parade out to the Reception, and the kissing begins; everything precisely as in the estimate.

Upstairs, on the wide balcony outside the Ballroom, are little tables with large blocks of ice; on the ice are cans of caviar and in front of them are warmed Peak and Frean crackers. Ten waiters stand about with trays of cocktails, the favorite being Orange Blossoms, a mixture of gin and orange juice, undrinkably sweet. The reception lasts half an hour, until the last guest has kissed the bride.

We had among the waiters here an old fellow whose name was Gustav, Gustl for short. He was happiest at these weddings, and whereas we had to call the others to come from behind the curtain, where they talked politics, to pass the cocktails, he was always ready, tray in hand. The reason was that he suffered from a mild nervous disorder, which he confessed to me when I caught him red-handed indulging it. As he moved about in the crowd, serving cocktails, I once noticed that the back of his left hand, every now and then, brushed past the hips of some of the women. When I got to know him better, he told me that in the beginning he would have had more pleasure if he could have used the palm of his hand, but he found that too dangerous, so that now, after many years of adapting himself, he had developed quite as much sensitivity in the nerves on the back of his hand. He loved Jewish weddings, there was such wonderful material for his hobby; and since he did no one any harm, I always put him in the thick of it. At an Affair he would be radiant, and sometimes he would come back to me and point out some particularly fine specimen in the way of curve and resistance. For dinner I would give him stations with round women, and it was charming to see how he could not do enough for them, serving them with all possible dispatch and hovering over the backs of their chairs. Gustl was not so happy at coming-out parties, the young girls having hardly anything to offer him. Sometimes he would slip a little in technique and an astonished Jewish matron with her mouth full of canapés would turn around on the crowded balcony as if stung by an insect; but when she saw dear old Gustl with his white hair and the lackey's immobile face, she would look at her husband beside her with 'Hey, hey, what's going on here?' eyes.

The eating at the wedding dinners was accomplished with noise and fat fingers, the individual broilers with plenty of gravy being cleaned to the bone. There was also a type of table talk which went exclusively with these wedding dinners. A wife would say loudly: 'You know what happened last time, Sam. You'll get sick to your stomach. Remember how sick you was? You'll take a physic when I get you home.' Then, while the orchestra played 'Les Millions d'Harlequin,' the conversation would become general and turn to the relative merits of various purges. Also they would exchange parts of chicken: 'Here take a taste of this.'

After the dessert, which is carried in as promised, in the dark and to the accompaniment of music, there is usually some singing. The family poet has written the words – they are about the bride and the groom – and they are sung to a tune that everyone knows. The song has been printed, along with photographs showing the bride as a 'tot,' the groom, and the scene of their meeting. The coffee is served and the cigars are passed around. The men take both the little and the big cigars, sometimes two of each, their wives encouraging them: 'Take another, Sam; they have to pay for it anyway.'

It is time for the photograph, and it is then that someone misses Grandpa, who has disappeared during the meal. He arrived in a tailcoat and egg-colored shoes, with unkempt whiskers and the hollow, unhappy face of the Jewish immigrant. He has a drivelly nose, red eyelids, and a little black skullcap, and he climbs all over the hotel like a baby. You can see him going down the stairs sideways, holding on to one railing with both hands. He walks into the ladies' washroom, into the outdoor garden, comes out of the elevator in the corridor of an upper floor, or appears in the kitchen, where the chef says: 'Qu'est-ce qu'il veut ici, ce phenomène?' Finally Mr. Sigsag finds him, takes his arm, and brings him back.

During the day, a photographer and his assistant, standing on a ladder, had concealed flashlights in white fireproof bags in the greenery overhead, and had focused their camera on a tripod up on the balcony so that it overlooked the room. Now the waiters leave the room, having no desire to have their pictures taken, while the guests straighten their neckties and the women wiggle in their chairs and tilt their heads. Everyone is asked to smile and face the photographer, who then sets off the flashes. Mr. Sigsag is in every picture, standing at attention in a corner, on his face a devout smile; he is a sort of trade-mark in them, the guarantee that he has personally taken care of all the details of the wedding, and he has an album full of these photographs. And when people later show the photographs they will point to him and say: 'And that's Mr. Sigsag, he's wonderful.'

The bride throws her bouquet from the balcony and disappears with the groom. Mr. Sigsag takes them up in the private elevator, running it himself, wishes them 'good night' and smiles coyly as he bows himself out. As the dancing begins downstairs, the mothers usually rush up for a last word with bride and groom – 'Be nice to her' – and weep and embrace them.

Below, them ladies pluck at the centerpiece, for flowers to take home with them. Mr. Sigsag sends for paper to wrap them up with. By midnight they are usually gone.

The father stays to the end. If the bill is ready he pays it then and there, and has the cash with him to leave a liberal sum, at least ten percent of the bill, for the employees as tips, and a large gift of money for Mr. Sigsag. There are rarely squabbles of any kind; they leave with many thanks for the good service, shake hands with all the employees in sight, and say again and again that everything has been wonderful and to come to the store to get that wonderful suit.

Improved Jewish Wedding

MR. SIGSAG had discovered a new kind of wedding, a sort we had never had before. They were celebrated by orthodox Jews who insisted on the strict observance of religious rules, and were brought to the Splendide by an energetic woman who took care of all the details herself. Mrs. Shallshah's mouth stayed open between words, and her eyes stared out from behind rimless glasses. Her hands hung loose on fat arms and rowed through the air as she walked all through the hotel in a coat such as butchers wear. She lived in Far Rockaway and had four sons, some of whom were studying at New York University to become lawyers.

In the beginning, she had some difficulties, as when the chef came up from below and had one of his attacks. 'No, no, keep this woman out of my kitchen, *sacré bon Dieu!* We are not going to have any of that, Monsieur Wladimar. *Mais ça ne va pas, cette vache . . .*' He repeated over and over that it did not go, this cow in his kitchen, out with her! Mr. Sigsag gave him a glass of wine, and talked of other things, for he knew that cooks must be treated like children and allowed to get used to new things.

For after her second visit, Mr. Sigsag and Mrs. Shallshah had become very thick friends. They sat together out in the large entrance hall on a little Adam sofa under a palm. Mr. Sigsag was so short that his legs, hooked together at the shoes, swung back and forth. He had his pencil stuck under his nose, his little fist clenched round it tightly, his posture one of closest attention. Occasionally he took out a folded menu, made calculations on the back of it, took down notes, and nodded in hearty agreement while Mrs. Shallshah, her lower lip hanging from her open mouth, her eyes shining, talked to him. They both became very quiet when anyone passed.

Von Kyling said: 'All right for this wedding, we have it on the books, but for God's sake get rid of that woman.' He ignored her, walked down the stairs when he heard her voice in the office, and never came near the party. But Mr. Sigsag talked to him for hours, showed him figures. He had a way of gaining his point, he was not to be thrown out with his ideas. Where any other person would have given up, he would start the subject all over again the next day, fresh and new as if it had never been talked about, and again the third day, and on the fourth it would be the same story, until von Kyling held his head and said: 'Yes, yes, yes, if only you leave me alone.'

And so gradually Mrs. Shallshah became a regular part of our business. She had a great circle of clients, among the Jewish people who lived in the West Seventies, along Riverside Drive, West End Avenue, and Central Park West. In a hotel like the Splendide, one's address is very important. Riverside Drive and West End Avenue are even worse than Brooklyn, and as for Central Park West, von Kyling used to say of it that in every house there lived an abortionist, a fortune-teller, or Roxy.

They all had money. Their weddings had hitherto been held in a small synagogue, the catering facilities of which had been under the supervision of Mrs. Shallshah. Now they were richer, business was good everywhere, and the synagogue had become too mean and little. They all wanted to come to the Splendide. Once the first family had been brought down by Mrs. Shallshah, all the others naturally followed.

Mrs. Shallshah sent in boxes upon boxes of material; a special room was put aside for her, the Genomies had to open the cases, the carpenters built shelves, while she stood in the middle of the storeroom, her arms hanging away from her sides, and directed the unpacking. In the cases were various glass services, from the five-and-ten-cent store. They were the kind that is not blown but comes out of a mould, the line where it is glued together clearly visible. One service was cloudy green: service plates, little plates, fruit cocktail glasses, all green and with a seam, a welt of glass, down the side and the stem. There were water tumblers and badly designed wine glasses, one big, one smaller, not the correct shape for champagne, or other wines, but just in two sizes. There were also badly formed glass swans – she held them up for Mr. Sigsag to admire – to be used for fruit cocktails, the body of the swan holding the fruit. After the green service, of which three hundred pieces of each kind were unpacked, came the red service – the same cheap glassware, again the larger plates, the smaller plates, and three hundred glass swans. Finally there were some ugly little glass dumplings with a hole in the top; these were candlesticks.

On a second truck came more cases. In them, carefully wrapped, were little trees of Bohemian glass, again in the bad taste which Mrs. Shallshah, Mr. Wladi Sigsag, and the customers, later on, found very beautiful. Stuck into little tubs, three inches wide and weighted so that they would not turn over, these artificial dwarf trees had their trunks wound round with silk, glass leaves attached to their branches, and flowers made of crude pieces of wired glass. There also came eight immense gilded tin horns on stands of bent metal, battered from being much carried and knocked about, and boxes of candles, in all assorted colors, with very exquisite ones for the bridal table, manufactured by an old Italian family of candle-makers. These bridal candles were big and stout and decorated with an ugly crust that was what Mrs. Shallshah called 'very dramatic'; they were scented, with a sweet perfume that hurt one's teeth.

Then came the menus, deckle-edged awfulness on imitation parchment, with a picture of the bride and groom in the center of the cover. Mrs. Shallshah had her own Rabbi, a leaning, inquisitive man in a worn coat and with a beard whose few hairs grew so far apart that it made him look unwashed. She also brought in several women to work in the kitchen, where the cooks stared at them; the chef had by then given up all resistance and just shook his head when he passed them. The last thing to arrive was a case of silver doilies, little pieces of perforated paper that were slipped in between the larger and the smaller glass plates. On top of the latter sat the glass swan with scooped melon in its body.

The glasses were put around, the Bohemian glass trees were placed in the center of the tables, together with the dumpling candlesticks and the deckle-edged menus. It was, Mrs. Shallshah said again, admiring it from near and from far, 'exquisite' and 'very dramatic.' The word 'dramatic' was just then appearing in all sorts of advertisements, for gowns, for mink coats, and Mr. Sigsag immediately added it to his party vocabulary, along with 'observance of dietary laws.' It was indeed dramatic. Beside it, the good service of the Splendide, the well-designed glass and china, the elegant menus, the lovely centerpieces of quietly arranged flowers, simply paled into plainness.

Mrs. Shallshah's sons were her florists, and in the afternoon her husband, too, appeared to help out – his regular job was selling cut-rate theater tickets at a Broadway drug store. On the day of the wedding, the sons went down to the wholesale market and bought flowers by the armful, with as much greenery as they could get thrown in. It was then stuck into the gilded horns and stood about the walls, and Mrs. Shallshah interlaced a few lilies in the bower of thin greenery built by our florist. The golden horns, after being used in the Orchid Salon below, were, while the bride was being kissed, rushed upstairs in a back elevator and carried through a service door into the Ballroom.

The candles were lit and the chandelier turned down as much

as possible. This again was 'dramatic' because it dimmed the light on the bare walls, and it was also 'cozy.' Down in the kitchen the Rabbi was supervising the making of soups and sauces and Mrs. Shallshah's three women were manufacturing canapés, soggy bits of toast smeared with pastes or covered with cream cheese with a spoonful of redcurrant jam in the center.

Besides the rental for the rooms, Mrs. Shallshah paid a set price for the menu, which she fought about for days, though on her own bill she added an equal amount as an 'extra charge,' as she called it, for the 'emerald' or the 'ruby service,' and for the silver and gold doilies. The music, which was charged for at the prices quoted for our best parties, was not half as costly to Mrs. Shallshah, who imported young men from Far Rockaway. On top of all this came her charge for 'personal attention to all the details.' There was even a profit in beautiful menus, a 'grand souvenir' to keep, and the wedding cake. Up to then all our wedding cakes had been made by a famous Fifth Avenue baker, but Mrs. Shallshah had a friend on Second Avenue, who made them for half the money, hideous mountains of sticky pastry, the base of which was made of wood that was used over and over again. She also brought her own champagne, a green, sweet, unripe California wine, that came in genuine bottles with well-imitated labels, and that had to be cooled for a whole day to keep it in the bottle.

During the service Mrs. Shallshah was everywhere in the way, as were her four sons and her husband. They mixed a syrupy cocktail made of liqueur and cream, and afterwards ate in our office, together with Mr. Sigsag, and drank their own wine. When the party was over, the sons got busy and packed away the remains of everything, whatever left-over food was portable, the glass trees, the flowers, the wedding cake – everything went to their place in Far Rockaway, where they had boarders.

The people who gave the parties were always pleased, paid their bill without a murmur, and left generous tips for the employees, which Mrs. Shallshah turned over in full to Mr. Sigsag. She brought many weddings to the hotel which we would otherwise not have had, and Mr. Sigsag saw to it that he got good prices in spite of all the haggling with her. Their worst feature was that these weddings took place on the few days in the season when the men might have had a rest, on Sundays.

Soon after our first improved Jewish wedding, Mr. Sigsag got hold of another storeroom, fixed it up with shelves, and filled it with boxes that came from the five-and-ten-cent store. We now had our own red and green swans, glasses, and plates, our own paper doilies, gold and silver; and one day the Italian candle-maker came with his two sons and was, first of all, engaged to make a huge candle with the Virgin on it and with scented crusts running down over it, to send to Mr. Sigsag's mother; then he was asked at what rate he could supply us with the rest of his art. The Bohemian glass trees followed. Of each of that kind, glasses, trees, and all, Mr. Sigsag ordered about a hundred; the rest were borrowed from Mrs. Shallshah's closet when she was not there, for our weddings were usually bigger than hers.

Mr. Sigsag had the 'dramatic' in his being now. The next time he had an appointment to discuss the details of a big wedding, he had three tables set up: one with the elegant service of the Splendide, the gilt-edged menus, and the chaste centerpieces; a second with the 'emerald service,' green swans filled with fruit, silver paper doilies, swollen candles, Bohemian glass trees, and the smaller deckle-edged menus; a third with the 'ruby service,' larger red candles, red swans filled with fruit, golden paper doilies, and the larger deckle-edged menu with a bigger bride and groom, an extra sheet inside, and a carmine ribbon.

The guests always chose the most dramatic ruby service; we hardly ever used the green, never the Splendide service. The investment in glass soon paid for itself – the 'extra charge' took care of that after a few parties. Mr. Sigsag shone with pride, but von Kyling gained several points: that the Rockaway orchestra must be eliminated, that the floral decorations must be left to real florists, that the wines must be bought through a reliable bootlegger. On the other hand, in another respect Mr. Sigsag improved even on Mrs. Shallshah. When the fruit cocktails came back from the tables, someone had to stand out in the pantry and fish out from between the larger and smaller glass plates the gold and silver doilies, which were then washed off, taken upstairs, and ironed so that they could be used over again.

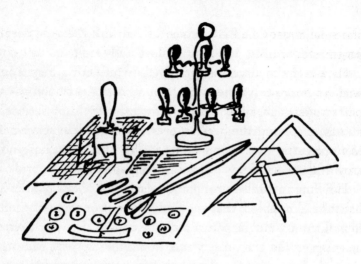

The Postmaster from Przemysl

HE WAS a postmaster in a little German-speaking village near Mr. Sigsag's home, but he had been a postal clerk in Vienna. All skin and bones, sideways built, he came to us soon after the arrival of the fabulous Mrs. Shallshah; it was a season of great improvements. Young and full of ambition, he was a distant relation of Mr. Sigsag; and the glory that Wladi Sigsag carried back to Przemysl every year had inspired Postmaster Rudolph Wenzeslaus to spend time and money studying English so that Sigsag could bring him to America.

He received a dress coat from Sigsag, much too short, the tails barely covering his seat, and a pair of trousers from von Kyling;

shoes he already had. Soon also he had inky fingers, turning postmaster again.

He was the shadow of Mr. Sigsag, carrying his papers around with an important lack of time for anything else. He was the perfect assistant, ready with any information Sigsag wanted – names, telephone numbers, amounts of money – and mirroring in his face the mood and temper of his master: they smiled, frowned, bowed, or were displeased together.

He wrote an excellent hand, and covered the labels on estimates, lists, and records with shadings and hairlines, arabesques and little illuminations. His signature was impressive. He had decided against the 'laus' in his name (in this one could see the fine instinct with which he adapted himself to the grace and elegance of his new surroundings); and the tip end of the 'l' in 'Wenzl' wound up very far away from that letter, among artful back-and-forth scribbling and with three little dots after its tail.

The secretary of the banquet department was an elderly pastry-quaffing woman who was an office fixture and who annoyed me constantly sending requisitions to the painting department to have the walls washed and repainted because they were 'full of drawings'; since everyone knew that the drawings were my work, and since a copy of this report went to Mr. Brauhaus, I thought she could just as well have said merely that the walls were dirty. Unerringly, Wenzl also became the devoted servant of this secretary, saw to it that she got plenty of coffee and pastry and, during the service, little dishes of ice cream, wrapped up left-over flowers for her to take home, and from the box of forgotten gloves picked out the right size for her puffy red hands. So, in a few weeks, Wenzl was an indispensable part of the department.

Soon he was having long conferences with Mr. Sigsag on the

Adam sofa under the palm, out in the lobby. If it concerned the good of the business, Mr. Sigsag would listen to anybody, for any length of time. He would follow carefully, take notes, and was willing to try anything. After these conferences, Wenzl brought the secretary her coffee and sat with her while she typed out, according to his neat designs, a stack of requisition slips, for the carpentry department, for the painters, for the stationery clerk, for the printer. These Mr. Wenzl then took around to the various departments himself, explaining their use.

A week later he had established himself in a closet, inside a room seldom used except as a museum for all of Mr. Sigsag's collected junk. By that time, too, he had persuaded Mr. Sigsag to isolate him from the other employees of the department, so that he could eat upstairs in the second-class officers' dining-room, where the cashiers, the head doorman, the bill clerks, and the rest of the hotel's middle class – the employees who could come in through the front door and did not have to punch the time clock – took their meals. He had a strong lock put on his closet door, and when it was open, he could swing to a little gate from the inside and let down a little wicket barrier with a cashier's opening, through which one could speak to him. He could shut that also, and then he was all one in his little post office again. Inside was a desk and many files and shelves, also a little metal tree with twenty rubber stamps hanging from it in a ring, alphabetical registers, bottles of ink in assorted colors, and an architect's drafting set. He was not to be had for any other work, but sat up there all day, wearing glasses, and when anyone stopped him outside, he would wave a piece of paper, say: 'Just a minute,' bow, and never come back.

Passing, one would hear: 'Thump, thump,' as he stamped his cards; he stamped everything with, first 'Hotel Splendide,' then

'Banquet Department,' then a little stamp for the date. He had green forms printed for the orders to the silver department, red for the china department, yellow for the glass pantry. All orders had to be completely filled out for every party, and every detail ordered in advance, from the demi-tasse spoons to the heavy six-armed candelabra, from butter plates to coffee cups, each item numbered and listed. Barrels of ice had to be ordered by kind, number, and the proper color of paper: fine ice for cooling wines, cube ice for water, large blocks of ice to set caviar in and cool orangeade with.

Next he drew elaborate maps, to be attached to the estimates, in which the entrances were shown and the position of every table. The latter he indicated by small designs of greenery in color, over which he wrote neatly: 'The Bride's Table,' 'The Parents' Table,' The Young People's Table,' 'The Speaker's Table,' or 'The Host's Table.' With Mr. Sigsag he sat over these plans and indicated the carpet on which the bride entered the room, filling it out in red ink, painting on it with blue: 'The Bride Elect enters the Ballroom here, and proceeds on the arm of the groom to the Bridal Table.'

'That's nice,' said Mr. Sigsag.

He also bought a home printing set, with a pair of pincers for picking up the type. He printed by hand the many signs that now hung all over the place, most of them outside his cage. They read: 'Gratuities will be paid Friday afternoon from three to four.' 'Errors must be reported at the cashier's window upon receiving tips.' 'Extra checks will be paid Saturday morning.'

It had been the custom up to then to pay the men their tips out of pocket, on the basis of a rapid mental calculation, or, at most, by referring to a quickly scribbled list that was then torn up. Once every week there would be a table full of money with Mr. Sigsag handing it out as if he were dividing loot. Now Wenzl had changed all that: his printing set, his signed receipts, the regular hour for paying out, and, above all, the stamping made it seem like Army pay day. It was less tip, and more honest pay. It was like dealing with a bank.

The waiters received an extra check for every party at which they worked. It was graduated according to the worth of the man and the hours he worked. A common waiter received a minimum of three dollars for dinner. If he came a little earlier, three-fifty. If he stayed to closing and helped clear away the dishes, four. At coming-out parties, when a man came early, worked for dinner and supper, and stayed for closing, his pay amounted to from nine to eleven dollars, not counting his tip and meals and whatever he picked up directly from the guests for small services. For the tips, the guests either paid a percentage of the bill or they had a list of the men submitted to them. At the largest parties these tips might come to several thousand dollars.

With his home printing set Number One, Wenzl had spent days upstairs in his heaven devising forms and slips and manifest sheets on which everything could be traced, and against which each man's card could be checked. After 'Hotel Splendide' and 'Banquet Department' and the date, came the name of the party, the hours of service, the amount of the tip, and the classification of the waiter: AA, A, B, BB, and, for the old men who came for the serving of meals only, D.

All this was very pleasing to Mr. Sigsag. Sometimes when we were having a glass of sherry together, von Kyling, Sigsag, and I, mostly at the quiet hour of five, Wenzl would bow and squeeze himself in. He would wiggle into a corner, unroll a graph, and announce: 'Did you know that Pommer, the bartender, made one hundred and fifty-seven dollars and thirty cents, this last week? And that Benedetto, a full-time AA waiter, made only two dollars less? Isn't that too much?' Von Kyling would chase Wenzl back upstairs, and then turn on Sigsag and tell him that we made plenty, and that we should live and let live. Outside, Wenzl would be waiting to apologize. 'I only wanted to let you know these things; I consider that my duty.'

'All right, all right,' said von Kyling.

Wenzl was never happier than when he saw the line of men standing in front of his cage. His face would tighten into importance as he handed out the cards, let them sign the receipts, and paid them out their money from a black tin cash box, after computing it on a second-hand adding machine. He also had a box marked 'Private,' containing large sheets on which one could see at a glance how many parties we had, what had been taken in, what paid out.

During the months of November, December, and January, it seems, sixty-five thousand dollars in tips alone were paid out. 'You didn't know that,' he says to Mr. Sigsag.

'No, I didn't,' says Mr. Sigsag, but von Kyling knew it very well.

'You know, Wenzl is wonderful, don't you think so?' Mr. Sigsag said to me. 'Look what he's done again.' Wenzl, it seemed, had gone out into the city and found some terrible place-card holders made of seashells, peanuts, and pipe cleaners in the shape of an animal between a grasshopper and a butterfly.

'Where did you get them?' Sigsag asked in admiration.

'Oh, you know, I just go around the city, looking here and there for what I can pick up, what might be useful.'

He now wears what he calls a 'Foreign Office' coat, wing collars, and striped trousers. And he has again changed his name to 'Monsieur Vincent.'

Dinner Out

ONLY ONCE did I go out to dine with Mr. Sigsag, and I never would again. One night we had no party at the hotel, and he said: 'Come on, I'll take you down to Luchow's. You'll like it there.'

This restaurant was in the center of a block on Fourteenth Street, close to the German theater on Irving Place. It was bathed in cigar smoke and beer smells, as such a restaurant should be and always is in Hamburg or Bremen. Antlers hung on the walls, and on its upper level, behind a mahogany banister, an orchestra – a piano, two violins, and a 'cello – played German restaurant pieces.

A red-faced captain, who had been in this restaurant for thirty years, leaned up against the banister with his hands folded over his stomach. He was very kind but beautifully ugly, and had a mouth and throat like an old toad. His eyes were half asleep, and when some of the guests smiled and waved at him and made faces, he would stick his fat tongue out at them, which made him look all the more like an old toad catching flies. Then he would wipe his hand over his face, smile, greet them with a bill of fare, which was much too big for comfortable reading, and go away for a little while only to return to the banister and lean against it again.

We came as the orchestra was playing an elaborate *Liebestraum*. Especially remarkable among the musicians was the pianist. As would a great virtuoso, he leaned back until he almost fell off the piano stool, with his eyes closed and his hair hanging down. Then he brought his nose down to the keys, close over his fingers which walked along the high keys in a calm passage. He sat sideways to reach the lower keys, pounded them, and looked up. For an encore he gave the 'March of the Wooden Soldiers.' Mr. Sigsag applauded both pieces.

Mr. Sigsag could not sit still; he twitched and turned, looking at what other people were ordering. In a little while he was out at the bar, where he found the manager, introduced himself, and brought him to our table. With critical eyes he went over the menu, looked at the prices, criticized the arrangement of it. When the waiter came, Mr. Sigsag told him who we were: 'I'm Monsieur Wladimir of the Splendide, and this is Monsieur Louis, and we want a little special attention here.'

The waiter got the captain, and Mr. Sigsag started to order. The table d'hôte dinner allowed a choice of either fish or meat, but Mr. Sigsag took hold of the captain's sleeve, and, with his red, yellow, and blue silver pencil, pointed at the card and said: 'Now you go out and tell the chef that it's for us, for Monsieur Louis here and for myself, and we want a little special attention. Now listen, instead of having one fish and one meat, we'll have one portion of each divided. First bring the fish for both of us, one portion, you know what I mean, and then the meat, also one portion served for two.'

'Well,' said the captain, 'that's easy. The waiter will bring one portion and two plates and then you divide it yourself.'

Mr. Sigsag was not in the habit of having his orders changed. 'Bring me the headwaiter,' he said, and then to me: 'I'm sorry about this, but we'll get service here in just a minute now.'

The headwaiter came and everything was all right. We received two full portions of fish and two of duckling. Then came a salad. On the dinner a plain lettuce salad was included, but under the salad list on the à la carte side of the menu Mr. Sigsag had noticed a celery root salad, of which he knew I was very fond. He called the headwaiter again and said: 'Could we have some celery root salad, instead of the plain lettuce? Because my friend Monsieur Louis, here, and I are very fond of it.'

'Yes, yes,' said the headwaiter and wrote out a slip. The captain sneered and the waiter was disgusted. The salad and the dessert eaten, Mr. Sigsag called for the headwaiter again. Now he wanted to see the kitchen, and I had to come along.

Out there he asked a thousand questions, and talked hotel memories to the chef. He went into the iceboxes and tried sauces and soups. He made comments about everything, honestly

124

and sincerely, and also suggestions: that a little shelf here would help, that the waiters should come in from that side and not from the other, that an attachment to pull kitchen smells out from over the service door would be better than their own arrangement. Now the chef was also mad; no chef likes his kitchen talked about.

At last I thought it was over and that we might get to the theater, for which we had two very good seats in the second row. But no. As we came out into the dining-room, Mr. Sigsag saw seated about a large table some Jewish wedding friends, people whose daughter had been married in the Splendide. They greeted him like a long-lost son. The mother almost kissed him. He had to sit by her side, and I got a seat on the other side of the table. We had to drink a glass of wine with them. 'Have you eaten? Eat with us. Order anything you want.'

Now the evening was completely ruined. Mr. Sigsag talked wedding, for they had another daughter; besides, they were going to send some friends. Although the last wedding was so very recent, Mr. Sigsag asked whether any happy events were in sight, and of course there were, in April.

He asked after Grandpa, after Grandma, as if they were his own grandparents, and all this time his eyes wandered about the room. 'Excuse me a minute,' he said, but not to go to the washroom; he had seen a customer trying to attract the attention of a waiter with motions of the hand and by saying: 'Psst.' The waiter, with folded arms, stood talking to another waiter.

'Come on, come on, you, wake up,' Sigsag said to him. 'Customer there wants to see you,' and the man went. If he hadn't, Sigsag would have upset the whole restaurant. He was eternally in business, and every hotel and restaurant in the world was his worry.

We finally left for the theater and arrived in the middle of the play. When we were seated, Sigsag turned to me. 'You know what they should have?' he asked.

'What?'

'They should have the pantry in front of the kitchen on the right, less cooking smell and the waiters don't run into each other, one door marked "IN" and the other "OUT," like this.'

And here in the second row, under Walter Hampden's nose, he designed the whole thing with his three-colored pencil on the menu which he always took along from every restaurant, as well as the wine card. He did not hear a word of *Cyrano*, but the next day he told everybody that we had seen a wonderful show.

The captain, the fat one who stuck his tongue out, told me about the founder, old Luchow. He was very strict with his men, but also very decent to them and provident of their old age. He had, like Otto Brauhaus, certain pet ideas. One was that his employees could drink all the domestic beer they wanted but never imported beer. He saw to it that they were well fed, but he did not like to have them steal food to eat, something that is, of course, done in every restaurant. His office was upstairs, and he had mirrors so arranged all through the rooms, that with their aid he could look into every corner of the restaurant from his window.

He had a Kellermeister, old John, who was with him for many years, and who was very fond of strawberry shortcake. He once swiped a big slice of it and began to eat it in a corner, but Luchow, who had observed him in his mirrors, came down. John tried to swallow as much as he could and threw the rest of it into a linen basket.

'John,' Luchow said to him, 'that was an expensive strawberry shortcake you had just now. It would not have been so expensive if you had eaten it all, but to throw it away into the linen basket here, that's not right; it's wasting things, and besides it's trying to make a fool of me. This strawberry shortcake will cost you five thousand dollars.' And when Luchow died, the Kellermeister received a legacy, and it was five thousand dollars short of what the others got. Another employee, a waiter, paid two thousand dollars for an imported Würzburger beer.

I went back to Luchow's many times – without Mr. Sigsag. I liked not only the generous service of food but also the cigars, which were well chosen and kept right, and the excellent beer that was never too cold. The clientele of this restaurant was made up of the people one might find in a good restaurant in Munich. There were many old people here and large families on Sundays, and Catholic priests, and many Jewish people. In a restaurant frequented by Catholic priests and Jewish families, one can always be sure of good ample cooking. That so many people had enough loyalty to it to continue to go all the way down to Fourteenth Street was nice, and another nice thing was that you could take your dog with you, and they would give him enormous roastbeef bones.

S. S. Zuider Zee

OLD GUSTL went back to Europe every year. He left in the spring and came back in the autumn, as many of our waiters did, working his way over on the ships when they were packed and needed extra help. This way, what with tips on board, most of the men earned their railroad fare for the other side and a few dollars extra, besides going to Europe without buying a ticket. In April and May they would begin to ask for a recommendation to the chief steward of some steamship line, and then, as our own business thinned and finally gave out, they left.

S. S. ZUIDER ZEE

Gustl was married to a Frenchwoman, and they had a little *pension* in Monte Carlo which his wife managed. He was a kindly, quiet person of much dignity. At weddings and coming-out parties he was one of our most reliable waiters, and at other functions he was placed at posts where his good appearance, his tact, and his patience were needed. He smiled beautifully, did not antagonize people, and was best in a corridor or on the stairs between the Ballroom and the Orchid Salon, when the two apartments were being used separately, to keep people from running into each other's party.

He was good as an usher, at receiving guests and showing them to their tables, and at helping them find names on the lists. He was placed at the door of the Orchid Salon to receive the children in the Tuesday morning dancing classes, to watch them dance and serve them icewater, for they liked him. He was also used when an announcer failed to appear, and he did that well. His sensitive face, the air of an old, trusted family servant, fitted him well for these duties. In such assignments he never made errors; the guests were always content.

Only he stole like a raven. He must have had eyes instead of buttons on the back of his dress coat. Sigsag watched him as a shooting dog does a bird, but Gustl would seem to dust away a fly from over a box of cigars, and half a dozen of them would be gone. I caught him at that several times. He also dropped things frequently, or upset trays of glasses or dishes. They would fall with a loud crash, but when I arrived, Gustl would be standing about six quickly taken steps away from the wreckage, looking surprised and accusingly out of the service door, or past a column, behind which the breaker of the glasses had presumably just disappeared.

It was just a sort of tenderness, for there was no charge for broken dishes. Others would stand and look stupid, but Gustl was averse to being caught, to being talked to. He knew that I knew that he had done it, broken or stolen something, and he knew, too, that I would do nothing about it, that I loved him; but he always went through the same play of sorrow, hurt, and condolence, looking down at the floor, beyond me, to the left and right of me, his eyelids working up and down. Then, when he was accused, he would paste the two lapels of his dinner coat down on his chest with the flat of one hand and say over and over again: '*Non, Monsieur Louis, mais non, mais non, non, non, non, pas moi, Monsieur Louis.*'

This would be followed by a thick explanation, not believable even to himself; I would have to laugh in the middle of it. Then, with a sweet expression, his lips pointed and his head held in an endearing pose, sideways and forward, he would give up, raise both hands to his sides, the fingers open, and admit it. I would pat him on the shoulder, because I was so fond of him, and what are a few cigars, dishes, or glasses? I came to like this performance so much that I accused him wrongly just to enjoy his upset. '*Mais non, nononon,*' he said, his face red in real anger, '*non, non, Monsieur Louis.*' He stamped his foot when he was innocent, and turned his pockets inside out. When I told him it was only in fun, he pleaded: '*No, you must not do that.*'

On going through the rooms, when we had no parties, to check up on necessary repairs and cleaning, I found him several times in the ladies' room of the Ballroom. He sat reading in the outer room, which was furnished with a dressing-table, a chair, and many mirrors, and his coat was hung in one of the six private compartments in the inner room. When there was no work, I discovered he practically lived here until he went home at night. He told me that his own room was near the elevated railway, that it was an ugly room, and that here it was nice and warm; he liked the mirrors and was near the help's hall where he ate. He said that this way he could save a little money, not having to take the Elevated home and back, or going to a movie.

'It's pretty late for him to start saving,' said von Kyling when he heard of this. He always used Gustl as the horrible example of what I would some day become if I did not reform. The conductor of the orchestra in the grill room of the Plaza, where he played some of the best dance music in town, had told von Kyling that he had seen me there often with a girl, dancing and drinking.

'The Plaza! The Plaza!' said von Kyling. 'Look at him there' – he pointed to Gustl, who was cleaning ashtrays – 'I had him on board the *Empress Catherine*. He was then a chef de rang; that was many years ago when restaurants on ships first became the fashion. He always made money, he could be retired today; but when we came to Hamburg, Monsieur Gustl dressed up, spats and gloves, walking-stick and ring, and went to the Atlantic, a gentleman, elegant, you should have seen him! The headwaiter bowed, the waiters ran, the music played his favorite pieces, and every whore in Hamburg sat in his lap. So now he's starting to save! And I can see you cleaning ashtrays thirty years from now, just like him; you have a talent for it, my boy.'

Then I looked down at Gustl, his fallen arches and his second-hand dress coat, on his white hair and the ashtrays in his hands, and for a second a cold shower of reason fell down my spine. Von Kyling, seeing me in a rare serious moment, went on: 'Now, tomorrow, you go to a bank, go to the second window and say:

"I want to open a savings account," and start with putting in all your money. No stocks, like Sigsag, no mortgages in Jersey, no tips on Wall Street, no margin business. Take your money and put it down, and then it's there and nobody can touch it or play with it for you.'

'The Plaza!' said von Kyling, every time he passed me from then on for a week.

When I told Gustl I was going to Europe, he said it was sinful to pay for passage when one could get across for nothing. Besides, he knew how to arrange it so that one did no work and ate like a first-class passenger. Gustl had much experience with ships; he liked best of all to cross on the *Zuider Zee*. He said this ship was not only very steady; it was also comfortable in other ways, and it landed you one morning in the middle of the beautiful city of Rotterdam. He took me down to the ship, where we looked over the accommodations, the nice broad decks, and the dining-room. It looked quiet, well furnished, just as Gustl had described it.

I wrote two letters of recommendation, one for Gustl and one for myself, and we were engaged on the *Zuider Zee* as emergency stewards, at one dollar in wages. We reported to a steward who fitted us out with uniforms, and when we had put these on, another steward showed us to our sleeping quarters. We walked down and down, past hatches and down companionways to the bottom of the ship, to a triangular room in which slept fifty or more men, in two tiers of bunks. Each man had a wooden box for his belongings, the one in front for the man on the lower bunk, the other for the man on the upper. We received two berths, a straw mattress, two blankets, and sheets and pillow cases.

Gustl said everything would be all right. 'Let's leave our things here. It's just, you know, Monsieur Louis, the way they do things here.'

Then we went above to report to the chief steward; it was almost time for dinner. 'Ah,' he said, 'the men from the Splendide.' He was glad to see us; he had a very fine job for us. A big stockholder in the company, Mynheer van Zoorn, and his family were on board, a party of eight altogether. They sat at the first table as one came in. Mynheer van Zoorn was a very exacting man, his wife was also difficult, and the Hoffmeester, as the chief steward is called on Dutch ships, was 'damned glad' we were on this trip; we would have no other work than to serve Mynheer van Zoorn and the family. 'But,' he said, holding up his two hands, and folding them as in prayer, 'attention, attention, attention.' He did not have one man in his whole crew who could look after them properly.

Gustl nodded, and the Hoffmeester gave us detailed advice as to what Mynheer van Zoorn wanted: above all, everything very hot, everything especially prepared for him, fast service, no talking. 'Never keep him waiting; he kicks up a terrible row, and I get it in the neck. So you know what I mean, give him service, Splendide service.'

Gustl nodded several times, looked very much interested, and asked the Hoffmeester to explain several things over again so that we would be certain of doing everything right. When everything was clear, we left the steward's room, and outside Gustl said: 'Don't worry about anything. I'll take care of this. Everything is all right, Monsieur Louis. It's always like this the first day on a ship, everything upset, you know. But leave it to me, I'll arrange everything.'

It was now the hour for the employees to eat, down in the

steward's dining-room. Here we found a long table with bread and butter on it and what looked like a dish of good soup. We only looked in; Gustl closed his eyes and strolled out, saying: 'This is not for us, Monsieur Louis, don't spoil your appetite. I just wanted to show you where the help eats.'

We went to the barber shop instead and looked over the copies of the *Saturday Evening Post* there, and waited until it was time to go up to the dining-room to polish the glasses and silver, lay the plates, and put the bread on the table. The lights were on, the first guests were arriving, and Gustl folded his arms and leaned against a pillar close to his table.

The Hoffmeester raised his eyebrows as a signal: Mynheer van Zoorn and his family had arrived. The Hoffmeester himself pulled out the chairs for a group of heavy people. They sat down, and the parents and children looked at us inquiringly, to see whether they would like us. We both wore our most frozen Splendide faces, and Gustl started doing something that no good waiter ever should. He chased flies off the table around Mynheer van Zoorn, his napkin slapping against the tablecloth.

The Hoffmeester, behind us, began cruising around the table in a wide circle, and it was hard to pretend seriousness as Gustl played the fool with a lovely talent and perfect control: repeating everything Mynheer van Zoorn ordered and very slowly writing it down, so that the man, who had selected a long list of dishes, became impatient and started looking from his wife's face to his plate and then with suspicion at Gustl. In the Kitchen Gustl stood around, watched the cooks, and waited. Then he went to the man who had the hors d'oeuvres to get a tray of them, but only just before the Hoffmeester came running and shouting:

'What's the matter with you men? I thought you were from the Splendide and first-class waiters or something?'

We continued to give terrible service; Mynheer van Zoorn's patience did not really break, though he received hot asparagus instead of cold, and mayonnaise with it instead of hollandaise. It was the chief steward who finally gave up, sent for two other stewards, and chased us out. He put us all the way in the back of the dining-room where inconsequential people sat, and assigned each of us to help an old waiter.

'Now that's better,' said Gustl; 'now just a little more patience, Monsieur Louis, and we will have everything in order.'

The two old stewards we were assisting were Dutchmen, as was old Gustl himself. They were not pleased at having to share their tips with anyone else; they made little enough money for their hard work. Gustl assured them that we did not want any of their tips, and that neither did we want any work. We would pay them five dollars apiece, just to let us hang around and maybe serve their guests with a little water and perhaps help them pass the vegetables, but that was all. They understood that right away, and were very pleased, especially when Gustl told them that if they ever wanted to get off the boat in New York, Monsieur Louis here, a very sympathetic man, was of great influence at the Splendide and would get them a job.

Then Gustl took a menu and asked me: 'What would you like to have for dinner, Monsieur Louis?' He explained: 'Pick out anything but soups or spinach. We must eat portable things, which we can put into our pockets.'

I was very hungry. 'Filet mignon?' I asked.

'Yes, that's all right,' he said.

'Pommes frites?'

'Yes, anything in the pocket. The filet rare or well done, Monsieur Louis?'

'Rare, please.'

'Good, come with me, please.'

In the kitchen, Gustl announced to the cook: 'Two filets mignon rare, two pommes frites.' We waited for them and carried them into the dining-room, past Mynheer van Zoorn, who was eating his second dessert, all the way back to the last station. Our service table was conveniently built against the back of one of the pillars. I held up the metal cover that kept the food warm while Gustl, with one eye on the Hoffmeester, fished under it as if he were catching a crab; he rubbed the two filets in the beurre *maître d'hôtel* that went with them, sprinkled a little salt and pepper on them, and asked: 'What kind of mustard?' In a second he had patted the mustard over the meat, never taking his eye from the mirror in which he could see around the pillar, swished his napkin over the filets, and they were gone, napkin and all, inside his pocket.

I followed him through the dining-room, out of a side door, past a metal shaft in which we heard the engines thumping, up several companionways, until we came out on deck in the forward part of the ship. He knew a sheltered place where we could not be seen from the bridge, and where the wind was broken by winches. After we found it, Gustl ran back down to the crew's canteen to buy two bottles of beer, brought them back, and we sat down to eat under the stars.

The food tasted much better than if we had paid for it. The *Zuider Zee* beer was heavy and just the right temperature, not too cold, and later Gustl went back to the dining-room for some cheeses to go with it. From then on we ate all our meals here, hard-boiled eggs for breakfast, and even griddle cake. After we were more at home, we carried sirup and mayonnaise for lobsters in demi-tasse cups in our trousers, and in a lifeboat we kept salt and pepper, a bottle of chili sauce, and mustard. We spent the time on deck in plotting how to get out something particularly difficult and how to eat it properly.

After our first dinner, Gustl said: 'You think we are going to sleep in that terrible hole, Monsieur Louis? *Non, nononon,*' he answered himself. 'Come with me.' I followed him through the backstairs part of the ship, passing an endless number of doors, ladders, stairways, sailors and stokers coming off duty from the firing-room. We went past kitchens and storerooms, all of them swaying up and down, pounding. Finally we came to another long passage, and here Gustl opened a cabin door. 'This will be twenty dollars for the both of us,' he said. It was an unoccupied third-class cabin which he had 'rented' from a room steward. Our baggage was already in it.

'Now let's dress and go dancing,' said Gustl. We found some nice young people in the tourist class, we ordered champagne, we danced. Naturally, when we left to go back to our cabin, our new acquaintances supposed that we were from the first class, which was true enough. As I lay in the upper berth, Gustl asked me whether I would like a little fruit, and when I said I would, he pulled out his traveling case, opened it, and showed me the contents of a complete fruit stand: grapes, apples, oranges, pears, and nuts, even the nutcrackers.

As we were eating the fruit, Gustl suddenly said: 'I don't know whether I should show you this, but you have always been my friend.' Unfastening a belt from under his pajamas, he opened a little pocket in it, and brought out a wide, heavy bracelet, twinkling with rows of large diamonds, sapphires, and emeralds. Several of the emeralds were missing; Gustl had sold them, each for three hundred dollars. The rest was a fortune. He had found the bracelet in the ladies' room where he spent most of his time.

'This is my last trip,' said Gustl. 'We have the little house in Monaco; now I can pay off the mortgage and live on the Riviera in peace.'

One morning, as he had promised, the city was right outside the ship, and the leaves of a tree looked in through the porthole of our cabin. It was as if the *Zuider Zee* had been pulled down a street in Rotterdam. Around us were houses, horses, and people, and there was hardly enough water on the other side of us to let pass the little boats and tugs.

We went to Brussels together. Von Kyling had told me tales of this city from his apprenticeship there; I had read de Coster's great book about Tyl Eulenspiegel and Lamme Goedzack; and I was eager to see it, and Brabant, Bruges, Malines.

Since Gustl knew Brussels very well, I asked him to take me to its best restaurant, where I would be his host. He held down his lapels in the old gesture and said: '*Nonononon non, moi, Monsieur Louis, moi.*' He would be the host, he insisted, or not even go in. The restaurant was the Poisson Doré, and it was a temple of good cooking. No bigger than an ordinary room, it was light and happy, white and gold, but on the ceiling were puffy cherubs in a bad rococo style, and from it hung an uncouth glass chandelier with arms, little arms on big arms, laden down with crystal, and with ruby and white frosted bulbs in its center.

There were as many *maîtres d'hôtel* and waiters and piccolos as there were guests, and the service was rapid and excellent. The best and worst thing about the restaurant was its proprietor, Jean Guillaume, an excellent chef. He looked like Toscanini, but younger, more like the man on the Eau de Quinine bottle, and he also assumed the gesture of that man when he spoke. He had taken over from the Tour d'Argent in Paris the very bad idea of tying on his fowls, before they came to the table, a tag with a number and the signature of the chef, as if it were a painting. So, attached to a roast capon that was magnificently cooked, well served, and taken to pieces with a surgeon's clean cutting, there was unfortunately a tag, given to us as a souvenir, signed by Guillaume, and reading: '*Le Chapon Jean Guillaume, Numero 1978.*'

On the cold buffet under the hideous chandelier was a wonderful display: white Brabant asparagus, jellied eels (for those who like them), Saint-Lambert strawberries, great dishes of puddings, galantines, cheeses. Indeed the entire menu read like music: *le lapin à la bière, les fricadelles sauce piquante, les choesels à la madère, la poularde rôtie, les carbonnades au lambic, les écrevisses, le rognon de veau, la tête de veau en tortue, le poulet sauté Sambre-et-Meuse, les tripes al djote, le cabillaud à la flamande, le maquereau aux groseilles, le pigeon à l'ardennaise, l'oie à l'instar de Vise, doreye de Verviers, les fromages de Huy, de Harzee, et de Herves.* One can hear the elegant hunger of Lamme Goedzack in de Coster's book.

All of it was good, but best of all was the melting *filet de sole Colbert*, the fish brought from Dover and not to be had better anywhere. If Monsieur Guillaume could have been made to stay in his kitchen, this would have been God's own restaurant. His prices were high, but one cannot cook with butter and use the best and not charge for it, and so that is as it should have been. But Monsieur Guillaume not only watched you eat, gluing himself to your table, wishing you good-day and good-by, he also pushed around his waiters, which should never happen, and at the end of the dinner came an unforgivable performance. He brought his three books, '*Mes trois livres de cuisine*,' and offered to sell them.

Gustl ordered some of the best wines with our meal, and in one other particular he was nice to be with. Waiters, *maîtres d'hôtel*, when they go out, always retain their professional behavior. For example, when they help you to something, they take fork and spoon in one hand and with an expert motion secure asparagus or other food as with a pair of forceps. Gustl was different. As if he had never worked in a restaurant, he took the fork in one hand, the spoon in the other, and carried the food from the dish to my plate with a careful degree of awkwardness.

Gustl left at six on the Paris Express, with his last bow, his eyes in a last apology for himself – *Nonononon!* – his bracelet in the belt next to his skin. To New York there later came letters and photographs from Gustl, pictures of the little *pension* in Monte Carlo that showed a life of vegetable gardening, laundry, and plain meals for which one does not allow room in mind when one thinks of that city. I showed the pictures to von Kyling. It's always wonderful when something altogether wrong ends right, without the help of either religion or the police.

The Good Son

'*MONSIEUR L'AMBASSADEUR, Messieurs: Vous vous souvenez tous de cette phrase chantée par notre admirable Massenet dans Manon: "Je suis encore tout étourdie." Moi, "je suis encore tout étourdi," mon cher Président, des fleurs que vous m'avez jetées. Je les prends, et je les envoie à travers les mers à la belle France que vous connaissez et que vous aimez. Je veux vous dire ici ma gratitude, gratitude que je dois à la générosité américaine. Ayant parlé depuis bientôt quinze ans de l'amitié franco-américaine, je ne veux plus en parler, c'est déjà un lieu commun.*'

It was the usual French speech, the answer to which always was: '*Nous sommes français par l'esprit, nous sommes américains par naissance, et nous sommes français et américains par le cœur.'* The word *'cœur'* was sung all the way up from the throat through lips thrown forward; it was stretched with indulgence all the way through a continuous nod to all the tables in the room and into the applause of the distinguished assemblage. Most of the guests were old gentlemen; their chairs were pushed back from the table; they listened with narrowed eyes, their hands folded into their armpits, their legs crossed. It was always the same and sometimes went on for hours.

During the first part of the speech, a waiter came running through the room. He was pale and out of breath when he came to me, took my arm, and said: 'Come quickly – hurry – run!' I went after him, down the Ballroom stairs, through the darkened Orchid Salon, through the kitchen, down past the pantries, the laundry, the bakery, and the employees' dining-room, down again to the locker rooms and the ice machines, down past the engineer's office, the dynamos, and the plumber's shop, all the way down to the bottom through the boiler room. It was where rubbish was burned; it was dusty, dry, and hot down there, and the floor was dirty: there lay discarded flower baskets, and dead brown palms, and empty boxes from fine fashion shops, and the piles of newspapers that collect in a hotel. It smelled of steam and rubbish, for the bottom of the elevator shaft was hot and dirty and close to the boilers. At the bottom of the shaft, six stories underground, on a blood-spattered cement block, lay Mr. Sigsag.

As we all did in the evening after the operator was gone, Mr. Sigsag had, during the speeches, himself run the express lift up to his dressing-room on the tenth floor. While he was in his room the linen man had taken the car up to the sixteenth floor, and Mr. Sigsag, always in a hurry, had opened the door and stepped into the shaft. Now they had laid him on a pile of old Sunday papers and empty bags, his arms and legs in curious positions, his face covered, while two men in white uniforms bent over him to put him on a stretcher.

When an ambulance clanks through the streets, it seems that it must always be for other people, never for our own. The car sped down Fifth Avenue, turned left on Forty-second Street and past the Grand Central Station, and went up a ramp to a hospital that is named, with lack of all kindness or consideration, the Hospital for the Ruptured and Crippled.

Two specialists were called, the wet X-ray films gave them no hope, there was no chance to save him, and on a little white wagon he was wheeled into a room, a screen was put around him and the door closed, so that he could die.

His small body was loosely marked off in the few folds of the sheet; his right hand still held in a firm grasp the three-colored silver pencil. They had not bothered to wash the hand; its fingers were dirty, as they had always been, from rummaging around in his 'museum,' in the cellar, from helping to put down carpets and move around palms and tables. When guests were about, he used to hide his dirty fingers under the tails of his coat, or by making a tight fist around his silver pencil, with the thumb hidden under the fingers.

The mind does not accept all at once the idea of death; it was at that moment only a shock and its meaning entered slowly in small fragments of thought. I took his free hand and then let it go; it fell back into a sickening angle, as if it were an empty hose, bending away from the middle of the arm between the elbow and the wrist, out, away from the body. He fell into that slow, laborious but even intake of air and the noisy exhalation that are the going of life.

At a few minutes after ten he was dead.

I walked back to the hotel. The housemen were carrying out tables, rolling up carpets, and making room for the setting up of tomorrow's wedding, the last party of the season. The men had Mr. Sigsag's last blue-and-red table plan in their hands; the party was still being directed by him. It was wonderful to see the hotel live on – the lights burning, the music playing, the plants being carried in, the bakers baking, and the waiters running – as if nothing had happened.

I called up an undertaking firm, the one whose advertised name came forward first in my mind. They sent down an intelligent, quiet young man, and I was surprised and glad at his decent handling of the business: he said and did nothing that was condoling or not absolutely necessary to the business. My vacation started the day after the last party, and I had already booked a passage for home during that week. So it seemed to me best to take Sigsag home to his people. He had to have a first-class passage, and three coffins – a sealed metal one, a lead coffin around this, and a wooden transport box around the lead. We found his passport and dressed him in a black suit, a shirt, a collar and tie, and a pair of evening shoes.

The new *Europa* was in its clean design more beautiful than any liner afloat. With its clear, wide decks and well-arranged public rooms, quietly decorated and well within the idea of a ship, it was like a yacht. The smoothness of the sailing was a joy to feel. The restaurant on the sundeck was smart, its cooking and service were excellent; and, indeed, in all things, one had the certainty, more than on most ships, that one was in good, able hands. Only its straitlaced discipline made one uncomfortable. The snapping of orders by the eternal sergeants came too close to the passenger. One felt sorry for the stiff little overworked steward who stood pale and worried behind one's chair. Of course, they need not adopt the ideas on discipline of American stewards, who are as likely as not to kiss a passenger when they serve her breakfast in bed, or to nudge one on deck and ask: 'Got a match, buddy?'; but on a vacation voyage one should never have to be sorry for anyone; it should be part of the service to have rested, contented employees who are at ease.

At night, when there were only a few people about, I walked on the wide decks. It seemed often that Mr. Sigsag was a little behind me, to the left, and that if I were to turn suddenly, I could speak to him. Again and again I forgot that he was no longer alive; it was then like reaching into the air for something, or bumping into a new piece of furniture in a dark room. He was down below in a refrigerated compartment, together with two other bodies, those of a British peer and a German industrialist.

I thought about death and the hereafter, while I stood in the bow of the ship, where the lights danced and the wind howled in the rigging and the masts swayed right and left through the stars. It was impossible, it could never be; a heaven for Mr. Sigsag would have to be so complicated a place. It would have to be like the Splendide with a few pet improvements he had always talked about, with weddings, with cocktails for the old scrubladies, with coming-out parties, Bohemian glass trees, and estimates. It would have to be an all-day round of excitement, with music, telephones ringing, people running around, tables being pushed about.

Mr. Sigsag's only pleasure outside of his hotel had been his old parents' house in the little village outside Przemysl, in whose uncobbled square he arrived every summer as a hero returned from conquest. The little fire department, with coils of rope, bugles, and small hatchets hanging from its members stood behind the burgomaster. A small girl in a starched white dress, the heels of her heavy, black polished shoes together, her yellow hair pasted down, stood in front of the burgomaster, recited a poem, and handed Mr. Sigsag a bunch of flowers. In the meantime, Mr. Sigsag's twelve or more bags were being taken out of the train. He had much trouble keeping them together, for each one was marked with different initials: they had all been left behind at parties and weddings and were now filled with junk from the 'museum,' party souvenirs, streamers, dolls, New Year's Eve trumpets, confetti, balloons, artificial flowers, old billiardcloth, and discarded decoration draperies.

The scene was always filmed and shown in New York. The priest was also there, and the peasants stopped their carts to look on while Mr. Sigsag kissed the little girl, thanked her for the flowers, and then helped his peasant mother into the village's one landau, and his father after her. Then he jumped up beside the driver, and the one horse pulled them home.

The last summer he was there, he had sent his parents away on a trip, and while they were gone, for the first time in their lives, away from home, the good son prepared to carry out plans on which he had worked all winter in the hotel. He stripped himself to the waist and led the working men into house and garden.

The farmhouse in which they lived was a thick-walled stone building, covered with a roof of mossy, hand-hewn shingles, and against the side of the house was a high water wheel which turned the machinery in the blacksmith shop and pumped the large bellows of the forge. The wheel turned slowly; it was of heavy, soaked wood, covered with a green film of watermoss, and it brushed down over the moist leaves of an old willow tree whose branches swam away with the water from the wheel and then came back again in one repeated motion. The water came over a dam from a sleepy green pond behind the house, a pond that mirrored a row of swaying poplars and the hill behind them. Fat carp rolled on their sides under the streamers of water plants; they were tame, and came to the edge, looked out of the water, and silently kept saying: 'Oh, oh, oh.' White barnyard ducks swam quacking among the water lilies.

The rooms of the house itself were low and irregular, white-washed; their flooring was of scrubbed pine boards. A tile oven stood in the corner of each room, and a bake oven was built into the hall. The beds were painted blue, and were simply straw sacks laid on boards between posters. The furniture was well designed, simple peasant pieces that went with such a house.

It took Mr. Sigsag four weeks of hard work, all his vacation, to ruin this beauty. With boards and rollers over the soft ground, he directed the installation of the new big turbine where the wheel had been. Trucks rolled in, with cement and sand and tiles. The pond was drained, the carp and ducks given away, the water lilies thrown out. The pond was cemented and made smaller, the sides tiled, and a spring-board was installed at one end. The roof was taken off the house and replaced by a geometric design in red and white which spelled out the name of the family; over the name was a cross and beneath it the year. From far away it looked like a checked tablecloth stretched over the roof of the house.

From the railroad station came crates and boxes with

materials from New York and Vienna; the village children's hair was full of excelsior as they helped unpack them. There was a flagpole for the American flag, steel casement windows, wild modernistic carpets and wallpapers, a radio, an electric icebox, an ice-cream freezer, glass coffee-machines, ashtrays, floor lamps to match in color and design a bridge table with its folding chairs. There was modern furniture, nervous easy chairs of bent steel tubes that suspended one in the air and were upholstered in glossy leatherette. A fireplace was unpacked, complete with a patented lamp that flickered under the glass coals, then twisted andirons, a poker to stir the glass coals with, and for the supposed ashes a broom and a shovel on a small rack made of 'antiquated' brass, with ornaments pressed all over them.

The peasant beds, old, worn, painted in most beautiful forget-me-not blue, with saints on them, were taken away, along with the chairs that had so much peace in them and lovely simple carving with the trace of handwork on every leg. In their place came beds with inner-spring mattresses and pressed headboards, immoral little satin boudoir chairs, white frilled curtains gathered up in art-metal tie-backs, and bedside tables with mauve lampshades, thin legs, and no closet for the big honest *pot de chambre*, which was, of course, carted away with all the other good, simple things.

When the bedroom was finished, it received a clock with chimes, a large, modern instrument with an immense dial and a deep, liquid bong-bong-bong tone that was much too big for the room, as if one had carried a church tower into the house. The final touch was a copy of Molière's *Le Bourgeois Gentilhomme*, in a beautiful old binding, which, when opened, contained cigarettes.

Outside the house a few men finished laying the flagstones, on which were to be put the steel garden furniture that Mr.

Sigsag had waiting. A canary in a gilded cage arrived just in time. Mr. Sigsag tried out the telephone and the radio; he put on a bathing suit and dove into the pond, now also a pool. The dynamo hummed, the telephone rang, the radio played; he was happy, and one of the last things he did was to blow up an Abercrombie and Fitch rubber swan and try it out first on this side of the pond, then on that. Then he sent the workmen over to the church and went to get his parents.

They were afraid to walk into the new house in their new shoes; indeed, they were afraid to walk in them anyway, lest they get them dirty or scratched, for they walked mostly barefoot and in the winter in wooden sabots, and the new shoes hurt. Mr. Sigsag's mother lifted her many skirts and took her husband's hand for protection, and thus, close together, they walked through the rooms as visitors might in a museum. They sat themselves down carefully in the suspension chairs and talked in whispers, expecting to fall over backwards or to be ordered out. They could not sleep on the inner-spring mattresses and they cried all night.

The next day they sat outside the wide umbrella and looked with suspicion at the terrace, the dynamo, the pool, at this new house that was not home to them, and they watched Mr. Sigsag shaking cocktails for them and passing them little hors d'œuvres after the Shallshah recipe, cream cheese with a little bar-le-duc on it. Afterwards they ate ice cream for the first time in their lives and from it got that hard cold headache up over the nose and between the eyes. It ended with their going to church.

The church had Mr. Sigsag's new bells and rang with them. It was also freshly painted in salmon-red, by his men and with his paint. There were new comfortable prayer chairs for his parents in the first row, velvet pillows, polished name plates. Over them at the side of the church was a large two-paneled stained-glass window with the father's and mother's patron saints in a landscape, below which, in big ruby letters, was the name of the family.

After church Mr. Sigsag left again, with his twelve bags of different initials, empty now. On the train he was photographed waving good-by, by the electrical engineer who was staying to show the father how to work the turbine. The engineer ran after the train and handed the film camera up to Sigsag, who kept filming the farewells of the villagers until the train went around a curve and was on its way to Vienna.

It is good that people can lose themselves in weeping, like children. The filthy performance that is a funeral began. I had taken him back here because it was in accordance with his wishes, because it would make it possible for his devout mother to go to his grave and pray for him. He had worked so hard in the Splendide. I had often made fun of him, saying that when he died he would be buried in a dress coat, shrouded in a tablecloth; that a *maître d'hôtel* would read the service, waiters be his pallbearers, and napkins and aprons hang from the corners of the hearse; and that before they put him in the ground, he would lift the lid of his coffin and change the floral arrangements.

He had died so, in his dress coat, and here was the hearse, drawn by two fat horses with black plumes and cloaks. The priest was a fat, common man in a shiny, worn soutane. Mr. Sigsag's bells tolled in slow measure while the peasants prayed in a low voice like the even droning of bees. The firemen came, then the veterans, and a singing society. One man with a sky-blue sash draped over his shoulder ran up and down the line of parade with the policeman, who wore white gloves, held his shako in his hand, and carried a saber. These two pushed people into place and arranged the order in which they were to march; they moved the teacher and the schoolchildren up ahead, argued with the band about it, and moved them back again.

When all was ready, the flags of the several societies up ahead were raised; they began to sway forward, and the people behind them stepped out as they got room. There were chickens and pigs in the streets and along the road to the cemetery. When the boys up in the church tower saw the procession start, they rang the bells with a stronger, louder, faster clangor; the peasants raised their voices, the priest raised his, and the few brasses in the band yelled a sad march.

It had rained through the night; the road was slippery and filled with puddles. The parents walked with a will-less stoop, staring ahead, and their monotonous sobbing never changed until it was broken by the mother's shriek when the coffin sank down between the wet walls of the small grave.

The burgomaster made a speech at the grave. He was a big butcher, clumsy, jovial, and bald. His thick red fingers were squeezed into black gloves which he could not quite get up over his hands to button, and he wore an ancient, unkempt, too-small top hat which sat insecure on his head. He began to weep in the middle of his speech, and that started all the men and women off, large tears running down over the peasant faces. The burgomaster became confused, and, in trying to place a big wreath on the coffin, he lost hold of his hat. The hat rolled down the wet earth and fell into the water that had collected at the bottom of the grave. When it was pulled out and handed him, he looked at it, holding it away from himself, and stopped crying, concerned now with his hat alone. He turned aside and tried to clean it, while the priest delivered his speech of praise of the good son, chanted a last farewell, and sprinkled the coffin.

Through all this, I had watched a child, a little girl who was completely happy and interested. Her slim sunburned feet reached out to the edge of the soggy earth that had been shoveled out of the grave, and she squeezed it in ribbons up through the spaces between her small toes and molded little pieces with her arches, bending her toes to hold more of the soft wet clay. In her alone was reason and comfort.

The wind bent the young trees; the delicate shadows of the almost transparent, new green leaves moved under them. Rows of daisies turned their heads away from the wind. With them, grass began to stand up again after the rain, and the cemetery sparrows sat with puffed feathers in the sunlight on the bars of large rusty crosses and the headstones of tombs of children. They drank out of the small holy-water kettles that hung at the foot of many graves.

The music started again, after the procession had once more been arranged in order outside the cemetery by the man with the blue sash, who ran up and down as he had before. Everybody seemed more lax now; they moved their necks in tight collars and twisted their shoulders in unaccustomed clothes. A few of the boys came out of line and laughed. The melody was now a military air; the peasants who were veterans, the postal clerk, and teacher, shouldered their umbrellas like guns and started to mark time with small steps until the line had drawn itself out again and they could take full, firm strides back to the village. There they ate and drank at Mr. Sigsag's last banquet while I took the train to Munich and Schliersee.

The Old Ritz

THE HOTEL I have called the 'Splendide' was really the old Ritz-Carlton, which stood on the corner of Madison Avenue and Forty-sixth Street. Albert Keller, president of the corporation, appears in the hotel stories as 'Otto Brauhaus.' He was all I said he was, in kindness and character. Theodore Titze, 'Victor,' was the *maître d'hôtel* of all time. He exercised an iron discipline on his underlings and operated with the charm of a Prussian sergeant. There were many nice people and many more awful ones. What was most valuable to me were the models the hotel provided: the most beautiful women, the most powerful men, judges that took gifts, savants who got drunk and turned into idiots. There were figures for every kind of play, in front and backstairs.

The Crystal Room (the main dining-room), designed by Warren Whitney, was of a grandeur and beauty no longer possible in New York hotel construction. Tall marble columns supported a concave ceiling. The decoration was in the style of the Brothers Adam. A balcony in four sections ran along the wall.

In my early days at the Ritz, I had to clear the dishes from the part of the balcony that was to the right of the entrance. At the beginning of lunch, when Armand Vesey's orchestra played, and the stately procession of people began, there were naturally no dirty dishes. There was butter to be brought up, and ice water, and rolls. The rolls were delicious and warm, and the butter was the best; in back of the screen that hid the service doors, there was a sideboard with an assortment of sauces. A roll there, with plenty of butter and a squirt of ketchup, was a good thing.

Next to the base of one of the marble columns was a stack of menus, the backs of which offered very good sketching surfaces. The palm there protected me, and I was fascinated by the beauty of ugliness for the first time in my life. Two of the restaurant's most esteemed and demanding clients, whom I called Monsieur and Madame Dreyspool, were my favorite subjects.

Another esteemed guest, who lived in the hotel, was a famous cartoonist. He was known for his generosity in tipping and for never looking at a bill. The entire staff from the *maîtres d'hôtel* to the chambermaids considered him a 'gentleman par excellence.' Spurred on by a waiter with whom I worked as a bus boy, I decided to become a cartoonist. By 1926, after years of work and countless disappointments, it seemed as if I had achieved my goal. I sat up in the cupola of the old *World* building with a group of funnymen: Webster, Milt Gross, Ernie Bushmiller, and Haenigsen. Walter Berndt, who drew 'Smitty' in the *Daily News*, helped me a great deal. There was constant laughter in that cupola.

Unfortunately, there were so many complaints about my strip, which was called 'Count Bric-a-Brac,' that after six months, during which no syndicate had picked it up, I was fired. It was a bitter time, for I had to go back to the Ritz; and the old cashiers and the *maîtres d'hôtel* said, 'Ah, Monsieur Bemelmans, who felt himself too good for this dirty trade, is back again. *Tiens, tiens* [Well, well].'

THE OLD RITZ

*

One day, I looked into one of the many mirrors of the Ritz. I was thirty-one years old. The rosy cheeks were more rosy than they had been when I arrived from Tirol, but this was due to indoor exposure. The capillaries had exploded from too much drinking. I had a stomach. I gasped when I walked up the stairs. Morally, I felt as disgusting as I looked, and I said to myself, 'How many more of these meals, how much more of this life before you look like Theodore, the penguin-shaped *maître d'hôtel* or, what is even worse, like some of the guests? You will be unhappy, useless, a snob, a walking garbage can. Get out, throw yourself into life. All you can learn here, you know.'

From the deluxe protectorate and refuge that the Ritz had been, I stepped out into the cold world, where you had to get up on a stand to get your shoes shined, carry your own shirts to the laundry, and eat in places that were Greek, Chinese, Italian, and German.

I had planned my change from fantasy to real life with terrible timing. After two weeks away from the Ritz, everything suddenly slipped out of place. Came the crash of 1929. Nobody bought any pictures, nobody had any money. My friend Ervine Metzl, a commercial artist, sat desolate in his studio, with nothing to do. I could not go back to the Ritz, and, as things went from bad to worse, I moved in with my former valet, Herman Struck, and his wife. They lived in Astoria, on the top floor of a house with a beautiful view of Manhattan and a cellar from which I carried the coal upstairs. We had a *gemütlich* existence together – lived on potatoes, kraut, dumplings, and sausages; looked at New York, evenings, and talked of the 'old days.' Money, there was none. Frau Struck did the laundry; occasionally, Herman brought home a bottle of wine or a cigar. The Ritz was running very quietly. I walked every day, to the tune of 'Brother, can you spare a dime?,' across the Fifty-ninth Street Bridge.

I never sold anything – never. And I had reduced my demands to the cost of paper. I sat for a while in a café and tried to draw people, but, when they saw themselves, they shook their heads. I came home, freezing, and with stiff fingers opened the door of the house in Astoria. There was a dreadful hour then – before Herman came home and while his wife was out shopping – when I was alone, just as the light of day waned. I sat thinking on the theme of ending it – how? Gas? No; Herman would come in and strike a match, and the little house would go up with a big bang. Poison? We didn't have any; besides, it's painful. Jump off the bridge? In the summer, yes; but now, into that ice-cold river? Thank you, no. In front of the subway? Messy. If we had a car, then I could put it into the garage, let the radio and the motor go, and die beautifully. But Herman had only a motorcycle with a sidecar – and, besides, the garage leaked; it was made of loosely nailed-together boards.

To hang oneself is always possible, for you need only a rope. We had a rope. When they redecorated the Crystal Room at the Ritz, all the old stuff was thrown away, or rather, it lay on the floor, and anybody who wanted something picked it up. So there was the old rope that had been used to hold people back at the entrance to the Crystal Room. This now was in the stairhall, to hold on to on the way up. It would be just long enough to go around the branch of the old tree in the yard. A chair to kick from under you was all that would be needed, and you were off to a better world. I thought it would be quite nice to have this last connection with the old Ritz – this soft, elegant, velvet-covered rope, in my favorite color, emerald green. I grabbed it with a feeling of security and friendship whenever I went up or down the stairs.

Herman's ambition had been to be a concert violinist. His father had been a restaurant violinist in Vienna and had given him instruction. But the son had not inherited his father's talent and had no ear at all for music, although he was the only one who did not know this. His favorite time of playing was towards evening. The music, which seemed to be composed by Schönberg, was extremely atonal, or anti-tonal.

I was in my room one evening, nailing a frame together to put some canvas on, when Frau Struck came in and said: 'Please, shh! Daddy is playing with the Philharmonic.'

Herman was sitting in front of his radio, accompanying the musicians in Liszt's *Hungarian Rhapsody*, when there was another disturbance – a knock on the door. Herr Keller, the manager of the Ritz, stood in the doorway.

'So here is where you live?' he said. The canary answered, 'Peep, peep.' He looked around, was given a cocktail, and stayed for dinner. At the end, wiping his mouth with his napkin, he looked around again and said, 'You might as well come back to the hotel.' He meant that everything there – the glasses, plates, curtains, candles, carpets, the rope in the stairhall – was from the Ritz.

Frau Struck resented this a little and said, 'All honestly come by, Herr Keller, if you please,' and she showed him the chips in the cups, the cracks in the glasses, the rips in the curtains, the cigar-burn holes in the carpets – all neatly repaired.

'*Ja, ja,*' said Herr Keller, '*ich weiss schon* [I know]. Is there anything else you need? Just tell me, and I'll see that it gets broken.' The good friend and benefactor left.

WORK

I didn't hang myself with the beautiful velvet rope, nor did I go back to the Ritz. I made a drawing in pen and ink of Herman playing with the Philharmonic and, with six other such simple efforts, sent it to the *Saturday Evening Post*, which bought and published all seven of them. That was my first toehold on the shaky ladder of success.

In a moment of optimism, I rented a studio in a house on Eighth Street. Within a few weeks, I again felt like a hopeless failure. A wave of black depression came over me. Outside my windows was a miserable view. I pulled down the shades and painted scenes of the Austrian Tirol on them. A lithographer, by the name of Tom Little, who had a studio in the same building, saw the shades and the room – I had painted on the walls as well. One evening he brought the second Mademoiselle who was to be very important in my life, and to whom I owe virtually everything in my career as an artist. She was Miss May Massee, the children's book editor at The Viking Press, and she said simply, 'Do a children's book on Tirol – make it just like the shades on the windows and the pictures on the wall.' She folded a piece of paper several times and explained, 'Here goes black and white; on these pages you can use color.' A few months later I handed in the manuscript for *Hansi*. Next came *The Golden Basket* and then the first book for adults, *My War with the United States*. Meanwhile I had met the third Mademoiselle, and it was in the pattern of my life that I should find and marry someone who had intended to become a nun but had left the convent as a novice. When Barbara was born, we were romantically poor – the garret kind of existence. My mother asked for photographs, but we couldn't afford any. However, I knew a photographer, and in the waiting room of his studio was a table full of baby pictures. I took one of these and sent it to my mother, who wrote how very close to me the likeness was.

At first Mama was not impressed by my success. Writers and artists were to her forever insecure, and there was nothing one could expect from them but unhappiness. On a visit to New York, she was especially shocked by seeing a manuscript of mine that Harold Ross of *The New Yorker* had sent back for corrections. All the way down the margin of every page, it said, 'What mean? What mean? What in hell mean?'

It precipitated a crisis and tears again. Mama sat with the manuscript in her trembling hands; it was exactly like many years ago when I came home from the *Königliche Realschule* in Regensburg with my composition all red with professor's ink.

'*O, mein Gott! O, mein lieber Gott im Himmel!*' she sighed, looking at Ross's margin notes. 'What does it mean, "What mean? What mean?"'

'It means that he doesn't understand what I have written means.'

However, at long last, she breathed easier. My father-in-law was the president of a bank in Mount Kisco. When I sold my first story to the movies, I deposited some money in a trust fund for Barbara. He was so overcome by this that he made me a director. My name appeared on the letterhead of the Trust Company of Northern Westchester.

I wrote a letter on this stationery to Mama; she carried it in her handbag for years. She had shown it around so much that it was worn off at the edges, and whenever I came to Regensburg, everybody addressed me not as they normally would, as '*Herr Bemelmans*,' '*Herr Poet*,' or '*Herr Painter*,' but as '*Herr Direktor*.'

Theodore and 'The Blue Danube'

DINNER WAS over, the room was filled with smoke and empty tables, the orchestra played 'The Blue Danube,' and a waiter cleared off the buffet.

'*Sale métier! Bande de voleurs!*' said Theodore Navarre *né* Navratil, the *maître d'hôtel*, and he thought of that dog Wenzel Swoboda, headwaiter many years back, at the restaurant in Vienna where he had served his apprenticeship ...

The tip of Theodore's nose was white with anger, he crumpled the list of reservations, tore a table plan into small pieces, and

walked up to his dressing-room. He counted the tips. Filthy money! Filthy profession! The end of 'The Blue Danube' came up the stairs and he had to think again of that specimen of a dog, Wenzel Swoboda . . .

Theodore had been young then, he had wavy blond hair and his first slim tailcoat . . . it was spring in Vienna . . . The

restaurant had a garden shaded with old chestnut trees that were in full bloom. Under one of them stood a buffet, a square table covered with a white cloth, and arranged on this were trays of pastry, peach, apricot, plum, and apple tarts, and a bowl of whipped cream with fragrant wild strawberries.

Wenzel Swoboda was the *maître d'hôtel* and to this restaurant came every day the not altogether young but American Mrs. Griswold Katzenbach. She always asked for Theodore; he served her under a large yellow umbrella.

One Friday afternoon a dark cloud floated past the hotel and stopped over the chestnut tree, water came out of it, and together

with the blossoms from the tree messed up the pastries, the tarts, and the whipped cream with the strawberries.

Swoboda saw this and looked for Theodore; Theodore leaned over Madame Griswold Katzenbach and pointed to the scenery.

The dog Swoboda danced to the table and kicked Theodore in the heel; then he himself pointed to the scenery and smiled at Madame Katzenbach, and while she looked he hissed at Theodore in Bohemian, 'Clear off the buffet – son of a swine,' and he kicked him again with more power and higher up.

The orchestra played 'The Blue Danube.' Theodore attacked the buffet, he cleared it with the speed of an acrobat, stacking tarts and pastries all over himself – in one trip he made the kitchen – strawberries and all – without dropping anything . . .

Ever since then Theodore had suffered when he heard 'The Blue Danube,' saw a buffet, or came upon a chestnut tree in bloom. As for Madame Katzenbach, she lives upstairs in this very hotel where he sat on his bed in thought. She talks to him for hours in the dining-room where he stands behind her chair. When she meets him on the street, she stares at a lamp post or looks into a shop window until he has passed, but then they were all alike – and besides in two more weeks they could all go to the devil! In this hope Theodore mumbled a litany that went: *'Que le diable les emporte – j'en ai assez, moi – pique-assiette, pique-fourchette, je m'en vais, moi, je m'en fiche – foutez-moi la paix, bande de sauvages, salauds!'*

Every year Theodore Navarre went to Europe, first class in a modest cabin on one of the slow boats, because none of the hotel guests ever crossed on them. He took the Orient Express but would change to a slow train in Salzburg. It took him to a little village on the shore of a quiet lake and he walked to the hotel Alpenrose, and there he took the cure for his soul.

As soon as he arrived at the Alpenrose he went up to his room – Number 5, with a balcony – waited for his trunks, and came down a changed man.

He took a bath in esteem and respect, and this started in the morning when he appeared at the table for breakfast. Stefi, the waitress, with soft round arms and flaxen hair, wished him a

loud and healthy 'Good morning, Herr Direktor,' and 'How has the Herr Direktor slept?' and 'What does the Herr Direktor want for breakfast?'

It would never do to live in this respectable hotel without a title. Everybody has one and Herr Theodore Navarre had written, where the register asked for his name, birthday, profession, domicile, and nationality – *Navarre, Theodore, July 6, 1878, Direktor, New York, USA.*

Dinner was at noon, at a round table. Most of the guests came here year after year and they were from left to right:

Herr und Frau Generalkonsul von Kirchhoff, Vienna
Herr und Frau Oberstaatsanwalt Zeppezauer, Vienna
Herr und Frau Professor der alten Philologie Leichsenring, Graz
Herr Direktor Theodore Navarre, New York

Supper was at seven, the ladies dressed in crêpe de Chine and chiffons; afterwards there were parties, once a week the peasant theater, quiet evenings at the hotel – Schubert *Lieder*, cards.

Herr Direktor Navarre was invited to play, to swim, to dance, everyone listened to him – no one called him Theodore, he sat on a chair and important men took off their hats when they met him on the street and smiled and said, 'Good morning, Herr Direktor – good afternoon, Herr Direktor – and good evening, Herr Direktor.'

Herr Direktor had a good deal of trouble getting on and off his bicycle, but he stopped, even on a curve, for a few words with the gendarmes. They saluted and spoke to him with their heels together, their hands at the seams of their green trousers – it was good medicine.

On his birthday Stefi decorated the table with crocuses and Herr Direktor ordered twelve bottles of the young heady wine that was the best he could find in the cellar of the hotel.

The Alpenrose did itself proud with lake trout *au bleu*, Wiener Schnitzel with cucumber salad, and a pancake, big as a garden hat. The Generalkonsul made a speech, the bottles were emptied, and Herr Direktor Navarre sang.

After dinner it was decided to hire a car and go all together to the other side of the lake and take coffee there.

The automobile arrived and slowly turned the lake for them. Herr Professor Leichsenring, who sat next to the driver, pointed at a dark cloud, but the driver said that it hung too high and would pass.

On this other side of the lake, a table had been set close to the water; two rowboats bobbed up and down. The restaurant 'On the Lake' was elegant; it had a waiter.

Herr Direktor Navarre stared at a loose button hanging from the man's shiny dress coat while he ordered Cointreau for the ladies and drank brandy with the men. On a painted platform played a small orchestra, zither, guitar, and fiddle. Frau Oberstaatsanwalt's cup was empty.

'Psst,' more coffee – Direktor Navarre turned in his chair and looked for the waiter with the loose button.

He saw a large chestnut tree; under it stood a buffet, a square table covered with linen. Arranged on it were pastries, apricot, pear, and plum tarts, Apfelstrudels, wild strawberries, and a bowl of whipped cream.

The zither player plucked his strings.

The wind leaned into the tree, it swayed, the dark cloud hung over it, rain started to fall and with it the blossoms of the chestnut tree, like rose-tinted popcorn.

Without knowing it, Herr Direktor Navarre left his table and rushed to the buffet, he stacked cakes and pastries all over himself, took along the whipped cream, the wild strawberries, and disappeared into the kitchen.

The orchestra finished 'The Blue Danube.'

'Herr Direktor!' said Frau Generalkonsul. 'Herr Direktor?' looked the others. . . .

He left with the first train, the one that carries peasants to Salzburg, and he never came back.

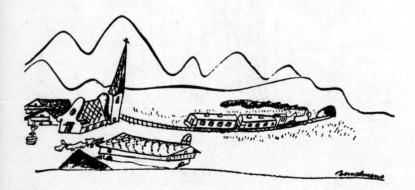

Play

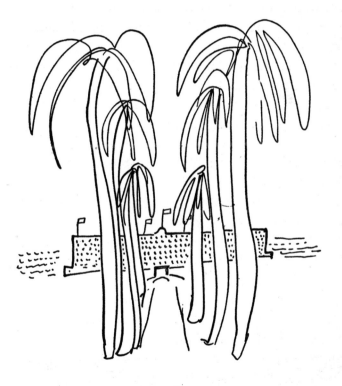

Dear General,
What a Surprise!

MY FRIEND Anthony produces plays. I meet him about once a year, usually on Times Square, running to or from a rehearsal in a sad, unbuttoned overcoat, which he has owned as long as I have known him and which he never takes off.

Last season we met on Forty-sixth Street. He slapped me on the back and pulled me out of the sidewalk traffic into a white-tiled grotto on whose walls were mats of artificial grass. Pineapples hung from the ceiling, and on a counter were a stack of cold frankfurters, a mountain of coconuts, and a radio, framed in mustard pots, playing a Toscanini concert. It was Saturday and late.

When Anthony says anything he smiles so widely that he has to close his eyes – big, black eyes, which when open interfere with the mask of complete happiness that announces all things, good and bad, alike. Anthony smiled and said, 'I'm doing an anti-Nazi play. There's a part in it for you. Wanna be an actor? It opens in three weeks. I'll send you the script in the morning.'

The play was in the next day's mail, bound in blue cardboard. Next to it was a small pocket-sized folder. Outside the folder was printed: 'German General.' Inside, held by a clip, was half a sheet of transparent typewriter paper and on this was written my part. It read: *The Germans enter. First a platoon of soldiers followed by a Lieutenant. The Lieutenant is followed by a Colonel. The German Colonel introduces himself to the Austrian officers.*

An orderly off stage: Attention! *You enter.*

The German Colonel: His Excellency Graf Ottokar von Sporentritt zu Donnersberg – Commanding General of the Garde Grenadier Regiment zu Fuss Nummer Eins. *You salute.*

The Austrian General's wife enters. Austrian General's wife: General – what a surprise!

You are surprised, you turn, bend over her hand, and kiss it.

You: Dear lady, I am delighted to see you again.

You mix with the officers.

A line under this ended my part.

I had barely spoken the lines a few times when the telephone rang and I was instructed to be at the Belasco for rehearsal at eleven o'clock.

Promptly at eleven, I sat at the edge of the ground cloth of the Belasco. A man came toward me, asked my name, nationality, the place of my birth, and for fifty dollars. He was from Equity and he made me a member.

After the Equity man had congratulated me and gone, another actor introduced me to the members of the company, and then we watched an earnest young man make chalk marks on the floor. He was the stage manager. When he had finished marking he sat down at a table at the side of the stage and opened the typescript of the play. The rehearsal began.

A newly engaged actor came late. He was to play the part of an American journalist, and as he took his coat off he said, 'Oh, they're on their feet already.' This meant that the rehearsals had progressed far enough for the actors to walk about and speak their lines or read them out of little folders such as I had left at home, for which there is a fine of five dollars. I also learned that 'Upstage' is in the back of the stage and 'Downstage' is in front, nearer the audience.

My friend Anthony from that day on always sat in one of the fauteuils in the first row of the orchestra. Behind him sat two men, one in gray flannel slacks, yellow shoes, and a tweed jacket, a long ivory cigarette holder in his teeth. The other man had a mustache. Both had pads and pencils, and most of the time they held their heads sideways in the position in which one admires a rare vase, a good picture, or one's cute child. These two men were the authors.

After we had rehearsed for two hours, Anthony sent out for ham on rye and a paper container of coffee. This was his diet for the next three weeks.

The authors, who came from Hollywood, went to lunch at '21,' the actors to a cheap lunchroom which seemed always to be directly across the street from the stage door of whatever theater we rehearsed in.

For three weeks we moved from one theater to another, into little and big theaters, theaters with plays in them and empty theaters, and most of the time I sat on a chair in the back of the stage and waited for the third act and my cue.

The chairs and boxes on which I sat were always broken and dirty, it was drafty and dark. Next to me on other broken chairs sat and whispered the other actors, who also waited for their cues.

Dear General, What a Surprise!

When the long rehearsals were over, the stage manager called the actors together and said, 'All right, you can go now. Be back here at eight o'clock,' or, 'You can go now. Be back here at eleven tomorrow. That's all.'

After the second week's rehearsals were over (there was no pay for the first), the actors all received envelopes with twenty dollars in them. I spoke to one of them about the twenty dollars being very little. He fished the money out of the narrow envelope with two fingers, caressed the bills, folded them carefully after counting the money, and then gave me a curious answer.

'My dear fellow, don't be silly,' he said. 'This is absolutely marvelous. Why, a few years ago we received nothing for rehearsals – not a penny for five weeks of rehearsals. This' – he unfolded the bills again – 'is extremely generous – it's wonderful!'

'Shhhhh!' said the stage manager.

My confidant, a gentle, precise Englishman, bent closer and whispered, 'There was a time, you know, when we had to buy our own costumes – wigs, gloves, and what not. Oh! I must tell you a funny story about a pair of stage gloves, about a pair of lemon-yellow gloves—'

'Quiet, back there!' said the stage manager.

My friend shrank a little and was quiet for a while, then he leaned over again and whispered into my ear, 'Years ago, in London, I played opposite a very important actor, comedy of manners, Haymarket Theatre. He played a lord. I was his valet. We had to furnish our own wardrobe. In the second act he called for his gloves, a pair of lemon-yellow gloves. He had to put them on so a lady would recognize him by them. We had a bit of a tiff over these gloves: he insisted that I buy them; I said it was he

who should, because he wore them. He pointed to the script where was written, "Valet enters with gloves in his right hand, hands them to Lord, who puts them on."

"'You can't come on without them," he said, "so you must buy them."

'He absolutely refused to do so himself. And, mind you, he was drawing twice my salary.

'Came opening night, and I taught him a lesson, the bounder! Last minute before curtain time I ran out to a fruiterer's, bought three bananas, peeled them carefully, and hung the skins out of my right hand. From out there, they looked more like gloves than real gloves. When he called, "Jarvis, my gloves – my lemon-yellow gloves!" I handed him the peels, hü, hü, hü!'

'Shhh! Quiet back there!'

'Cured him,' added my friend almost inaudibly, as if under the protective bedcovers of a nursery.

A few days before the opening of our anti-Nazi play we started to rehearse the third act. I walked up and down in the wings and tried my lines.

'Dear lady, what a surprise!' – no – 'Dear lady, I am delighted to see you again.'

My cue came, I marched in, saluted, looked surprised, bent to kiss her hand, kissed it, and said, 'Dear lady, I am delighted to see you again.' With my most elegant gesture I pulled a chair that stood a little to the right, for the lady to sit down on.

The play stopped the moment I touched the chair. The stage manager ran in from the wings. He stuttered, waved in the air with both hands, and when he had found his breath, yelled, 'For God's sake don't touch that chair! Don't ever move that chair again! Don't move anything! You'll throw the whole play out of gear.' He took the chair back again and carefully placed it on its chalk marks.

The actors looked at one another and shook their heads, in an oratorio of surprise, shock and pity. The authors had come down out of their second-row chairs, leaned over the footlights like two worried mothers watching a child drown. Anthony shook his head and looked at his watch. The stage manager wiped his head and said, 'All right now, that's all. You can go now. Be back at three o'clock.'

After everyone had left, the famous actress who played the lead, the role of the Austrian General's wife, smiled, walked

toward me, took my arm, and said, 'Look, dear, watch me carefully, slowly repeat after me, "I am delighted to see you, dear lady" – or how does it go again?' I told her, 'Dear lady, I am delighted to see you again.'

She said it for me once more, effortless as music. As liquid pearls on a string the words came from her lips. It was a superb reading of my part and I repeated it after her three times. 'That's much better,' she said.

'Now look, darling,' she said in consoling tones, 'never, never, never move anything on any stage. That, my dear, is the first thing for you to remember. Secondly, don't twitch, don't dance, don't wiggle or move, don't start talking, until I have crossed over to your side. Acting is timing.

'Don't mind this, dear, but I feel someone must tell you this. You see, the audience out there, they are like little children. If you move a finger, they take their eyes from me to your hand. They want to see what you are going to do next, and I might as well not be on the stage. It kills my lines.

'Just now, when we rehearsed it, you walked on my lines, dear. Watch your timing. Now let's try it again.'

Anthony, wrapped in his overcoat, sat out in the audience with his ham on rye and his nose in the container of coffee.

'Oh, another thing,' said my mentor, 'don't ever play with your back to the audience – don't ever!'

We tried it again.

'Oh, General – what a surprise!'

I turned and looked surprised. She walked across the stage, lithe and free as Le Gallienne in *The Swan*. I bent over her hand and kissed it, counted to five, and said, 'Dear lady, I am delighted to see you again.'

'You see,' she said, 'it's very simple.'

We went out to celebrate the simplicity with lunch at the Algonquin and even sat at a table next to George Jean Nathan's. At three o'clock we went to another theater to continue rehearsals.

The stage manager made chalk marks on the floor, the authors came backstage, and the one with the cigarette holder asked me to step aside with him. The other author waited in the gangway. One was to my left, the other to my right.

'They'll never hear you out there. Louder, much louder,' said the one with the hunting jacket. 'You're a general, see? You're the big cheese. When you come on like this, see, with your chest

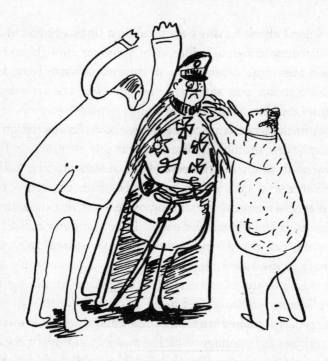

out, you walk in as if you owned the place. They're all scum as far as you are concerned – a lot of weaklings. You're taking the place over, you're headman. Know what I mean?'

'More schmaltz,' the other said.

'But you're also a gentleman,' added the first, 'so when you see her, you kinda drop the military air a little. You're surprised, like this, pleasantly, but not too friendly.' The author showed me on his face how a German general is pleasantly surprised. Both of them stood aside to let me try it.

'Dear lady, I am delighted to see you again.' I did it with gestures and pantomime.

Both of them shook their heads and looked worried, and one

said, 'I don't think he was cut out to be a German general. Too soft.' Turning to me, he added, 'Not Prussian enough, and you haven't the right accent. Try it this way: "Dear lady, I am delighted to see you again."' He screamed in the accents and voice of Lew Lehr of the newsreels.

They both escorted me to the ladies' room. An electrician was called to turn the lights on and I was left to practice. I had several visitors during the rest of the afternoon. The authors came twice and said, 'Much better.' The famous actress came and said, 'Remember the timing.' The Englishman with the yellow-glove story came and said, 'I hope you don't mind, but I feel I must tell you this: when you speak your lines, look at her face, not at her navel. Otherwise your words will drop on the floor – blup, blup, blup – and die there.' Last of all, Anthony came: 'Louder, still louder! You have to project yourself. You'll never get across. They won't hear a word in the fourth row.'

After the stage manager had dismissed us that night, I took a bus. I must have said loudly, 'Dear lady, I am delighted to see you again,' because everybody looked at me and the woman next to me said, 'Why I have never seen you before!'

I excused myself, explained that I was an actor going over my part. The woman got up and went to another seat.

The next day we moved to the theater in which we were to appear. The scenery was up. In the flies above hung the scenery of another anti-Nazi play that had folded up there a few days ago. 'You can have it for two bucks,' said the stage-door watchman; and he added that the producers of that play had not enough money left to have the scenery carted away.

Our theater had been rented out to a theatrical society from the Bronx who had bought out the house for a preview that night. In the dressing-room which I shared with my colonel hung my uniform – a splendid garment, its breeches bearing the wide, carmine stripes of the general staff, the coat laden with the Iron Cross first, second, and third class, and the order Pour le Mérite. There was an exquisite pair of boots and an elaborate cavalry saber with golden belt and chased buckle. Over all I wore a cape weighted down by a sable collar four feet wide. My colonel was only slightly less magnificent; his cape had a mink collar one foot wide.

All day the first and second acts were rehearsed, the actors were let go one hour sooner, at six, and we were back at eight to make up and dress.

My colonel hung up his street clothes, took off his old shoes, and, sitting in his underwear, showed me how to smear grease paint over a layer of cold cream. He himself used olive oil out of a small bottle for a base because, he said, it lasted longer and was cheaper and if the play closed you could make salad dressing out of it, or use it to cook. He showed me how to put blue shadows over and under my eyes, and finally he traced my eyelids with an eyebrow pencil so worn down that he had to hold it between his fingernails.

We helped each other button up the tight uniform collar, slip on the boots, and tighten belt and spurs. Then we went down and stood in the wings to watch the first two acts.

Everybody wished everyone else good luck. The slim German girl who played the heroine spat three times – toi, toi, toi! – on my sable collar, the Continental actors' way of wishing good luck. She also said, '*Hals und Beinbruch!*' – a phrase that skiers and acrobats shout to each other as they go up into the snowfields or to their trapezes.

The curtain was still down. Outside was a humming sound like

a swarm of bees flying past, a dangerous noise punctuated by the sound of seats being pushed down and the rustling of programs.

The stage manager said, 'All right, first act.' The actors walked on the stage. For most of that act the American journalist had to hide in a telephone booth and spy. The actor who played that part went into the booth and closed the door. My colonel leaned down and whispered, 'Poor fellow! It's all right now, but it will be hell in there next summer.' The curtain went up, the play was on.

The first two acts went by, the third act and my cue came on with the speed of a car that is going to run you over. My feet and legs left me, my mouth was filled with cotton, and I repeated over and over, 'Dear lady, I am delighted to see you again – don't touch that chair, don't wiggle, you're the big cheese, timing, don't walk on her lines – Dear lady – ' The gentle Englishman squeezed my hand and said: 'Go out there and give it to them!' Then came the cue: 'His Excellency Graf Ottokar von Sporentritt zu Donnersberg, Commanding General of the Garde Grenadier Regiment zu Fuss Nummer Eins!'

Somehow I was on the stage, saluted, kissed her hand, 'Dear lady, I am delighted to see you again—'

But it would not have mattered what I said. From the moment I came on, the audience hissed, booed, and stamped their feet.

We had never had time to rehearse what I was to do after I had said my lines. I said them in the center of the scene, almost at the footlights, and I would have remained there, but for my English friend. He came and took my arm with a patrolman's determined grip and said something about going out into the garden, because the audience had just begun to listen again, and he carted me to the back of the stage and out.

'You walked on my lines again, dear,' said the actress, wagging a finger. 'And, darling, on opening night please don't wiggle that sword. You'll ruin everything. Everything depends on you in this scene.'

I went home. I could hardly speak. I had shouted myself hoarse. The next morning I had a fever, but I thought, 'The play must go on!' and went to gargle and took some quinine, until I read in *The Times* that I had laryngitis and that another actor would take my place and play the General at twenty-four hours' notice.

Dear General, What a Surprise!

That evening, like a murderer to his victim's burial, was I drawn to opening night, to hear another man say, 'Dear lady.' He did it very well, with perfect timing, without walking on her lines or wiggling his sword.

After the show, I went backstage. The famous actress put her hand on my shoulder. 'But I tried to tell you how to play it, dear,' she said.

The press agent said, 'You shouldn't hang around here. You should be in bed, for Christ's sake.' And he added, 'What the hell you care? Be glad you're out of it. It's a flop. This is a coffin, this theater. Anybody wants to be an actor is nuts.'

The play lasted one night.

When it was over and the audience had left, I looked for Anthony. He sat in the last row of the orchestra in his old coat – cold and alone, like a wet mouse. He has the theater for an illness. With his eyes closed, he smiled his wide grimace and said, 'I guess I'll have to look for another play.'

The authors had left, one for Jersey, to shoot pheasants, the other for Hollywood. They had not said good-by, even to Anthony.

Up in our dressing-room my colonel, who had worried a little while ago about the summer's heat in the telephone booth, packed up, put on shoes with their heels worn off. His threadbare coat hanging from his shoulders, he stuffed the little bottle half full of olive oil, the eyebrow pencil stub, his dirty powder puff, and the rest of his make-up into a battered biscuit tin and then walked out.

On the dressing table we had shared was an envelope, torn open with his name on it. Some figures were written on the back of it. It was the twenty dollars for the last week's rehearsal, and deducted from it was the cost of two tickets for opening night, seven dollars. That left him thirteen dollars.

Dog Story

FOR MANY years our summer vacations were spent in an old peasant house, and everybody who came to see us was breathless, partly on account of the beauty of the scenery, but chiefly because the house stood atop a steep hill, overlooking a village on the shore of a remote Austrian lake.

The landscape was as simple as bread and water. A ring of dark, green mountains which anyone could climb reflected themselves in the silent lake. At one side of this lake, a string of gay rowboats shifted back and forth in the currents of the green water. Each boat had the name of a girl painted on its side, and from the end of the pier to which they were tied I went swimming while Wally, my dachshund (she was so small that I carried her home in my coat pocket whenever we had walked too far), slept in one of the boats, in the shade of the bench that spans the center. Wally disliked both sun and water.

From the pier one walked into the garden of the White Horse Tavern, a cool space, filled with yellow tables and chairs, shaded by an arbor of wild grapevines.

Here usually sat a man of good appetite; he was a butcher and Wally's best friend, a plain fat man with a round shaven head, a large mustache, the caricature of a German, and certainly a butcher. He owned the house to the left of ours, on the hill.

After he had finished eating and laid knife and fork aside, he

would take a piece of bread, break it into two pieces, call for Wally, and, mopping up the rest of the sauce on his plate, carefully feed it to the dog.

He paid his bill, said good-morning, blew his nose into a large blue handkerchief, finished his beer, and took his cane from a hook, put on an alpine hat, and in a wide circle walked around the baroque, salmon-colored church.

Next to the church was a fountain, with a statue of St. Florian, the patron saint of firemen, standing on a tall column above it. As the butcher passed this fountain, the lower half of him was always hidden by the wide basin and only his hat, coat, and arms – rowing in the air – seemed to walk up the street. In a while we followed him up the hill.

The sounds of this remote place were as comfortable as its panorama. In the morning twilight, Wally was at the garden gate, barking at the cattle that were driven up to the high meadows. From their necks hung bronze bells suspended from heavy, quill-embroidered leather straps. The bells clanged away into the distance, and their place was taken by the church bells below calling to early mass at about seven.

The little motorboat that zigzagged back and forth over the lake had another bell, which announced its first departure half an hour later. The bell on the schoolhouse rang at eight.

As the sun rose over the high wall of mountains it changed all the colors in the valley and lit up the underside of the clouds that hung in the thin clear air above. Children sang in the schoolhouse, the birds in the trees, carpets were beaten in gardens, and the cobbler started hammering.

At half-past ten followed the screech of the small wheels of the daily train from Salzburg as it slowed down to negotiate the sharp curve which carried it into the village. At this sound Wally sent up a long, high flute-like cry. She took that up again for another sound that came from the same direction as the train, the tearing howl of the whistle which announced that it was noon in the sawmill at the far end of the lake.

The worst sound, one that made the little dog's hair stand on end and sent her for protection under a couch, was the music that started at one, Mozart, Bach, Haydn, Schubert, and Beethoven. It came from the house on our right. In its living-rooms, little girls, in one-hour shifts, glared at études, cramped their small fingers into claws, and performed awful concertos on two old Bechstein grand pianos.

This went on until four. When the last of the little blonde girls had left, Frau Dorothea von Moll, the music teacher, came out of the house, held her temples for a moment, and then walked slowly up and down in her kitchen garden. She wandered between even rows of spinach, kohlrabi, beets, celery, peas, and carrots and the large leaves of rhubarb.

She wore a severe black costume, on cold days a mantle trimmed with worn Persian lamb, an old gray bonnet, and a watch on a long thin golden chain. She looked like someone deliberately and carefully made up to play the role of a distinguished old lady in reduced circumstances.

She went out little; a few gentle, little old ladies formed a group that met in her garden house on Thursdays. She entertained them with coffee and Gugelhupf, a native cake, and with anecdotes of musicians and the great people she had known

when her husband, the famous pianist Arnulf von Moll, was still alive.

As soon as the pianos were stilled, Wally ran down the steep stairs that led to Frau Dorothea's garden as if to thank her because the terrible concert was over. Wally see-sawed down the incline – front legs first, back legs after. Then she squeezed through an opening in the fence and attended the Thursday teas, eating cake and drinking milk. On other days she just walked up and down between the rows of vegetables, behind Frau Dorothea.

Wally's initial cost was very small, notwithstanding the fact that her father was the Bavarian champion Hasso von der Eulenburg, and that she personally was entered on her distinguished pedigree as Waltraut von der Eulenburg. However, she became expensive almost immediately.

One Sunday morning she pulled the cloth off the breakfast table and with it every cherished cup and saucer of a Sévres tea set. The hot water from a falling pot scalded her, and Wally walked about for a week wrapped in bandages. As soon as this was forgotten, she ate a box of matches, and when she had recovered from that experience and come back from the

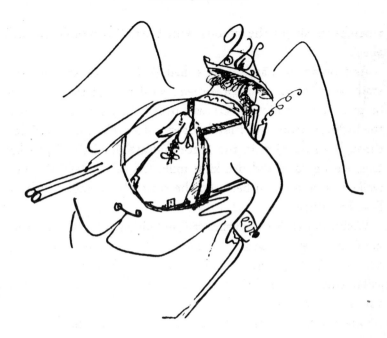

veterinary, she worked a whole night to rip the satin cover off a Biedermeier love seat, took all the horsehair carefully out of it, carrying small tufts of it all over the house, down to Frau Dorothea's, and over to the butcher's garden.

There were many more nice things in this old house of which we were very fond, and it seemed best to send Wally away to be trained. One day a forest ranger, who had trained many dogs, took her away in his knapsack. To this experience I owe the knowledge that dogs can recognize a picture, a fact often disputed.

The forest rangers are government employees; they wear green mountain uniforms and faded felt hats with plumes. Most of them have Santa Claus beards, and usually they smoke long

pipes that hang down the middle of the beard and end over heavy silver watch chains that are weighted down with old thalers. They carry knapsacks and over their shoulders hang double-barreled shotguns.

This forester found Wally more stubborn than any dachshund he had ever trained. He was very strict with her, rubbed her nose on the floor whenever she had done indignities to his clean house, gave her a few slaps on the backside, and threw her out into the forest.

Wally came back to us a few weeks later a completely changed dog. A model dog. Soon after her return a new tobacco was put on the market. It was called 'Forester's Cut' and was wonderfully and widely advertised. Large posters were pasted up everywhere; on them appeared a package of 'Forester's Cut,' and the picture of a forester smoking it with delight. He wore the rakish hat with the plume, the grass-green uniform, the white beard, the shotgun, and was just such a one as Wally had been living with.

Whenever Wally saw this picture, she went for it. She strained on her leash, the little hairy chest became a bellows and started

to work in and out, the lips were pulled up from over her teeth, and long rolls of thunder came from her throat. She shook with anger and looked like an old woodcut of the devil in a peasant Bible. She did nothing about the picture when it was shown to her in magazines, where it appeared in full colors but was

reduced to half a page, nor did she recognize it when she saw a poster that was life-sized but printed in black and white.

At the end of that summer's vacation, we took Wally to America with us. It was not a happy idea and we should have followed the advice of Frau Dorothea, who wanted to keep Wally for us until our return. Wally hated the big liner. She was in a good kennel and had the company of two theatrical black poodles, good-natured animals, used to travel, and able to ride a bicycle and to count up to ten. The food was excellent, the sailor who took care of her a friendly fellow. But Wally remained curled up in a corner of her compartment, an unhappy, defiant coil of dachshund. She looked with mistrust at the ocean, with despair at the masts, the funnels, and the ventilators of the ship. She never played with the other dogs and stopped trembling only when she was wrapped up and resting on my lap in a deckchair.

Wally did not like New York any better than the ship. Her memories were a nightmare of fire-engine sirens, revolving doors, backfiring automobiles, the absence of grass and bushes, the rarity of trees. We decided the next summer to leave her with Frau Dorothea, who took care of our house while we were away.

This was also a sad arrangement. Frau Dorothea wrote that Wally came home only for meals, that she ate little, became thinner and thinner, sat in front of the closed door of our house, and that even her friend the butcher, leaning over the fence from his side of the garden and holding up choice pieces of meat, could not console her. Once she almost bit him when he came up to the house to speak to her.

We asked a dog specialist for advice and he suggested that we send her some piece of personal wearing apparel. A pair of old slippers, an old skiing mitten to which I had lost the mate, and a sweater with a few holes were dispatched with the next mail.

This helped a good deal. We read in happier letters that Wally now had a basket on the porch of our house and busied herself packing and unpacking it. She carried the slippers or the glove proudly through the garden, slept inside, under, and on top of the sweater. She still sat on the porch waiting for us until dark, but she ate now, slept at night in Frau Dorothea's house, and the butcher was allowed to come into the garden, was welcome, with a bone, or even just as he was.

We did not open the house the next summer; it was the year of the Anschluss. From letters we gathered that the village was not noticeably disturbed; a new strategic highway was being built along the lake, new songs were being sung, some people had become very quiet and others too loud, and a few places had

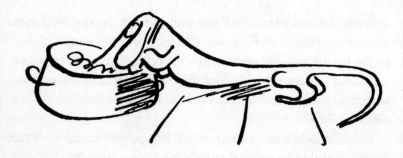

been renamed; but to a dog, Hermann Göring Strasse and Adolf Hitler Platz are as good as Heinrich Heine Strasse and Dollfuss Platz.

Early the next year, Frau Dorothea had a visitor at whom Wally barked. He was a portly, serious businessman from Salzburg and he offered to buy her house. The man's name was Hermann Brettschneider.

Frau Dorothea said that she loved her home, had no reason to sell it, and would certainly never sell it at the price he offered her. She told him that our house was for sale. He did not want our house. He left.

A few weeks later he came back again, this time in the parade uniform of a captain of Storm Troopers, the medal of the Order of the Blood, highest Nazi decoration, on his chest. He sat a long while in her garden house and talked, and he left finally, red in the face. Frau Dorothea still did not want to sell.

Soon after he was gone, the piano lessons stopped, the little blonde girls were forbidden to come. The old ladies also sent their regrets and stayed away on Thursdays. One night windows were broken, and then the butcher was arrested because he had come out of his garden to beat up a young man in uniform. The young man in uniform had been busy with a pail of red paint and a brush; he had lettered on the wall of Frau Dorothea's house, 'Get out of town, Sarah – make haste, go back to Jerusalem.'

On the first of the next month the house was newly painted, the windows repaired; the balcony broke out in Nazi bunting, and Herr Hauptmann Brettschneider gave a garden party bright with uniforms.

Frau Dorothea moved out of the village, to a house near the sawmill, and during the daytime she stayed indoors or in her little garden.

Wally, of course, was Aryan. She could run around and she made the long run to our house twice a day. She climbed to the terrace, unpacked the dirty slippers, and carried the skiing glove about. The butcher was in a concentration camp, but the Brettschneider housekeeper gave Wally occasional pieces of ham, ends of sausages, cuts of pork. Storm Troopers keep good kitchens.

When it was time for her to come home, late at night, Frau Dorothea usually walked to meet her in the dark. It was a rather dangerous place to walk. It was a freightyard of a place; its contours were an uncertain smudge, much like a charcoal

drawing. There was a lamp about sixty feet from the spot where the railroad track crossed the new cement highway. It was here that the wheels of the train screeched at half-past ten in the morning. The highway entered the village in a blind, sudden turn, something the engineers would have liked to avoid, but the alternative would have been to drill a tunnel through two mountains. At the side of the highway, on its outer curve, the ground was soft and the terrain dropped down to the rocky bed of a river, the outflow of the lake. About where the lamp was, the water thundered down over a dam. It was an ideal setting for accidents, this place.

The accident happened on the night of March 7, 1939. A battery of tanks was being rushed to the Eastern Front – Front is the right word, for Germany was in a state of war – and came to the sawmill somewhat ahead of schedule, at the moment that Wally was about to cross the highway.

The beams of the strong headlights, the hellish clatter and tumult of the machinery, and the apparition of terror that a tank is, must have frozen the little dog to the middle of the road.

The driver of tank Number 1 tried to avoid her. He suddenly put on the brakes, that is, he retarded the left tractor belt and advanced the right. Four of the tanks behind him piled into one another, and his had turned too far, left the highway, and rolled over three times as it went down into the river bed.

It went into the shallow water (the sawmill closes the locks at night, to have more water for the turbine the next morning) right side up, and the two men in it, in overalls, loosened their belts and climbed out of the machine. Tanks Numbers 2, 3, 4, and 5 were somewhat damaged.

From the tower of tank Number 6 jumped a baby of a

lieutenant with his first mustache. The men had climbed out of the other tanks and stood in a ring about Wally. The lieutenant picked her up, patted her head, spoke soft words to her, and held her to his cheek.

When Frau Dorothea came forward he clicked his heels, saluted, and smiled. 'Dear lady, so sorry,' he said, and gave the dog to her. While the mechanics set to work repairing the damaged tanks, the young lieutenant lingered a moment or two, asking the dog's name and talking to Frau Dorothea about her. Then he went over to the edge of the highway.

At his direction, pulleys and spades appeared. Chains and cables were carried down the embankment. As two bugs might pull another, a dead one, under a leaf somewhere to eat him, two of the tanks above, without effort or strain, dragged the tank up out of the river bed and set it on the road. The lieutenant waved at Frau Dorothea and Wally as he got into the top of his machine. Tank Number 6 started forward, then the other tanks fell into line, one by one, and the procession continued on its way to the Czechoslovakian frontier.

Bride of Berchtesgaden

AT EVERY hotel and inn we stopped at that summer in Bavaria we were put into the bridal suite, because I always wrote on the register, 'Bemelmans and Bride.' It was good for a laugh; Bride was an old mountain guide and he would come into the place after I had registered, carrying our baggage and followed by his two dogs.

Bride had a carrot-red beard, wore buckskin breeches and hobnailed boots, and carried a guitar under his arm when he wasn't climbing mountains. He looked like a souvenir-postcard picture of a Tirolean. He was a famous guide and usually hung around the crags of the Ortler, Grossglockner, and Watzmann

Mountains. He was my friend, and one of God's outstanding creatures. The last time I was with him we climbed for a week and then came down to Berchtesgaden, where I intended to try to arrange an interview with Mr. Hitler the next time he came to his mountain hideaway. We stopped at the inn, in the bridal suite.

It rained for three days and three nights. We stayed indoors all the time, read over and over the two magazines the clerk had,

and looked out of the windows at the water that fell every-where. Drifting fogs obscured the mountains and the roofs of the houses. Raindrops danced in the puddles, small rivers ran down the streets, and Mr. Hitler stayed in Berlin.

The fourth day, we watched the proprietor of the inn play cards for an hour with the teacher, the local pharmacist, and the stationmaster. Then we looked out of every door and window at the rain, and then we began to drink beer. We had some in the dining-room and some in the lobby, where the card game was going on, and some in our room. We had a good deal before it was anywhere near time for lunch. In our room, Bride ransacked all the drawers in the bureaus, looking for anything, and found an almost empty bottle of American nail polish. He asked me its use. I explained it and then took off my shoes and fell asleep on the couch. When I woke up, Bride had just finished painting my toenails and was sitting on the floor in a corner, humming and accompanying himself on his guitar. I turned over and slept until two o'clock.

It was gray and cold, and we went down to the dining-room again. That room was an immense, vaulted hall on the side facing the street. Raised a few feet from the floor was a balcony. On a nice day, we could have sat there and looked out of the wide windows, over the valley and toward the high mountains. Now we turned the other way and looked at all the empty chairs and tables. Zenzi, the waitress, brought us *Glühwein*, a good drink for such a day. It is red wine served heated in a big goblet, with some herbs in it. We drank slowly, dipping pieces of bread into it. Later we just drank it and smoked cigars. We did this for hours. Bride's two wet dogs slept under the table all the while, and stank.

Toward nightfall a porter came in and dusted and straightened a picture of Hitler which hung at the far end of the hall, and then went out and came back with two large Nazi flags. He draped these around the picture. Another porter came in and together they carried out most of the tables and arranged all the chairs facing the picture, as if for a lecture or an entertainment of some kind. Then two young men came in pushing a wheel-barrow stacked with wreaths and garlands made of pine branches, and with these they decorated the room. It began to smell like Christmas. Finally a radio and a loudspeaker were brought in and connected up. The loudspeaker was placed under the picture of Mr. Hitler.

The proprietor of the inn came to look things over and we called him to our table on the balcony. He told us that all this was in celebration of a National Socialist holiday, that Herr Hitler was arriving in Berchtesgaden that afternoon, and would make an address from his mountain villa at eight o'clock. 'Tomorrow will be a beautiful day,' he said. '*Der Führer* always brings good weather with him when he comes to Berchtesgaden.'

Around seven-thirty the hall began to fill with men. We had each had our seventh *Glühwein*, and I could not see them very clearly, but I heard the sound of their heels coming together in sharp greetings, the scraping of chair legs on the wooden floor as they sat down, and a sound of conversation – a deep murmur that came to my ears like the word 'Rhubarb, rhubarb,' repeated over and over. Bride seemed to be asleep. A song started the festivities and I asked some men sitting a few yards from us if we should leave, but they said no, very cordially, and invited us to stay.

The Führer's address came over the loudspeaker and lasted for an hour and a half. Then the *Horst Wessel Lied* was sung, and when the men sat down again the local head of the Nazi Party stood before Hitler's picture and addressed the assembly.

His address was shorter than Hitler's. Toward the end of it he told how proud all of them were to be privileged to breathe the same clean German mountain air as the Führer himself, how honored they felt at being here in beautiful Berchtesgaden, so close to their Adolf Hitler, 'who is right up there behind us.' At these words, the speaker pointed in the general direction of Hitler's mountain villa. It seemed to me at the time that he was

pointing directly at Bride and myself. As he did so, the members of the assembly turned around in their chairs, looked at us, and applauded.

In an ashtray on our table was a cold cigar butt about the size and shape of a small mustache. I stuck it under my nose, rose to my feet with great effort, and gave the Nazi salute. I also made a short speech. I can't remember what I said, but I screamed some words of encouragement in that hysterical tone, that falsetto pitch familiar to radio listeners all over the world.

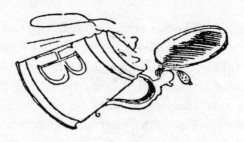

There was a moment of silence when I sat down again; then the leader shouted, '*Schmeissen Sie das Schwein 'raus!*' and a beer glass sailed past my right ear. The next one must have hit me, for the rafters in the ceiling, the table, the uniforms, and Zenzi's big white apron all became an uncertain black-and-brown picture. I remember that both of Bride's dogs barked and that Bride was carrying me somewhere, like a baby. I woke up the next morning in the bridal suite. Bride and his dogs and his guitar were gone.

It was, as the proprietor had promised, a lovely, sunny mountain morning. I put a cold towel on my head and walked out on the balcony. Down the street, behind an immense flag, came little girls marching in military formation and singing. At the far end of the street a rheumatic old prelate hobbled in haste to reach a side street to avoid having to salute the flag. I felt a hand on my shoulder, and when I turned around I saw two young men in civilian clothes. One of them identified himself as a member of the Gestapo and said, 'Herr Bemelmans, come with us – very quietly and without attracting any attention whatever.'

We walked through the town as friends would, without attracting any attention. We went straight to the railroad station, where one of the young men bought two tickets, second class, to Munich; the other stayed behind, I learned later, to call up Munich and tell somebody we were on our way. After the train was rolling, the young man with me pulled a small notebook from his pocket and asked me to help him with his English. He was studying English, he said, to help advance himself in the service of the Gestapo. I helped him with it.

In Munich we went to the headquarters of the Gestapo, which is in what used to be the Wittelsbach Palace. Here I had to surrender my American passport. I was asked some questions, and after an hour's wait, was taken to a prison in the center of the city by another young man in civilian clothes. Again we walked like friends and attracted no attention. He carried in his hand a large envelope on which was written in red ink, 'Foreigner – Urgent.' He seemed to know about my case. 'I am ashamed on your behalf, Herr Bemelmans,' he said to me on the way. 'Why don't you like Germany? Don't you see how fine everything is? Have you seen one single beggar? Have you seen anyone badly dressed or in want? Have you seen anyone hungry or idle? Has a train been late for you? Other foreigners who come here and look around are full of praises for the Third Reich, and for its Leader. You should be ashamed, Herr Bemelmans!'

At the prison I was handed over to an official in uniform, who took me to a cell in which sat a small, pale fellow who introduced himself to me as the former editor of a Catholic publication. He told me he had been in solitary confinement for six months. He was very eager and jumpy and talked fast. 'You are, dear sir,' he said, sitting close to me and taking hold of my hand, 'the first person I have spoken to in all this time. I have been in this nice, bright cell only since yesterday – I think my case has come up for trial. Up to now I have not been informed of the charges

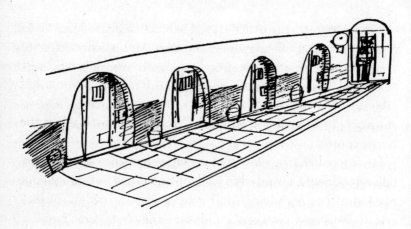

against me. I have no lawyer; I don't even known what has become of my wife and my three children, but I am thankful to have someone to talk to.'

He asked me why I was there. I told him my story and he said, 'You won't be here long. An American citizen – how enviable, how fortunate for you! They will not dare to lock you up for long. You will walk on the streets this evening, or tomorrow evening, and hear the bells of the tramways and see people and eat in a restaurant and listen to the music playing. Of course you will get out – by seven o'clock tonight, I should think.

'But if anything should go wrong,' he went on, gripping my shoulder with his hand, 'and they lock you up alone as they did with me, then make yourself sit still, for heaven's sake. Don't start walking up and down, for you will walk around the earth in your cell; you will never be able to rest again. Another thing I will tell you that will help you: somewhere in your cell, on a wall, on the ceiling, perhaps on the floor, in some corner, at some time of the day or night when the light casts just the right shadows, you will find a place where an irregularity in the cement or the paint, a patch on the repair work, will outline for you the face of someone you love – your wife, your child, someone. It will take some imagination in the beginning, but after a while it will be there for you, strong and clear whenever you want it, to help you when the trembling starts, when the terror comes.'

He seemed embarrassed by his own vehemence and stopped talking suddenly. I wanted to walk up and down but sat still out of deference to his advice. After a while a key turned in the lock and he whispered, 'You see? I told you – they have come for you.'

The keeper had my envelope under his arm. He took me to a waiting car and we drove to another prison of the Gestapo in a suburb of Munich – a dirty old building with sweaty walls. I was handed over to the warden and he ordered a keeper to examine me.

An examination in a German prison is most thorough. The room in which it took place was as bright as a photographer's studio, with floodlights around the ceiling. There was a glass-covered table in the room, with a powerful light under the glass, and as I took off coat, vest, and trousers the keeper stretched them out on the table and examined the cloth, the lapels, every seam and pocket with the light shining through them. He asked for my shoes and almost took them apart. With a flashlight, next, he looked into my mouth, at the roof, then under the tongue, and into the spaces between the cheeks and the teeth. Then he asked for my underclothes. Finally he asked for my socks; I took them off and stood in front of him and the warden with my painted toenails.

The warden looked at me intently and then laughed. He pinched my cheek, called me 'darling,' and ordered that for the other prisoners' protection I be locked in a solitary cell. Doing a lopsided fandango, with one hand on his hip, the fingers spread fanwise, the warden danced out, shouting 'Yoo-hoo!'

I was locked in a solitary cell.

In an hour I got something to eat. Through a small opening in the iron door came a ladle; I turned, and from it a heavy lentil soup, with small disks of sausage in it, poured into a battered tin bowl which I held under it. A hand reached in and gave me a large slice of black bread. Both the soup and the bread were good.

The light began to change after an hour or two more and I began to look for a patch on the wall, an irregularity in the floor or ceiling. Against the Catholic editor's advice, I had walked up and down several miles. Then the door opened and the warden told me that he would have to release me, that the American consul was downstairs in his quarters with an official from the Gestapo.

I was released, and the consul advised me that I was to report to the State's Attorney the next morning. I got there promptly at nine. The State's Attorney was an affable, academic young man with a left cheek divided into six irregular fields by saber cuts. He received me in the outer room of a suite of offices under the inevitable picture of the Führer, but instead of the obligatory '*Heil Hitler!*' he said comfortably '*Grüss Gott!*' and offered me his hand in greeting. A one-armed secretary, a veteran with many decorations, brought my envelope and laid it on a desk. The State's Attorney pulled two chairs up to the desk, gave me a cigarette and lighted it for me, and waved the secretary out of the room. He began to speak, punctuating his sentences with a short, explosive, nasal 'Ah-eh!'

'Ah-eh!' he said. 'Disagreeable business, regrettable incident, Herr Bemelmans. Understandable, of course. A glass too many. Can happen to any of us. Ah-eh! Your – shall we call it pantomime? – should have been ignored, of course. Some of our people, Herr Bemelmans, in a sincere effort to – ah-eh! – serve the Party, are sometimes overzealous. You chose, however, a particularly awkward spot, Herr Bemelmans. Berchtesgaden is – ah-eh! – is the last place for such a – but let that pass.

'This affair has, however, gone too far simply to dismiss it. The Party – that is, the State – cannot let you go – ah-eh! – unpunished. The police cannot admit having made – ah-eh! – a mistake. In order to put this matter out of the way, I have permitted myself to make some calculations with which I hope you will find yourself in – ah-eh! – agreement. There is a very

good train for Berchtesgaden, leaving Munich Hauptbahnhof at seven-forty tomorrow morning. They've reported the first snowfall in Berchtesgaden; there's some excellent skiing around there; Berchtesgaden is enchanting in late September. Ah-eh! While you are there, Herr Bemelmans, I suggest that you go to the District Court – I have written the address on this slip of paper for you. It is only a few steps from the station. In return for a small fee you will receive your passport there.

'Ah-eh! As for the amount of the fine, what do you think of, say, a hundred marks, Herr Bemelmans? Not too much – very little. Ah-eh! A bagatelle for an American, what?'

I went back to Berchtesgaden, paid my fine at the District Court, and got back my passport. Coming out of the building, I saw Bride and his two dogs walking up the street. They were a block or so away and I stuck my fingers in my mouth and whistled. Bride turned and the dogs stopped in their tracks. He had his guitar under his arm and, standing against the background of snow, he looked, as always, like a souvenir-postcard picture of a Tirolean. It was my last glimpse of him. Bride's arm began to rise involuntarily as if in greeting, and then all at once he had turned and was running up into his mountains, his dogs after him, as if they had seen the devil.

I Love You, I Love You, I Love You

SHE CAME over and into my bed and leaned her ash-blond head on my new *framboise*-colored twelve-fifty Saks-Fifth Avenue pajamas, and then in the cadences of Leslie Howard, with her eyes on my lips, in three distinct shadings, soft, softer, and the last words in an almost inaudible whispered tone, she said, 'I love you, I love you, I will always love you.' And she added, 'I hope you will take me back to Paris when the trouble is over and when the *Normandie* is painted new again.'

I said that I hoped I could soon, that I hoped all the boats would be painted new again soon, and to myself I said that I hoped also that she would be able to say, 'I love you, I love you, I will always love you' exactly as she had said it, on the stage, because then she would be a great actress. But I am afraid that, instead, my daughter Barbara will be the pen pal of some future desperado, or, if we're very lucky, the chatelaine of Alcatraz or Sing Sing.

Barbara was then three and a half years old; most of her life has been spent in Europe; she has also been in Chile, Peru, Ecuador, and Cuba. She knows the captains of at least half a dozen liners. Everywhere she has met nice people and left them nicely alone – and everywhere, with the nose of a retriever, she has found out and attached herself immediately to some socially maladjusted individual.

In Paris, Barbara formed an underworld friendship with a backstairs Villon whose name was Georges. We had two friends by that name. One was bon Georges, the other bad Georges. Bon Georges is Georges Reyer, the novelist and writer for *Paris-Soir*; he had introduced me to bad Georges, who was in the words of bon Georges, '*un chef de bande sinistre*.' Bad Georges was my guide to Paris at night, and he assisted me in some reportage. -

Once, after a long all-night tour, we were sitting in my room about nine o'clock when there was a knock at the door. Barbara was up and came in and said that two men were outside looking for Georges. Georges's hand closed around my wrist, and he said, 'Remember, I have been with you all night.' The men came in, and I told them truthfully that Georges had been with me all night.

They were surprised and said to me to be very certain of that; then they said, '*C'est une affaire extrêmement grave*.' The one with the beard who said that seemed to love this phrase – he repeated it several times. They left without taking Georges with them. Georges said a prayer after they were gone and offered me back my watch, a watch which I had missed since the first day I met him. He said he had been sorry about it all along. I thanked him. Barbara said that it was 'une affaire extrêmement grave,' and Georges said, 'Ah, you are so right, most extrêmement grave.'

I wanted at the time to get a nurse for Barbara, to take her to the park and to watch out for her. Several applicants came, but Barbara did not want a nurse. Georges, who was always with us, could be her nurse, she said. I told her that men were not nurses, but she said they were; she had seen the little daughter of an Indian maharaja who lived in the hotel go out with a nurse who was a man, wore a turban and a beard, and played with the little dark-skinned child in the Champs-Élysées. Georges said he loved no one better than Barbara, but I said no.

We walked out of the Ritz on the Rue Cambon side, up toward the Madeleine. On the right-hand side there is a toy shop. In this shop Barbara saw a small statue of Napoleon on horseback, brightly painted in the manner of a toy soldier. Immediately she wanted it.

Barbara has methods of stating a claim that put the propaganda of *Doktor* Goebbels to shame. Here is the work she did on Napoleon: 'Papa promised Barbara a toy – please buy a toy for Barbara, Barbara wants a toy, a toy for Barbara, Barbara wants the little soldier on the horse, please buy the soldier – Mamma said Barbara could have a toy, please buy a toy for Barbara.'

This nasal singsong text, wailed off-key like reedy, Oriental beggar music, is repeated for three hours. It is like having two

peanut whistles tied to your ears; after a while one does not hear the words any more, just the music, but there is also a grip on the trousers, pushing and pulling, and tears are in readiness for the final effect.

'All right, Barbara, we'll go back and buy the little soldier if you only stop this, if you promise to be quiet.'

'Don't be a fool,' says Georges. 'Don't be a fool and buy it. I will steal it for her.'

We had arrived near the Madeleine, and I asked whether we could sit down and have a drink and an ice cream before we went back to buy the Napoleon. Barbara weighed this for a moment and then agreed. Georges said he had to go somewhere and excused himself. He was back by the time I paid the bill, and sat down and ordered another drink. He gave the Napoleon to

Barbara under the table, and, with both hands and tilted head, cut my protest short. 'It is nothing,' he said.

Georges was thin and small, he wore a cigarette on his right ear and a cap, his jacket was tight as a brassière and rode up over his hips when he walked. He was continually pulling it down. He looked like an advertisement for a *bal musette*. The arrangement for taking Barbara out was made at the end of a three-and-a-half-hour filibuster that went something like this: 'Barbara wants to go with Georges, Papa promised that Barbara could go with Georges, Georges wants to take Barbara to the park –'

Georges reported every day, and he was an ideal nurse. He took Barbara to the Luxembourg, walked around with her while she rode the little donkeys, sailed boats for her in the Tuileries, took her to the Jardin d'Acclimatation, and out to the Restaurant Robinson in the trees.

The first time they came back from a Punch and Judy show, I was not there, and they both sat in that long corridor of the Ritz which is lined with show-cases. Georges's eyes were on the rings, bracelets, pendants, and wristwatches in the show-cases.

Olivier, the *maître d'hôtel*, passed and saw him, and he called the doorman and the reception clerk and asked everyone, '*Qui est ce phénomène-là?*' Somebody had seen Barbara before, so they asked her, and she said that Georges was a friend of Papa.

'And who is Papa?'

'Papa has no hair,' said Barbara by way of explanation, and then she added, '*C'est une affaire extrêmement grave.*'

'*Ah – oui, ah oui, alors,*' said Olivier, '*extrêmement grave.*'

Even the maid was worried and said it would end very badly and I would be sorry the rest of my life for letting Barbara go out with this creature. There is, she said, such a think as '*le kidnap.*'

The next day, after they had gone, I was a little worried. I looked down out of the window. The Place Vendôme was filled with chauffeurs and the municipal shade of green that was on its freshly painted lamp posts and auto-buses. Usually buses do not run here, but the Rue Royale was being torn up to be recobbled, and the buses that usually go to the Madeleine passed in front of the hotel. A Senegalese Negro, with feet like two *pains de ménage*, climbed across the square.

On one corner stood two men, one carrying a big easy-chair, the other a bouquet of pink and white tulips stuck in mimosa. They waited for the traffic to pass; and when this got tiresome, one put down the chair and the other sat down on it and smelled his bouquet. A sailor, with some teeth missing, was making love to a girl leaning on a lamp post; a couple crossed the center of the square with three black poodles.

In front of the Palais de Justice stood a German tourist in shirt-sleeves and *Lederhosen*, held up by embroidered suspenders. He had a green hat with *Gemsbart* on it, a cigar, and a Baedeker. The greatest charm of Paris is that here in this bright light no one paid any attention to a couple with three black poodles, to the man in the easy-chair with his bouquet, or to the man in a Tirolean costume. The view from a Paris window is never monotonous.

After a while Georges and Barbara came out of the hotel right under my window; they walked to Schiaparelli's store. Barbara stopped and looked at the stuffed white doves that hang in it,

suspended from thin wires, and Georges lifted her little white dog Fifi so that the dog could see them too. Then they walked on to Cartier's. I was afraid – they had a gold-and-pearl elephant clock in the window which Barbara wanted. I thought for a moment that she would ask Georges for it. I could just hear her say to him, 'Papa promised an elephant for Barbara, please buy the elephant for Barbara, Barbara wants an elephant –'

She did. Georges ground a few centimeters of cigarette under his heel, pulled down his jacket, looked around, and then shook his head. I looked around, too, and was greatly relieved – there were three *agents de la Sûreté*, with their eyes on Georges. Two of them followed him and Barbara down to the park. There was no need to worry – Barbara was the best-guarded child in Paris.

Star of Hope

THREE INFANTRYMEN, their arms interlocked, came up the Boulevard Raspail. My friend Georges leaned over the marble-topped red table and said, 'I am ashamed whenever I see such soldiers! Look at them, walking arm in arm like girls! When they are far away they look blue, then they slowly get dirty, and when they are close to you, you can observe that their uniforms never, never fit. They are like horse blankets with a bandage wrapped around the middle.

'Look at them – how they wear the cap, and the cigarette hanging out of one corner of the mouth! And the shoes! Too big!

And not shined! And the uniform always dirty! The Germans are too clean, and the English walk with their hands in their pockets, but the American soldiers – that is something else. I love America!'

The three soldiers, now hanging together with their elbows around each other's necks, had turned the corner and were going down the Boulevard Montparnasse. They sang, and one looked back at the legs of a woman who was emptying a pail of water into the street.

A waiter came and spoke a few words to Georges, using his hand as a screen between his mouth and Georges's ear. Georges got up and walked to the rear of the café and spoke to a girl. She had a young, obedient face and raven hair. She gave him something, or he gave something to her. Georges sat down at the table again, and the girl passed by without stopping and went out on the sidewalk.

'I must be very careful,' said Georges, and looked around. 'I must be very careful. One can never tell, because if they recognize me and catch me, it is good-by. I will go to prison for long, stupid years – and in France prison is not a club like in America.

'But I don't think they will catch me. The French police are very dull. They make their round-up always at the same time, always the same police. I know them from far away. Every child knows them. It is not fun to elude them – just tiresome and a matter of watching the clock.'

A stout policeman with a Hitler mustache, his cloak draped

over one shoulder, the thumbs of his round hands stuck in his belt, slowly passed in front of the sidewalk café.

'Look!' said Georges. 'Look at him! Look at the face! You have police like that in America? I don't think so. You have G-men, not police to laugh at!'

Georges drank some black coffee, then he turned and watched two women who had sat down a few tables away from ours. They were large and well dressed. One of them talked very loudly. 'My cousin Jaqueneau,' she said, 'owns the property. It's an original grant from the king of –'

'Fake!' said Georges. 'Fake jewelry. Yes, the jewelry is certainly fake. I can see that from here even without glasses.

'The ring and the brooch are fake too,' he added, leaning forward.

'And so are the earrings,' he concluded, and turned away.

'Of course, there are always the traveler's checks. Don't look now, but her bag, on the chair, is open. Inside, in the little black folder, there are the traveler's checks.

'They are a nuisance, traveler's checks. Lately they come in very small amounts – five dollars, ten dollars, seldom higher. You have to sit up all night and practice the signature or, what is worse, teach a girl to sign them. Then you must run to some nightclub in Montmartre, sit and drink a while, and, when it is late enough, cash them and get out. I prefer money, or jewels.

'Paris has changed,' he sighed. 'Oh, how Paris has changed! I lie awake at night trying to think about new ideas, but it is all for nothing, everything has been tried.

'It is almost impossible to live here any more, and I am one who is alert and willing to work hard, but – ' He snapped the

sentence shut, shrugged his lean shoulders, and with his hands said, 'What is the use!'

'In America you have at least the hold-up to count on. But the French people, they don't believe in it, they don't believe in it at all. They don't think that the gun can be loaded! They don't believe it can be dangerous because nobody in France has ever been shot in a hold-up. You can go in, anywhere, ask for the proprietor, and when he comes, point a gun at his stomach. You know what happens? You know what he will do? He will argue with you!

'If some intelligent people would only get together here, hold up fifty or sixty people and shoot them, then perhaps they would begin to take it seriously. But we have no co-operation here. That is why I love America.

'Of course there are other things. There is the casino. For a while I made a little money playing roulette, but I became very nervous. I placed my bets on the colors. When the color was right, I left my bet. But when I lost, I quickly snatched it back, in a split second's time. Sometimes the croupier would start a scandal, but then I would say, "Ah, sorry, I thought I still had time." Sometimes they made me march to the director's office, and the director tore up my card of admission and the casino telephoned to all the other casinos not to let me in. I had to change my name and get a new card. But eventually they begin to remember the face, and then the game is over.

'Once I had a little business, in the Gare St.-Lazare. It was a telephone business, and it was good as long as the calls cost one franc. I had twelve telephones in this station. I went every morning and put a little cotton in each one of them. When people want to get their money back after calling a wrong number, and move the hook up and down, the franc falls down, but it does not come out. During the afternoon hours I returned and collected, sometimes eighteen francs, sometimes twenty – not much, but it was a steady income. I wanted to include the Gare du Nord too, but just then they changed the telephones.

'In the quiet months, when there are no tourists, when things are very bad, when I am altogether broke, then I have to work very hard to make twenty francs.

'As a last resort, I go to a rooming house, late at night. I look very respectable and serious in a dark suit, and I ask for a room with a wide bed, because it is much easier to get rid of double-size sheets. I pay for the room in advance, for one night's lodging. I notice immediately, as I walk in, whether or not there is a little carpet. If there is none, then I explain to the woman that I am a peculiar fellow and that I like a little rug in front of my bed; also that I cannot stand towels with holes or frayed edges. In the middle of the night I get up, pack the little rug, the

sheets, the pillowcases, mirror, towels, and curtains in my bag, and leave quietly.

'I go directly to a place where the complete outfit is bought at the regular price of thirty francs. Deduct from that the ten francs paid in advance, and you have left twenty francs for one night's work! Oh, I am so tired of this country!'

Georges ordered another glass of coffee. The girl who had spoken to him earlier in the rear of the restaurant passed in front of the tables with a man. Georges went on: 'The mentality of the French people is awful. They mistrust everybody. You could lie here in the street like a dog and they would leave you there. No one will turn a hand to help you, and if they find out that you have done something bad, then they will kick you on top of it!

'In America, in the United States, do the people there have a nice mentality and not think that everybody is a thief and a crook? Do they behave nicely? Do they give you hospitality? Do you think if I arrived there with two or more nice girls – you know, *goût américain* – that I could do a little business?

'Not on the sidewalk like here, of course. I mean a *salon*, on Fifth Avenue, with a maid in a white cap and a little apron, a few bottles of champagne, everything very nice, and the right connection with the government. It would take a lot of money of course, the passage, the furniture, the government, and the girls.

'I could have made a good deal of money here last night,' he said, 'enough for all the expenses and more for a small reserve capital. Last night they sold sixteen thousand francs' worth of heroin, right here.

'Turn around and look at the bar. Over the bar you see some light fixtures, glass tubes with light in them, neon lights. One of the tubes you see is without light. That is where they keep it, inside the tube. The *maître d'hôtel* here is in this business also.

'I don't like to deal in it regularly. It's too dangerous. But once in a while, for a good supper, a nice present for someone, for a vacation in Deauville, or to help out a friend – then it's all right.

'The price changes. Now we sell it to the girls on the street for fifty francs the gram. They sell it again for perhaps seventy-five.

'The profit is in the Americans. They pay more – at least a hundred and fifty francs – and for that they get just a little bit of heroin. We mix it for them – seventy-five percent bicarbonate of soda and twenty-five percent heroin.

'They love it, but they are good for only one sale. The next day they go to Versailles. But no matter what price you ask, *OK, Georgie*, they say, and pay. Oh, I love America!'

Little Bit and the America

'LOOK, WHAT a lovely day we have for sailing,' I said, pointing my pen toward the lit-up greenery outside the open window. The birds sang in the trees, and the sun shone on a deck of brightly colored luggage tags which I was filling out. Under 'S.S. *America*' I had carefully lettered my name, and I answered the gay question of 'Destination?' with 'Cherbourg.'

I was about to fill out a new tag when I noticed Barbara's silence. She was standing at the window, staring at me. I saw clearly the symptoms of wanting something, symptoms long known to me and always the same. I remembered that the day before she had said something about a dog, but I had been called away before I could talk about it at length.

For the most part, Barbara is a sweet and normal child; when she wants something, she changes. The child is then under great stress. A trembling of the lower lip precedes the filling of the beautiful eyes with tears. I am allowed to see these hopeless eyes for a moment, and then, as a spotlight moves from one place to another, she averts her gaze and slowly turns, folds her arms, and looks into the distance, or if there is no distance, at the wall. The crisis is approaching. She swallows, but her throat is constricted; finally, with the urgency of a stammerer, and with her small hands clenched, she manages to convey a few dry words. The small voice is like a cold trumpet. The last word is a choking sound. There is a long, cold silence.

On the morning of sailing I recognized the first stage of this painful condition that overcomes her from time to time. I could tell it by her eyes, her mouth, the position she stood in, the peculiar angles of her arms and legs. She was twisted in an unhappy pose of indecision. Not that she didn't know precisely what she wanted: she was undecided about how to broach the subject.

After the tears, the gaze into the distance, the silence, Barbara blurted out, 'You promised I could have a dog.'

I steeled myself and answered, 'Yes, when we get back from Europe you can have a dog.'

An answer like that is worse than an outright no. The mood of 'I wish I was dead' descended on Barbara. She stared coldly out of the window, and then she turned and limply dragged herself down the corridor to her room, where she goes at times of crisis. She closed the door not by slamming it, but with a terrible, slow finality. One can see from the corridor how she lets go of the handle inside – in unspeakably dolorous fashion; slowly the handle rises, and there is the barely audible click of the mechanism. There is then the cutting off of human relations, a falling off of appetite, and nothing in the world of joy or disaster matters.

Ordinarily the comatose state lasts for weeks. In this case, however, Barbara was confronted with a deadline, for the ship was sailing at five that afternoon and it was now eleven in the morning. I usually break down after three or four weeks of resistance. The time limit for this operation was five hours.

She decided at first to continue with standard practice, the manual of which I know as well as I do the alphabet.

From the door at the end of the corridor came the sound of

heartbreaking sobs. Normally these sobs last for a good while, and then, the crisis ebbing off, there follows an hour or two of real or simulated sleep, in which she gathers strength for renewed efforts. This time, however, the sobs were discontinued ahead of schedule and were followed up by a period of total silence, which I knew was taken up with plotting at the speed of calculating machinery. This took about ten minutes. As the door had closed, so it opened again, and fatefully and slowly, as the condemned walk to their place of execution, the poor child, handkerchief in hand, dragged along the corridor past my room into the kitchen. I never knew until that morning that the pouring of milk into a glass could be a bitter and hopeless thing to watch.

I am as hardened against the heartbreak routine as a coroner is to postmortems. I can be blind to tears and deaf to the most urgent pleading. I said, 'Please be reasonable. I promise you that the moment we get back you can have a dog.'

I was not prepared for what followed – the new slant, the surprise attack.

She leaned against the kitchen doorjamb and drank the last of the milk. Her mouth was ringed with white. She said in measured and accusing tones, 'You read in the papers this morning what they did in Albany.'

'I beg your pardon?'

'They passed a law that all institutions like the A.S.P.C.A. are to be forced to turn dogs over to hospitals, for vivisection – and you know what will happen. They'll get her and then they'll cut her open and sew her up again over and over until she's dead.'

'What has that got to do with me?'

'It has to do with the dog you promised me.'

'What dog?'

'The dog that Frances wants to give me.'

Frances is a red-headed girl who goes to school with Barbara.

'I didn't know Frances had a dog.'

Barbara raised her eyebrows. 'You never listen,' she said, and as if talking to an idiot and with weary gestures she recited, 'Poppy, I told you all about it a dozen times. Doctor Lincoln, that's Frances's father, is going to Saudi Arabia to work for an oil company, and he had to sign a paper agreeing not to take a dog, because it seems the Arabs don't like dogs. So the dog has to be got rid of. So Doctor Lincoln said to Frances, "If you don't get rid of her, I will." Now you know how doctors are – they have no feelings whatever for animals. He'll give her to some hospital for experiments.'

I resumed filling out baggage tags. When I hear the word 'dog' I see in my mind a reasonably large animal of no particular breed, uncertain in outline, like a Thurber dog, and with a rough dark coat. This image was hovering about when I asked, 'What kind of dog is it?'

'Her name is Little Bit.'

'What?'

'Little *BIT* – that's her name. She's the dearest, sweetest, snow-white, itsy-bitsy, tiny little toy poodle you have ever seen. Can I have her, please?'

I almost let out a shrill bark.

'Wait till you see her and all the things she's got – a special little wicker bed with a mattress, and a dish with her picture on it, and around it is written "Always faithful" in French. You see, Poppy, they got Little Bit in Paris last year, and she's the uniquest, sharpest little dog you've ever seen, and naturally she's housebroken, and Frances says she's not going to give her to anybody but me.'

I was playing for time. I would have settled for a Corgi, a Yorkshire, a Weimaraner, even a German boxer or a Mexican hairless, but Little Bit was too much. I knew that Doctor Lincoln lived some thirty miles out of the city, and that it would be impossible to get the dog to New York before the ship sailed.

'Where is the dog now?' I asked with faked interest.

'She'll be here any minute, Poppy. Frances is on the way now – and oh, wait till you see, she has the cutest little boots for rainy weather, and a cashmere sweater, sea green, and several sets of leashes and collars – you won't have to buy a thing.'

'All right,' I said, 'you can have the dog. We'll put it in a good kennel until we return.'

The symptoms, well known and always the same, returned again. The lower lip trembled. 'Kennel,' she said – and there is no actress on stage or screen who could have weighted this word with more reproach and misery.

'Yes, kennel,' I said and filled out the baggage tag for my portable typewriter.

'Poppy –' she started, but I got up and said, 'Now look, Barbara, the ship leaves in a few hours, and to take a dog aboard you have to get a certificate from a veterinary, and reserve a place for him, and buy a ticket.'

To my astonishment, Barbara smiled indulgently. 'Well, if that's all that's bothering you – first of all, we're going to France; the French, unlike the English, have no quarantine for dogs, and they don't even ask for a health certificate. Second, you can make all the arrangements for the dog's passage on board ship, after it sails. Third, there is plenty of room in the kennels. I know all this because Frances and I went down to the U.S. Lines and got the information day before yesterday.'

I stared into the distance. At such times I feel a great deal for the man who's going to marry Barbara. With all hope failing I said, 'But we'll have to get a traveling bag or something to put the dog in.'

'She has a lovely little traveling bag with her name lettered on it, "Little Bit."'

The name stung like a whip. 'All right then.' I wrote an extra baggage tag to be attached to the dog's bag.

Barbara wore the smug smile of success. 'Wait till you see her,' she said and ran out of the room. In a moment she returned with Frances, who, I am sure, had been sitting there waiting all the while. The timing was perfect.

Little Bit had shoebutton eyes and a patent-leather nose and a strawberry-colored collar; she was fluffy from the top of her head to her shoulders and then shorn like a miniature Persian lamb. At the end of a stub of a tail was a puff of fluff, and other puffs on the four legs. She wore a pale blue ribbon, and a bell on the collar. I thought that if she were cut open most probably sawdust would come out.

A real dog moves about a room and sniffs its way into corners. It inspects furniture and people, and makes notes of things. Little Bit stood with cocksparrow stiffness on four legs as static as her stare. She was picked up and brought over to me. I think she knew exactly what I thought of her, for she lifted her tiny lip on the left side of her face over her mouse teeth and sneered. She was put down, and she danced on stilts, with the motion of a mechanical toy, back to Frances.

I was shown the traveling bag, which was like one of the pocketbooks that WAC colonels carry.

'We don't need that tag,' said Barbara. 'I'll carry her in this. Look.' The pocketbook, which had a circular opening with a wire screen on each end for breathing purposes, was opened; Little Bit jumped into it, and it was closed. 'You see, she won't be any bother whatever.'

The bag was opened again. With a standing jump Little Bit hurdled the handles of the bag and stalked toward me. Tilting her head a little, she stood looking up, and then she again lifted her lip over her small fangs.

'Oh, look, Barbara!' said Frances. 'Little Bit likes your father – she's smiling at him.'

I had an impulse to sneer back, but I took the baggage tags and began to attach them to the luggage. Then I left the room, for Frances showed signs of crisis; her eyes were filling, and the heartbreak was too much for me. Little Bit was less emotional. She ate a hearty meal from her *Tourjours fidèle* dish and inspected the house, tinkling about with the small bell that hung from her collar.

It was time to go to the boat. The luggage was taken to a taxi, and Little Bit hopped into her bag. On the way I thought about the things I had forgotten to take care of, and also about Little Bit. It is said that there are three kinds of books that are always a success: a book about a doctor, a book about Lincoln, and a book about a dog. Well, here was Doctor Lincoln's dog, but it didn't seem to hold the elements of anything except chagrin. I wondered if Lincoln had ever had a dog, or a doctor, or if Lincoln's doctor had had a dog. I wondered if that side of Lincoln, perhaps the last remaining side, had been investigated as yet or was still open.

We arrived with Doctor Lincoln's dog at the customs barrier, and our passports were checked. The baggage was brought aboard. In our cabin we found some friends waiting. Frances and Barbara, with Little Bit looking out of her bag, inspected the ship. The gong sounded, and the deck steward sang out, 'All ashore that's going ashore!' The passengers lined up to wave their farewells. The last of those that were going ashore slid down the gangplank. Good-by, good-by – and then the engine bells sounded below, and the tugs moaned and hissed, and the ship backed out into the river.

There are few sights in the world as beautiful as a trip down the Hudson and out to sea, especially at dusk. I was on deck until we passed the Ambrose Lightship, and then I went down to the cabin.

Little Bit was lying on a blotter, on the writing desk, and watching Barbara's hand. Barbara was already writing a letter to Frances, describing the beauty of travel and Little Bit's reactions. 'Isn't she the best traveling dog we've ever had, Poppy?'

The cabins aboard the *America* are the only ones I have ever been in that don't seem to be aboard ship. They are large – more like rooms in a country home – a little chintzy in decoration, and over the portholes are curtains. In back of these one suspects screened doors that lead out to a porch and a Connecticut lawn rather than the ocean.

I put my things in place and changed to a comfortable jacket. I said, 'I guess I better go up and get this dog business settled.'

'It's all attended to, Poppy. I took care of it,' said Barbara and continued writing.

'Well, then you'd better take her upstairs to the kennels. It's almost dinnertime.'

'She doesn't have to go to the kennels.'

'Now, look, Barbara – '

'See for yourself, Poppy. Just ring for the steward, or let me ring for him.'

'Yes, sir,' said the steward, smiling.

'Is it all right for the dog to stay in the cabin?' I asked. The steward had one of the most honest and kind faces I have ever seen. He didn't fit on a ship either. He was more like a person that worked around horses, or a gardener. He had bright eyes and squint lines, a leathery skin, and a good smile.

He closed his eyes and announced, 'Dog? I don't see no dog in here, sir.' He winked like a burlesque comedian and touched one finger to his head in salute. 'My name is Jeff,' he said. 'If you want anything – ' And then he was gone.

'You see?' said Barbara. 'And besides, you save fifty dollars, and coming back another fifty, makes a hundred.'

I am sure that Little Bit understood every word of the conversation. She stood up on the blotter and tilted her head, listening to Barbara, who said to her, 'You know, Little Bit, you're not supposed to be on this ship at all. You musn't let anybody see you. Now you hide, while we go down to eat.'

There was a knock at the door. Silently Little Bit jumped to the floor and was out of sight.

It was the steward. He brought a little raw meat mixed with string beans on a plate covered with another plate. 'Yes, sir,' was all he said.

Barbara was asleep when the first rapport between me and Little Bit took place. I was sitting on a couch, reading, when she came into my cabin. By some magic trick, like an elevator going up a building shaft, she rose and seated herself next to me. She kept a hand's width of distance, tilted her head, and then lifted her lip over the left side of her face. I think I smiled back at her in the same fashion. I looked at her with interest for the first time – she was embarrassed. She looked away and then suddenly changed position, stretching her front legs ahead and sitting down flat on her hind legs. She made several jerky movements but never uttered a sound.

Barbara's sleepy voice came from the other room. 'Aren't you glad we have Little Bit with us?'

'Yes,' I said, 'I am.' I thought about the miracles of nature, how this tough little lion in sheep's pelt functioned as she did; with a brain that could be no larger than an olive, she had memory, understanding, tact, courage, and no doubt loyalty, and she was completely self-sufficient. She smiled once more, and I smiled back: the relationship was established. Life went on as steadily as the ship.

On the afternoon of the third day out, as I lay in my deck chair reading, Barbara came running. 'Little Bit is gone,' she stammered with trembling lower lip.

We went down to the cabin. The steward was on all fours, looking under beds and furniture. 'Somebody musta left the door open,' he said, 'or it wasn't closed properly and swung open, and I suppose she got lonesome here all by herself and went looking for you. You should have taken her up to the movies with you, Miss.'

'She's a smart dog,' said Barbara. 'Let's go to every spot on board where she might look for us.'

So we went to the dining-room, to the smoking-room, the theater, the swimming pool, up the stairs, down the stairs, up on all the decks and around them, and to a secret little deck we had discovered between second and third class at the back of the ship, where Little Bit was taken for her exercise mornings and evenings and could run about freely while I stood guard.

A liner is as big as a city. She was nowhere.

When we got back the steward said, 'I know where she is. You see, anybody finds a dog naturally takes it up to the kennels, and that's where she is. And there she stays for the rest of the trip. Remember, I never saw the dog, I don't know anything about her. The butcher – that's the man in charge of the kennels – he's liable to report me if he finds out I helped hide her. He's mean, especially about money. He figures that each passenger gives him ten bucks for taking care of a dog, and he doesn't want any of us to snatch. There was a Yorkshire stowing away trip before last; he caught him at the gangplank as the dog was leaving the ship – the passenger had put him on a leash. Well, the butcher stopped him from getting off. He held up everything for hours, the man had to pay passage for the dog, and the steward who had helped hide him was fired. Herman Haegeli is his name, and he's as mean as they come. You'll find him on the top deck, near the aft chimney, where it says "Kennels."'

At such moments I enjoy the full confidence and affection of my child. Her nervous little hand is in mine, she willingly takes direction, her whole being is devotion, and no trouble is too much. She loved me especially then, because she knows that I am larcenous at heart and willing to go to the greatest lengths to beat a game and especially a meany.

'Now remember,' I said, 'if you want that dog back we have to be very careful. Let's first go and case the joint.'

We climbed up into the scene of white and red ventilators, the sounds of humming wires, and the swish of the water. In yellow and crimson fire, the ball of the sun had half sunk into the sea, precisely at the end of the avenue of foam that the ship had ploughed through the ocean. We were alone. We walked up and down, like people taking exercise before dinner, and the sea changed to violet and to indigo and then to that glossy gun-metal hue that it wears on moonless nights. The ship swished along to the even pulse of her machinery.

There was the sign. A yellow light shone from a porthole. I lifted Barbara, and inside, in one of the upper cases, was Little Bit, behind bars. There was no lock on her cage.

No one was inside. The door was fastened by a padlock. We walked back and forth for a while, and then a man came up the stairs, carrying a pail. He wore a gray cap, a towel around his neck, and a white coat such as butchers work in.

'That's our man,' I said to Barbara.

Inside the kennels he brought forth a large dish that was like the body of a kettledrum. The dogs were barking.

'Now listen carefully, Barbara. I will go in and start a conversation with Mr. Haegeli. I will try to arrange it so that he turns his back on Little Bit's cage. At that moment, carefully open the door of the cage, grab Little Bit, put her under your coat, and then don't run – stand still, and after a while say, "Oh, please let's get out of here." I will then say good evening, and we both will leave very slowly. Remember to act calmly, watch the butcher, but don't expect a signal from me. Decide yourself when it is time to act. It might be when he is in the middle of work, or while he is talking.'

'Oh, please, Poppy, let's get out of here,' Barbara rehearsed.

I opened the door to the kennel and smiled like a tourist in appreciation of a new discovery. 'Oh, that's where the dogs are kept,' I said. 'Good evening.'

Mr. Haegeli looked up and answered with a grunt. He was mixing dog food.

'My, what nice food you're preparing for them. How much do they charge to take a dog across?'

'Fifty dollars,' said Mr. Haegeli in a Swiss accent. There are all kinds of Swiss, some with French, some with Italian, and some with German accents. They all talk in a singing fashion. The faces are as varied as the accents. The butcher didn't look like a butcher – a good butcher is fat and rosy. Mr. Haegeli was thin-lipped, thin-nosed, his chin was pointed. In the light he didn't look as mean as I expected; he looked rather fanatic, and frustrated.

'How often do you feed them?'

'They eat twice a day and as good as anybody on board,' said Mr. Haegeli. 'All except Rolfi there – he belongs to an actor, Mr. Kruger, who crosses twice a year and brings the dog's food along.' He pointed to the cage where a large police dog was housed. 'Rolfi, he is fed once a day, out of cans.' He seemed to resent Rolfi and his master. _

'You exercise them?'

'Yes, of course – all except Rolfi. Mr. Kruger comes up in the morning and takes him around with him on the top deck and sits with him there on a bench. He doesn't leave him alone. There is such a thing as making too much fuss over a dog.'

I said that I agreed with him.

'He tried to keep him in his cabin – he said he'd pay full fare for Rolfi, like a passenger. He'll come up any minute now to say good night to Rolfi. Some people are crazy about dogs.' Mr. Haegeli was putting chopped meat, vegetables, and cereal into the large dish. 'There are other people that try to get away with something – they try and smuggle dogs across, like that one there.' He pointed at Little Bit. 'But we catch them,' he said in his Swiss accent. 'Oh yes, we catch them. They think they're smart, but they don't get away with it – not with me on board they don't. I have ways of finding out. I track them down.' The fires of the fanatic burned in his eyes. 'I catch them every time.' He sounded as if he turned them over to the guillotine after he caught them. 'Ah, here comes Mr. Kruger,' he said and opened the door.

Kurt Kruger, the actor, said good evening and introduced himself. He spoke to Mr. Haegeli in German – and Mr. Haegeli turned his back on Little Bit's cage to open Rolfi's. The entire place was immediately deafened with barking from a dozen cages. The breathless moment had arrived. Barbara was approaching the door, but the dog-lover Kruger spotted Little Bit and said, 'There's a new one.' He spoke to Little Bit, and Little Bit, who behaved as if she had been carefully rehearsed for her liberation, turned away with tears in her eyes.

Mr. Kruger and his dog disappeared.

Mr. Haegeli wiped his hand on his apron and went back to mixing the dog food. The chances for rescuing Little Bit were getting slim.

'Where do you come from, Mr. Haegeli?'

'Schaffhausen. You know Schaffhausen?'

'Yes, yes,' I said in German. '*Wunderbar.*'

'*Ja, ja*, beautiful city.'

'And the waterfall!'

'You know the Haegeli Wurstfabrik there?'

'No, I'm sorry.'

'Well, it's one of the biggest sausage factories in Switzerland – liverwurst, salami, cervelat, frankfurters, boned hams – a big concern, belongs to a branch of my family. I'm sort of a wanderer. I like to travel – restless, you know – I can't see myself in Schaffhausen.' He looked up. He was mixing food with both hands, his arms rotating.

'I understand.'

'Besides, we don't get along, my relatives and I. All they think about is money, small money – I think in large sums. I like a wide horizon. Schaffhausen is not for me.'

'How long have you been traveling?'

'Oh, I've been two years on this ship. You see, I'm not really a butcher but an inventor.'

'How interesting! What are you working on?'

At last Mr. Haegeli turned his back on the cage in which Little Bit waited. 'Well, it's something tremendous. It's, so to say, revolutionary.'

'Oh?'

'There's a friend of mine, a Swiss, who is a baker, but you know, like I'm not a real butcher, he is not exactly a baker – I mean, he knows his trade but he has ambition to make something of himself – and together we have created something that we call a frankroll.' He waited for the effect.

'What is a frankroll?'

'It's a frankfurter baked inside a roll. We've everything here to experiment with, the material and the ovens. I make the franks and he makes the rolls. We've tried it out on the passengers. Mr. Kruger, for example, says it's a marvellous idea. I might add that the experimental stage is over. Our product is perfect. Now it is a question of selling the patent, or licensing somebody – you know the way that is done. You make much more that way.'

'Have you tried?'

Mr. Haegeli came close, the inventor's excitement in his eyes now. 'That is where the hitch comes in. On the last trip I saw the biggest frankfurter people in America – they're in New York. Well, the things you find out! They were very nice. The president received us and looked at the product and tasted it. He liked it, because he called for his son and a man who works close to him. "I think you've got something there," said the old man. I think with him we would have had clear sailing, but he had one of these wisenheimers for a son.'

As Haegeli talked he forgot completely about the dogs. He gesticulated with hands that were sticky with hash, using them as a boxer does when he talks with his gloves on. Standing close to me, he held them away lest dog food soil my clothes. He stood exactly right, with his back turned to the spot where Barbara was slowly reaching to the door of Little Bit's cage. It was all foiled again by the return of Mr. Kruger and Rolfi. Mr. Kruger kissed his dog goodnight and stood waiting while Rolfi slowly walked into his cage. He said to Rolfi that it was only for two more nights that he had to be here, he wished us a good night also, and after a final good night to his dog he went.

'Where was I?' said the butcher.

'With the frankroll, the old man, and the wise-guy son.'

'Right. Well, the son was looking at our product with a mixture of doubt, so he took a bite out of it, and in the middle of it he stopped chewing. "Mmmm," he said. "Not bad, not bad at all. But – " He paused a long time, and then he said, "What about the mustard, gentlemen?"

'I said, "All right, what about the mustard?"

'So the wise guy says, "I'm a customer. I'm buying. I'm at a hotdog stand. I watch the man in the white jacket. He picks up the frankfurter roll that's been sliced and placed face down on the hot plate – he picks it up in a sanitary fashion – and he takes the skinless frank with his prong and puts it in the roll and hands it to me. Now, I dip into the mustard pot, or maybe I decide on a little kraut, or maybe I want some condiments or relish. Anyway, I put that on the frank – " He held out his hand.

'So I said, "What's all that got to do with our frankroll?"

'So Junior says, "A lot. Let me explain. It's got no appeal. Practical maybe, but to put the mustard on the hot dog the customer would have to slice the frankfurter bun first, and that leads us straight back to the old-fashioned frankfurter and the old-fashioned roll. The frankroll may be practical, but it's got no sizzle to it. No eye appeal, no nose appeal – it's no good."

'Well, the old man was confused, and he got up and said that he'd like to think about it, and then he said he'd like to show us the factory. Well, you'd never think how important a thing a frankfurter is. There are two schools of thought about frankfurters, the skin frank and the skinless. These people specialize in skinless ones – because the American housewife prefers them without skin – but did you know that the skinless comes with skins and have to be peeled? This factory is spotless. There is a vast hall, and at long tables sit hundreds of women, and music plays, and they all have in their left hand a frankfurter, and in the right a paring knife, and all day long they remove the skins from the frankfurters – an eight-hour day. And at the end of the room is a first-aid station, because at the speed at which they work there is a great deal of laceration. The man in charge –'

'Oh, please, Poppy, let's get out of here!' Barbara broke in.

'The man in charge explained that in spite of elaborate safety precautions there was a great deal of absenteeism on account of carelessness. They had people who were working on a machine to skin the frankfurters. "Now if you could invent a frankfurter-skinning device," said the old man to me, "you'd be a millionaire overnight." Well, we're not licked yet. The beauty of working on a ship is that you have everything on board. One of the engineers is working with us on a skinning machine, and I have another outfit lined up for the frankroll.'

The light in Mr. Haegeli's eyes faded. He wiped his hand again on his apron, and I shook it, and slowly we walked out on deck and down the first flight of stairs to A deck. I said to Barbara, 'Run for your life, for by now he has discovered that Little Bit is gone.'

We got to the cabin. Little Bit smiled on both sides of her face, and she bounced from floor to chair to dresser. There was a knock on the door – the thrill of the game of cops and robbers had begun. Little Bit vanished.

Barbara asked innocently, 'Who is it?'

It was the steward. 'Did you find her?'

Barbara smiled.

'You got her back?'

Barbara nodded.

'Well, for heaven's sake, keep her out of sight. That crazy butcher is capable of anything – and I got a wife and family.'

'From now on the dog must not be left,' I said to Barbara. 'She must go with us wherever we go, to the dining-room, on deck, to the lounge, and to the movies. And you can't carry her in that bag – you have to cover her with a scarf or have her inside your coat.'

Barbara started going about as if she carried her arm in a sling. The steward averted his eyes whenever he met us, and he didn't bring any more dog food.

Mr. Kruger said, 'The kennel man suspects you of having removed the dog from the kennel.'

'We did.'

'Good,' said the actor. 'Anything I can do, I will.'

'Well, act as if you didn't know anything about it. How is Rolfi?'

'Oh, Rolfi is fine. You know, he's never bitten anybody in his life except that kennel man.'

Mr. Kruger offered to get Little Bit off the boat. He had a

wicker basket in which he carried some of Rolfi's things, and he would empty that, except for Rolfi's coat, and in that he would carry Little Bit off the *America*, for the butcher would follow us and watch us closely, and if he didn't find the dog before he'd catch us at the customs.

'Isn't he a nice man – Mr. Kruger? People always say such mean things about movie actors,' said Barbara.

Camouflaged in a scarf, Little Bit rested on Barbara's lap during meals. On the deck chair she lay motionless between my feet, covered by a steamer rug. She traveled about under Barbara's coat, and she took her exercise on the secret afterdeck, while I watched from above.

After the morning walk, the next day, the steward knocked. He looked worried. 'The butcher was here,' he said, 'and went all over the room. He found the dish with those French words and the dog's picture on it, on the bathroom floor.'

'How could we be so careless?' I said, my professional pride hurt.

'And of course he saw the bag with *Little Bit* printed on it. I said I didn't know nothing about any dog.'

We doubled our precautions. Little Bit's mouth was down at the edges with worry. I contemplated what to do. After all, there were only two more days, and if the worst happened we could sit upstairs with Little Bit, the way Mr. Kruger sat with Rolfi. I said to Barbara, 'Perhaps it would be best to pay the passage and have it over with.'

The symptoms were back. 'No, you can't do that. Think of the poor steward and his family!'

'Well, we could settle that, I think, with the butcher. I don't like to cheat the line – '

'Well, Poppy, you can send them a check afterward, if that

worries you, or drink a few extra bottles of champagne, or buy something in the shop.'

Knock on the door.

'Who is it?'

'The purser, sir.'

'Please come in.'

The door opened. Behind the purser stood Mr. Haegeli.

'Just wanted to look and see if everything is all right. Are you comfortable, sir?'

'Everything is fine.'

'By the way, sir, we're looking for a small white dog that's been lost. We wondered if by any chance it's in here.'

'Come in and look for yourself.'

'That's quite all right, sir. Excuse the intrusion. Good evening.' The purser closed the door.

'What a nice man!' said Barbara.

The butcher was excluded from pursuing us in the public rooms of the ship; he couldn't follow us to the movies or the dining-room. But he seemed to have spies. 'What a lovely scarf you have there, Miss,' said the elevator boy, and after that we used the stairs. The butcher came on deck in a fatigue uniform and followed us on the evening promenade around deck, during which Little Bit sat inside my overcoat, held in place by my right hand in a Napoleonic pose. We made four turns around deck. I leaned against the railing once, holding Little Bit in place, so that I could stretch my arms; Barbara was skipping rope, and the maneuvre fooled him. He ran downstairs, and we caught him as he emerged from near our cabin – he had made another search. We saw his shadow on the wall near the stairs several times. He seemed to be nearing a nervous breakdown. Mr. Kruger told us that he had sworn we had the dog and meant to find it at any cost. There was one more night to go, and the next day the ship would dock.

At ten Barbara would deliver Little Bit to Mr. Kruger, and we would fill the bag in which she traveled with paper tissue, tobacco, soap, extra toothbrushes, razor blades, dental floss, and other things, which can all be bought in Europe but which for some droll reason one always takes along.

Little Bit was fed from luncheon trays which we ordered for ourselves in the cabin instead of going down to lunch.

The steward was shaking. 'I don't know,' he said, 'when that guy butchers, or when he takes care of the other dogs. He's hanging around here all the time. I hope you get off all right.'

On the last afternoon on board I became careless. Some passengers and a bearded ship's officer were watching the last game of the deck-tennis tournament, and others were lying this way and that in their deck chairs, forming a protective barricade. Barbara had checked on the butcher – he was busy aft, airing some of his charges.

I thought it safe to take Little Bit out of my coat and place her on deck, so that we all could relax a bit. She had been there but a moment when I heard a cry. 'Ha,' it went. It was the 'Ha' of accusation and discovery, chagrin and triumph, and it had been issued by Mr. Haegeli, who stood with both arms raised. Fortunately he was not a kangaroo and was therefore unable to jump over the occupied deck chairs. I gathered up Little Bit, and we were safe for a few seconds. By now I knew the ship's plan as well as the man who designed her. We went down two decks on outside stairs, entered through a serving pantry, climbed one inside service stair, and then nonchalantly walked to the bar. I sat down and rang for the steward. I ordered something to drink. In a little while Barbara, with her lemonade in hand, said, 'He's watching us through the third window!'

I swept my eyes over the left side of the room, and his face was pressed against the glass, pale and haunting. He kept watch from the outside, and ran back and forth as we moved around inside.

We went down to dinner. When we came back I got a cigar. He was outside the bar. As I went to the saloon to have coffee he was outside that window.

'Don't give Little Bit any sugar,' Barbara said. 'He's watching us.'

The floor was cleared for dancing, and we got up to walk back to the library. There is a passage between the main saloon and the library off which are various pantries and side rooms, and it has no window. In a corner of it is the shop, and on this last evening people stood there in numbers buying cartons of cigarettes, film, small sailor hats, miniature lifebelts, and ship models with 'S.S. *America*' written on them. Here I suddenly realized the miraculous solution of our problem. It was in front of me, on a shelf. Among stuffed Mickey Mice, Donald Ducks, and teddy bears of various sizes stood the exact replica of Little Bit – the same button eyes and patent-leather nose, the fluff, the legs like sticks, the pompom at the end of the tail and the blue ribbon in its hair.

'How much is that dog?' I asked the young lady.

'Two ninety-five.'

'I'll take it.'

'Shall I wrap it up, sir?'

'No, thanks, I'll take it as is.'

'What are we going to do now, Poppy?'

'Now you keep Little Bit hidden, and I'll take the stuffed dog, and we'll go into the library.'

There we sat down. I placed the stuffed dog at my side and

spoke to it. The butcher was on the far side of the ship, but he almost went through the window. He disappeared and ran around to the other side. I had arranged the toy dog so that it seemed to be asleep at my side, partly covered by Barbara's scarf. I told her to take Little Bit down to the cabin and then come back, and we'd have some fun with the butcher.

When she came back Barbara took the toy dog and fixed its hair and combed the fluff. Then I said, 'Please give me the dog.' We walked the length of the ship on the inside. The butcher was sprinting outside, his face flashing momentarily in the series of windows.

At the front of the ship we went out on deck. I held the dog so that the pompom stuck out in back, and I wiggled it a little, to give it the illusion of life. It took the butcher a while to catch up. He walked fast – we walked faster. He almost ran – we ran. He shouted, 'Mister!' I continued running. As we came toward the stern I asked Barbara, 'Can you let out a terrible scream?'

'Yes, of course,' said Barbara.

'One – two – three – *now*.'

She screamed, and I threw the dog in a wide curve out into the sea. The butcher, a few feet away, gripped the railing and looked below, where the small white form was bobbing up and down in the turbulent water. Rapidly it was washed away in the wake of the *America*.

We turned to go back into the saloon.

We left the butcher paralyzed at the stern. He wasn't at the gangplank the next day.

Little Bit landed in France without further incident.

Cher Ami

TO WORK for me, to live with me, is hard. I am composed of disorderly habits. I live the way William Saroyan thinks people live, and it's not so funny off the stage. Normally, I am filled with the greatest good-will toward my fellow men, and I manifest this with generous gestures in all directions. I stop and smile at children, and I spread breadcrumbs for the pigeons on the stairs of Saint Patrick's, but the next day I would like to kick them all in the shins.

My habitat is mostly bars and restaurants, hotels and depots, and the lobbies and entrances thereof. In normal times I am found on the decks of steamships, and on the shores of tropic isles. I arrive suddenly, somewhere far away, and once there I haunt the piers and terminals and curse if there isn't a boat or plane to take me back immediately. I get homesick as soon as I am away from where I've gone – going it's for New York, coming back it's for where I've left. To share such a life, one needs a mobile servant, adaptable as a chameleon, shock- and surprise-proof, a person who gazes into your face as into a crystal ball and then knows whether to come close or stay away from you the rest of the day. The coin is not too good, either.

The ideal servant for me is a kind of Sancho Panza, a companion and friend with the melancholy kinship of an Irish setter. The run-of-the-mill retainer won't do at all; no Treacher type, no Admirable Crichton for me. I'd rather have him inept as far as service goes, but let him make it up with perfection in all the other departments. Above all, let him be someone curious and different. My ideal would be an ex-sergeant of the Foreign Legion, or a bankrupt banker, a retired road-company leading man who could mug Hamlet and Shylock, or a third-rate Karloff. Give me a burglar, or even a dismissed G-man, anything, but not the meek soul whose life is a monument to a million polished teapots.

My wishes are usually fulfilled with miraculous promptness, sometimes with such dispatch that I get scared at the prompt benevolence that hovers over me.

For example, I wished for this fol-de-rol butler, and not very hard either. I did not go to any employment agency to look for him; I did not even put an ad in the paper, nor did I ask anyone if they knew of such a man. I just wished, and he came.

I met him in Haiti last winter. For a while I lived in the *dépendance* of a small hotel, the rooms of which were like the cells in an exquisitely run insane asylum. Every compartment had its own precise garden of tropical greenery. Planted in the exact center of each of these eight-by-twelve-foot gardens was a tree, not large enough for anyone to use it for climbing in or out of the garden, but with enough leaves to shade a rattan *chaise longue*, and with four branches for birds to sing on in the twilights of morning and evening. Each of the gardens was enclosed by a white high wall.

The floor of the bedroom was a mosaic of black and white tile, and in its center stood a bed with tortured cast-iron ornaments, small knobs, and buns, spirals and little brass blossoms stuck and twisted on its head- and foot-boards. During the day, the design of the bed was somewhat diffused under a tent made of mosquito netting, which was attached to the ceiling by a rope and pulley. At night, one was under the tent, and then the fancy ironwork was beautifully clear.

The morning after the night when I wished for the companion, I beheld on awakening the outline of a man outside the mosquito tent. It seemed that he had stood there for a long while. He was in a state of repose, leaning on the wall, and he threw the butt of a cigarette out into the garden when he saw me sit up. On his head was a Chevalier straw hat. I lifted my netting, and, leaning out of bed, I observed that my visitor was barefoot and sunburned, and that his hat was honored with the bright colors of a Racquet Club band. He had a lean, generous face, and looked somewhat like a skiing teacher or a derelict tennis pro. Over his lips lay a black mustache, and his shirt was without buttons. The sleeves were torn off half-way between the elbow and the shoulders, offering ventilation to his chest.

He sat down at the foot of the bed and told me that he was my friend. He told me his name and informed me that he was one of a group of escaped prisoners from Devil's Island, and that he was taken care of, with his companions, by the good *Sœurs de la Sagesse*. He and the boys lived at the convent . . .

He corrected himself and explained that he and the others were not escaped criminals in the strict sense of the word, but

that since the Vichy Government was unable or unwilling to pay the upkeep of the prison or the salaries of the administrators and guards at Guiana, the prison doors had simply been left open, and whoever wanted to, left.

'I,' he continued, 'was a *doubleur*; that is, I had served my sentence, but had to stay on the Island. We left French Guiana, my friends and I, in a sixteen-foot *canot*. No one tried to stop us. We were twelve when we started. The hardest part was to get straight out to sea past the reef which is called the Frenchmen's Grave. To pass this, you have to go over sand-bars in a straight line for about thirty-five kilometres, and then you turn left.

'That takes courage. We did it all with the aid of a map, which we had copied, and with the aid of a Greek, a seaman who knew the stars. We also had a small compass with us, and we got as far as Trinidad. It was easy. A captain of a ship must find a port; we only tried to find the land. The Governor of Trinidad gave us eighty dollars to buy a bigger boat, and with that we got as far as Jamaica. Now we are here and thinking of going on to Cuba. We have a tolerably good life here. Twice a week we watch the plane come in, that is where I saw you arrive. We sit in the convent garden or along the water most of the time, and the *bonnes sœurs de la Sagesse* take care of us as if we were little birds, but it's not a life for a man.

'*Cher ami*,' he said, 'do something for me. I am a pastry cook, I have been a hotel director. I know how to drive a car and how to fix it. I can write on the machine. I can steer a boat. I am ready to go anywhere, and I am afraid of nothing. Give me a little food and pocket money, and I am your man, your servant, your friend for life.'

He lounged back on the bed, lit a cigarette, spread his toes fanwise, folded his hands in back of his head, and looked up at the ceiling, waiting for my answer.

'I wanted to talk to you last night,' he added after a while. 'I followed you from the cinema up to your hotel, but I thought you might get scared or nervous, so I came this morning.'

He broke the few moments of silence, in which I thanked that particular department of Providence that concerns itself with me, by remarking that if I was worried about his past he could put me completely at ease. He confessed that when he was young, he had made a mistake – he had disemboweled his mistress. Ah, Simone was a very beautiful girl, but she had been unfaithful, and he was not sorry.

I told him he could start in right away. He could pack my trunk and take it to the ship; and as soon as he got to New York, there were several people I would like to have disemboweled, but nicely, and I would give him a list every Monday. I gave him a small advance, and then I said that the only thing I was worried about was how he would get to New York, past the immigration authorities, the police, and J. Edgar Hoover's sharp-eyed and resourceful young men.

'Bah! Leave that to me,' he said. 'I shall be in New York – let me see – it's the middle of August now; give me until the end of September. It's child's play. About the twenty-fifth of September, I would say. Where do you live?' I gave him my address, and that afternoon he arrived with a boy to carry my trunk which he had neatly packed. On the way to the boat, he stopped the car at the *Magazin de Mille Cent Choses* and bought a pack of razor blades, which he said I needed; and then he said good-by and *au revoir*. He slowly shook my hand and lifted the Chevalier straw hat. He waved it so hard when the ship pulled out that the Racquet Club band came off and fell into the bay. A native boy dove after it, and he gave him a coin.

'Wonderful, wonderful,' I said to myself and missed him immediately. Stretched out in my deckchair, I thought how very fortunate I was. When I got home, I was still gloating over the fact that I had found the perfect man.

One morning soon after my return, I found a letter. It started: 'La Havane, Cuba. *Cher ami*, I have the honor to address these few words to you, to inform you that, after a sudden departure from Haiti in a boat which I and a few of the others who shared my idea procured along the waterfront, we proceeded for Cuba. The beginning of the voyage was without incident. One night,

however, we had some difficulty holding our direction, as a violent wind caused our leaking shell to dance an infernal sarabande on the waves.

'Without the sail and the mast, and also without the man who steered the boat at the outset, without a rudder even, the wind delivered us to the eastern shore of Cuba, and, to make our *misère* perfect, into a nest of waiting gendarmes from whom we were too wet and exhausted to flee. My companions and I find ourselves detained at the *Centre d'Émigration*, and I regret to inform you that my departure from here can only be effected by the immediately-sent sum of one hundred dollars. I will consider the hundred dollars in lieu of six months of service.'

I sent him the money. I have faith in such characters, and they have never failed. Neither did *Cher Ami*.

In the middle of one night when I lay awake, I had one of my rare moments of worry again. Suppose, when he turns up, I said to myself, he's the perfect servant, butler, and companion, and besides, a good pastry cook. Suppose he's out in the pantry one day squeezing many happy returns on my birthday cake when there is a knock at the door, and it's the police. Then follows the story of the body of a young woman, partly decomposed, found crammed into the luggage compartment of my convertible coupé . . . O.K. take him away; but he won't come quietly . . . smack, smack, *klunk*; I hold the door open while they carry him out. Then I have to get hold of Leibowitz, but Leibowitz has turned judge, and Arthur Garfield Hays is out of town. And then the trial and the conviction and the pictures in the paper, and then the visit up the river, and the last mile. It's all absorbing, stirring, and excellently done, but it's not much fun, riding back alone from Ossining with a cold friend up there.

The morning after the night that I wished he wouldn't come, he didn't come, but there was a letter from him, one of the nicest documents I have ever received and certainly worth a hundred dollars.

'*Cher ami,*' it said, 'I have the honor to address these few words to you, wishing to keep you informed of my condition. I have the honor to inform you with my deep personal regret that I will not come to America. Dishonesty is not my game. The money you so generously sent to me is paid out in the most splendid of causes.

I have used it to obtain for myself and for a friend who shares my idea, passage to Jamaica, from which isle this communication is addressed to you. We have come here to enlist in the forces of General de Gaulle. This is attested by our pictures and the text which you will find under them in the accompanying clipping from the Kingston *Star*. It's not patriotism, *cher ami*. France has not been a good mother to me . . . But it's the quickest way to become a man again. Please accept my respectful salutations.

André Pigueron.'

The Morale of the Natives

HE APPEARED before me every morning, across a three-foot garden wall, somewhere between an acacia tree in full bloom and some lotuses that grew close to his balcony. He was nude at about nine in the morning and a small monkey sat on his fist; he sang, and then lay down on a couch to take a sunbath.

A little black boy in a white coat brought him his breakfast, rubbed him with some lotion, and then stood by to chase the flies away. At ten he went into his house and then appeared after short interludes, first in his underwear, next stuffing his shirt into his trousers, and eventually fully dressed. He tied his cravat in the sun; his song had no melody, it was a formless tra-la-laa, a noise made of the pleasure of living, completely thoughtless, without beginning or end. For the rest of the day, when he was home, Captain Alastair Monibuy shouted at his servants, played with his animals, and took pictures with a Leica – pictures of anything and anybody.

He had arrived in Quito in the old Rolls-Royce, making the perilous journey from Babahoyo, driving himself, a high testimonial to the motor and the chassis of the old car.

In the back of the car he had stowed several Louis Vuitton suitcases and a dozen polo mallets, a rifle and fishing gear, a saddle and a case of gin – gin was his favorite drink. His eyes were like two round emeralds, and when he drank they shone with hypnotic brilliance. He stood always tense, one leg a little ahead of the other, the upper body erect, shoulders back, one hand in his trouser pocket, playing with keys or change, and the other holding the glass tightly.

The whole little man was closely packed into good clothes, so tight that one felt the buttons on his suit or shirt would pop off any minute.

He first lived at the Metropolitano, but later found a little villa in the Mariscal section of Quito, an inexpensive livable house with a large garden and a garage, and a place where he could keep his zoo. He had a monkey and two tigrillos. (A tigrillo is really an ocelot, but having no tigers of their own, the Ecuadorians have elevated that animal to the rank of tiger, using the diminutive.) He had also a macaw and two parrots. His ménage was sloppy, as was his person. There was a drawer full of bottles of Geneva gin in the living-room; cigarette butts and matches accumulated in the washbasins of all the rooms, and somewhere there was always a stack of empty bottles. Broken glasses in the fireplace, and a long blond hair or dandruff on his coat. His hair was sticky and dirty.

He had trained an Indian boy as a servant, a very attractive mulatto as a cook, and the mulatto's twelve-year-old daughter to make the beds and clean the house. He smacked them all across the backside with his riding crop whenever they passed by him, and then laughed a hearty ha-ha-ha-ha-ha, a furious signal that also escaped him after every short, loud and deliberate sentence. He did not speak, he telegraphed his ideas and observations, leaving out all unnecessary words – the telegram always came in faultless English. He had been to Sandhurst, he said.

After he had asked me for lunch one day, he showed me how he had decorated his house. Nailed on the wall in the living-room hung a uniform in which he had flown for Franco, and next to it was a large frame in which, behind a glass, he had arranged an assortment of letterheads, with most distinguished addresses printed on them. There were about thirty of them and the best were: the Château de Gande, the Athenæum, Chequers, Ten Downing Street, the Horse Guards, etc.

Each of these letters started with 'Dear Bimbo,' as he was known to his intimates; but the text in every case save one was hidden by the letter next to it. In the center of all these expensive papers, in cream and oyster hues, was a note from Hilaire Belloc, with text and signature showing, acknowledging the gift of a book. Once, when he added a new letter and had the whole correspondence laid out on the table, in order to arrange it anew, some of the other letters were laid bare. The one from the Athenæum requested the return of a loan; two others were regrets.

On the opposite wall hung another frame, into which he had written 'My Passions,' and this contained photographs: a string of polo ponies, a Savoia-Marchetti seaplane, a yacht and a sail-boat and several girls, all British and pretty and blonde, with their hair loose on top of their heads; every one of them had signed herself 'With love to Bimbo.'

He knew everybody and he had several kinds of behavior and fitted himself into almost any group. He never said anything, but his loud ha-ha-ha-ha followed every word he said and was infectious. People laughed and did not know why. He was the only completely happy man I have ever known; he lacked the capacity to worry.

266

Bimbo rode well, was a generous host, made compliments to the old ladies, and hopped from table to table. The doors of all good houses were open to him; he had, when he was in need of them, passable manners, and he had so ingratiated himself that he was permitted to come late everywhere and even sit down to dinner in riding clothes and mud-caked boots. Many a father thought that at last a man worthy of his beautiful but still unmarried daughter had arrived in Quito; dressmakers worked, florists were busier, wine merchants, butchers, and even saddlemakers felt the presence of Captain Alastair Monibuy.

One day he gave a cocktail party at his villa. He stood at the entrance playing with the change in his trouser pocket, pounding guests on the shoulder as they arrived, and roaring cheer.

The villa was filled, every room loud with conversation, long past the time when people usually went home. A dinner was hastily put together, some extra drinks made. It lasted late into the night. When almost everyone had finally departed, there was a scream from above, and then a body fell down the stairs.

It was the Armenian Minister, Gerard de Kongaga. This diplomat of good family and most amiable disposition had clamped himself to the banister, after talking to himself in the corner of the corridor above for half an hour, and then he had let go.

Kongaga had spent most of his life in Schönbrunn in one of the famous retreats of Professor Lorand, a healer who believed in occupational therapy. Kongaga had built so much garden furniture and so many birdhouses that he had become an expert carpenter and painter.

Since his arrival in Ecuador, however, he had never been

sober. When he came to parties it was in the manner of a blind man who had lost his god: he saw people where none stood, and offered them his hand in greeting. That day, as he came up the stairs, he passed the host, mistook the Papal Nuncio for the French Minister, embraced him, and told him dirty stories. He recognized the host later on and went up to him, held on to Monibuy to steady himself for a while, and then turned and looked into the room full of people. One could see him calculate his moves; he narrowed his eyes and surveyed his chances. There was a table filled with glasses to the right; a few feet away, opposite that hazard, stood a statue on a tabouret, and beyond this was a chair with a lady in it, the British Minister's wife. Wanting to say something nice to that lady, and observing that next to her was a vacant chair, he decided to sit down. He smiled at the Papal Nuncio, let go of Monibuy's hand, stood straight up, buttoned his coat, and then – one, two, three, – he started off . . . The lady was not there; it was a tall vacant Jacobean chair, upholstered, that had looked occupied. The chair next to it was there, so he took the armsrests into his hands and, with the dolorous mechanism of a paralytic, sat down – between the two chairs – pulling both down over him. He was rescued with great effort and seated in the chair on the left, and then he was quiet until the people who had lifted him up turned away and began to talk again. Then he plotted again and thought up a new and perfected excursion – which ended up in the fireplace.

He never became violent, his gentle face expressed nothing but a mild disappointment; he liked everyone and everyone liked Gerard de Kongaga. The women openly regretted that the rich, good-looking, and gallant man had few sober moments. He fell loosely like an acrobat and seldom came to grief. At

Monibuy's cocktail party he had fallen well again, and the host, the mulatto cook, and the Habsburg dragged him upstairs to the guest room and covered him up.

When the party finally began to break up, Bimbo decided that he could not sleep and wanted to go to the Ermitage, the El Morocco of Quito. The Ermitage was located in an old house. The policeman on duty in the street outside, the Carabinero No. 18, made himself useful opening and closing automobile doors, smiling at people, and acting as the doorman. In his faded greatcoat with the big saber at his side, he had gone better with the place when it was called Volga Volga. Like all the policemen in Quito, he was a half-breed. He had an old handkerchief tied around his face to protect nose and throat from the cold; but he kept this in his pocket on mild evenings and amused himself by imitating the songs of various birds, for he was an accomplished whistler. The rooms of the Ermitage were low and dim and so badly upholstered that when a patron sat down on one of the imitation leopard-skin banquettes, the patrons who sat to his left and right bounced up and down several inches. Cheap glass and crockery were on its tables, badly painted Russian murals with troikas and snow and the cathedral of Kazan painted on the walls, left over from the days when the place was under White Russian management. From that period also remained a large glass glove which showered the room with snow effects when the lights were turned low. The place was managed by two Frenchwomen, Lydia and Tamara, each with a friend in the Government and excellent business acumen. One smoked from a long cigarette holder; the other sat on a high stool, and twice an evening she played a guitar and sang such ballads as '*Ma femme est morte*.' Champagne was compulsory, the prices were out of reason, the music was native, and when they tried to play such things as 'St. Louis Blues' or 'South of the Border,' two of their favorites, it took a while to recognize the tune; and then the flutes pulled your scalp tight and made your ears wiggle. But late at night, when they played their own music, their native music which is in somewhat the same beat as a two-step, they played with fine rhythm. The *crème de la crème* of Quito assembled here; it was particularly crowded on Fridays, the shoddy linoleum dance-floor half set with chairs and tables.

At midnight on the day of the cocktail party, when Bimbo and the Habsburg were driving to the Ermitage, after taking off a door of the car coming out of the gate of the villa, they heard a voice from the back seat. It was Gerard de Kongaga and he said: 'You fellows aren't mad at me, I hope.' They stopped the car and told him that they were not mad at him, that they were very happy he had come along. The old Rolls-Royce squeezed itself through the streets of Quito with its loud special horn going tati-tata all the way to the Ermitage.

Kongaga crawled out of the car into the arms of his friends, and the three of them entered the room and advanced to the bright light where Tamara had just finished singing a couplet. Everyone became wide-eyed, Lydia quickly rushed to dim the room and turned on the snow effect, and the ladies looked the other way. Gerard de Kongaga stood in the center of the dance-floor minus his trousers. The room was darkened, the music started, and a waiter ran out for the policeman-doorman.

When the Carabinero No. 18 came in, he laughed and tried to be very friendly. He stood in front of Kongaga and tried to hide him from the audience with his big coat. Kongaga was busy twisting at the only button which was left on the policeman's coat; little pieces of thread hung empty where the others had been and the coat was held together by the belt from which the saber was suspended. The policeman tried to make himself part of the fun and hooked his arm into Kongaga's and said: '*Vamos!* Come on, let's go! Let's go home – no?' and started to pull him slowly from the room. This did not go well with Captain Monibuy. He looked hard at the policeman and then tore him away from Kongaga. 'Take your hands off that man instantly – let go now! Do you know who that is? That is His Excellency the Armenian Minister' – but the little policeman said again, '*Vamos* – let's go home,' and pulled on Kongaga's sleeve once more. Monibuy drew his shoulder back and hit the policeman so hard that he fell, spun, and disappeared – all but his small feet – under a ringside table. There was quiet again and the Habsburg dragged Kongaga out to the Rolls-Royce and they drove him home.

The next day Monibuy was in his little summerhouse in the garden. He came out in a bathrobe, and he shouted over the wall: 'You know, I wore out a suit last night; they ripped the sleeves out of my dinner coat.' His boy brought a bloater and he drank some tea. He sat in the morning sun for a while and his boy rubbed him down. At about eleven a car drove up, a policeman appeared and announced that the Chief of Police was in the car, and asked whether he might come in. The Chief came and put his cap and saber away, took off his gloves, and had some tea. He leaned back in his seat and looked up at Pichincha and over at Cayambe and said: 'What a lovely day. It was . . . you love my country? Ah, I am glad, is beautiful, no? And such lovely weather.' He changed his tone and kept his hands busy snapping his gloves together and taking them apart again. Then he watched the labor of some ants on the garden wall and said wearily: 'I am a very busy man, I am perhaps too serious. So many things happen, stupid things, and everybody comes to me with their troubles. I think there was some trouble last night – I do not go out much, I do not know much of these places – I hear in a place called the Ermitage, and somebody – I have not heard the name – I think with perhaps a little too much to drink, comes there, without proper dress . . . and there is a fight. Nothing important – it happens all the time, it happens everywhere – but I wish people would not hit our policemen; it is so bad for the morale of the natives.'

Benitin and Eneas

IN THIS village, in Baños, is a small restaurant called the American Country Club. It used to be run by two men who were partners in this enterprise, one named Benitin and the other Eneas.

Benitin and Eneas are the Spanish names of Mutt and Jeff in the American comic strip which appears in translation in the newspaper *El Comercio* in Quito. The restaurateurs were known by these names because one was tall, the other short, and also because their real names – they signed themselves Vorkapitch and Sasslavsky on all official documents – were too difficult for the Castilian ears of their clientele.

The general equipment of a restaurant in this land demands no great amount of capital. The local painter makes a sign for it, and you need in addition a strong padlock for the door, four tables, twelve chairs, a few glasses and plates new or old, tinware and a corkscrew and two salt and pepper shakers and a bottle of imitation Worcester sauce – and the dining-room is taken care of. At the bar is a box for the ice which the Indians bring down from the glaciers, a kind of hard, sooty snow, and the light comes from one weak bulb, without a shade, that hangs on a wire in the precise center of the room together with a sheet of flypaper. The flypaper acts as a sail, so that whenever the door is opened the light is carried to the left or right, and in a busy restaurant, in consequence of this, the shadows of every object are constantly in motion.

There is some kind of oven in the room and a pan to wash dishes. To divide kitchen from restaurant a curtain is hung, and with two pots and pans, the kitchen is ready.

What lifted the American Country Club into the rank of a *restaurant de grand luxe*, however, was that Benitin had invested in a music machine – a highly polished smooth cabinet with a slot into which a sucre could be dropped. When this happened, the instrument began to hum for a while, lit itself up in brilliant rainbow hues, and then rendered six pieces of staccato music to which people danced, while the Indians sat at a respectful distance outside the club and listened until the doors were closed.

Eneas, the other partner, had come through with an equally elegant contribution: he had installed two water-closets, one for caballeros and the other for señoras. The advertisements of the American Country Club featured both 'dancing' and 'confort moderne.'

The room was small and usually crowded, and warm. The ceiling was low. Benitin and his music machine were out in front. He attended to the four tables there and kept watch over the two dozen bottles of assorted spirits which comprised the cellar of the club.

Eneas and his investment were behind the curtain. He crouched over a low inadequate oven, cooked, made ham and chicken and club sandwiches, and talked to himself.

Eneas was not satisfied. The place was the only restaurant in Baños, it was in an excellent position facing the plaza, and it did good business for luncheon, dinner, and late into the night. He stood behind the curtain all day long until closing time; he did most of the work while the other one hung over the bar out front, laughed and talked with the customers, poured himself drinks, and listened to the music.

'Why,' said Eneas to himself, and to anyone who came behind and listened to him, 'why should I work like a dog and split the profits with him? This town can stand another restaurant.'

The next time he found himself in bad humor, he took advantage of a routine dispute with his partner and declared in his native Czech that he was through being a poodle, that he wanted his share of the business and also the water-closets.

A water-closet in this remote valley is a rare convenience. It is not only a testimonial to the initiative of its owner; it costs a good deal of money. Once ordered, its arrival is problematic; landslides will delay it, bridges may be washed away, there is the chance of breakage or of total loss. The time that passes between the day it is ordered and that when a donkey finally brings it to the door is one of chagrin and suspense.

It is easy to understand why Eneas insisted on taking his investment with him to his new restaurant. The new place, which was immediately next door, was higher; it had once been a Government building, sported two Ionic columns and a coat of arms over its door. It had fallen into neglect, but Eneas had painters busy for a week, put a carpet on the floor, built a solid division between dining-room and kitchen, and hired an artist from Ambato to decorate the interior.

At the entrance next to the columns he placed two large palms, and from the ceiling he hung Japanese paper lanterns with red 75-watt bulbs in them. He even entertained the idea of having an electric sign made with 'Salon Hollywood' flashing on and off.

After the 'confort moderne' was properly installed to the left and right, Eneas hired a native cook and he himself put on a chef's hat and supervised the preparations of the specialties of the house.

His tables, in accusing contrast to the American Country Club, were covered with clean chequered tablecloths. For most of the day Eneas now stood out in front waiting for his guests, his new waiters in a semi-circle around him, alert as pointing dogs.

It was all in vain.

Next door, without even whitewash on its walls, the American Country Club was crowded; people laughed and danced to the music of Xavier Cugat and Enrique Madriguera, corks were pulled and glasses broken, the noise went on until dawn. But Eneas continued to stand alone among his empty tables and chairs. At long-spaced intervals a hurried customer came running from next door, ordered a drink, and asked Eneas to turn on the light in the back, but the rest of the time his place yawned with emptiness and failure.

A month after he had opened it, Eneas closed the Salon Hollywood. The chairs and tables he sold to Benitin. The 'confort moderne' he decided to take with him.

Four donkeys inside the Salon Hollywood stood loaded with the heavy porcelain, the fixtures, pipes, and water tanks. Eneas gave his last instructions to the Indian who was to deliver the cargo in Ambato, and then he sat down under a striped new awning on one of his own chairs, in the midst of his tables and palms, which now were all part of a sidewalk café in front of the American Country Club. His former partner Benitin served him some rice and mutton. Eneas took a half-hearted bite and then pushed the plate away and stared out into the plaza.

This square is formed by three rows of houses half fallen apart, maroon, yellow, green, and black. Two have no roofs and moss grows on the tiles of the others. The doors, the balconies, the stones at the entrances have all been shifted to conflicting angles by earthquakes, and there is one balcony that makes the heart stop beating. It is high up and has no railing, just three short beams coming out of the house with two pieces of rotted gray board laid over them; and out on this platform a baby crawls every day to play and listen to the music of the American Country Club.

A few feet north of the center of the square stands an immense, fanciful tree. Its wide branches carry stout green leaves the shape and color of laurel. The trunk of the tree is bent and twisted, and it is as if it were hammered out of dull silver. Most of the leaves hang down over a fountain, a severe octagonal basin which, like all the stone in this humid valley, is soft and enchanting under a coverlet of fan-shaped miniature greenery. At the side where the water spills over the stone hang long beards of dripping grass, and from this grass the water flows down across the wide steps that encircle the fountain. The water quietly enters a large puddle that is in the exact center of the square. In this dark brown water a white church reflects itself, making the fourth side of the square. On days when the sun shines, shadows heavy and black, like blankets of indigo, lie under the tree; the water in the fountain is black and the only light comes from a basket full of lemons spread in front of an Indian woman sitting under the tree, and from the ponchos of besotted customers over in the native tienda across the square.

Into this scene Eneas looked for the last time. His donkeys, loaded with the 'confort moderne,' passed the tree and their gray hides were reflected in the puddle. They drank from the fountain and one of them raised his head, showed his teeth, and began his peculiar song. The church bell clanked and a sudden wind shifted the spray of the fountain. More water spilled and ran down over the side.

The Salon Hollywood was boarded up, the shutters nailed together. Eneas, with an Indian carrying his belongings, walked to the bus for Ambato and soon was gone.

But the tragedy of Eneas repeated itself in Baños soon afterward, with disturbing similarity in details.

When one walks under the big tree on the plaza and looks into the water, one sees a small red flame burning in the water. It is the cloak of the Lord who sits outside the old church. He faces the square on a small table covered by his fiery velvet cloak and shaded by a small and broken black umbrella.

His face is cut out of polychrome wood; the agonized glass eyes are turned heavenward; his mouth is half open, showing a row of small real teeth behind his blue lips. His body is a ghastly mess of wounds and running blood. He is covered with them all the way down to the toes, which the Indians kiss all day long.

The statue is not without merit; it is Spanish baroque, vulgar, done in the spirit of butchery, but the modelling of the face, hands, and feet is exquisite work. It is very old.

On the poor head, above the crown of thorns, they have put a wig taken from a doll, a wig such as Shirley Temple dolls wear. Two long flaxen curls hang alongside the face, the rest down over the cloak behind. At the feet is a strong-box, and from the shoulders on a string dangles a sign which asks for alms: 'Give me something for my temple.'

The Indians bend the knee before him, give him their coppers and realitos; but they love much more the Madonna who sits inside the church. To her they pray and sing, 'Santa María, Santa María, salve regina.'

Even for the *misa del gallo*, the earliest mass, this church fills up. It is an adobe building with some stone here and there, ordinary windows, and a low roof. It is a church only because it is blessed and has a bell tower, otherwise it is just a long room divided into a place for the congregation and spaces for the altar, the confessional, and a small stone pulpit from which the padre preaches. It is lit by candles which the Indians buy, and they also bring from the surrounding fields the flowers which decorate the altar – mostly large white, sweet-smelling lilies.

Besides the padre there is a sacristan, a trembling, chalk-faced, ancient frater who never looks up and always prays so silently that one hears only 's–s–s–ps–ps–s–s–s' when he passes.

The Madonna between the altar and the confessional is the statue of a beautiful young girl, without sorrow. She is life-sized, painted in the ever-fresh tones of church statuary. She wears a forget-me-not-blue cloak over a snow-white dress, she is smiling, and all in all she looks as if she had just come out of a bath. The Indians have been told that she arrived in the middle of a very dark night, riding on a black donkey. The animal with its sacred burden pushed open the door of the church and walked in. Inside, it trotted up to the sacristan's bell, took the cord in its teeth, and – dingaling, dingaling – rang it until the sacristan and the padre were awakened. The Indians love the story and must hear it over and over; the old sacristan tells it to them once a week, standing in front of the Madonna. On the back of the statue, pressed into the stucco of which it is made, one can read that the Madonna came from very far; it says there: 'Gebrüder Pustet, Fabrik Kirchlicher Geräte, Leipzig' and 'Made in Germany No. 186432.'

The old church in Baños was built by the Dominicans. They had rented it to the Franciscans and these brothers were not very happy with the arrangement. They said to each other that Baños could stand a second church, and that it was folly to pay rental to the Dominicans.

Not far from the old church they decided to build their own. The new edifice was high and entirely of stone. It was lit by electricity, had three altars and six confessionals. The pews were of costly woods, elaborately decorated; there was a runner down the center aisle for high holidays, and windows of stained glass. The main altar housed in its lower part a relic of Saint Francis, and in its tower hung three new bells.

The church was opened with processions and ringing of all the bells – with every ceremony known to the church. Hot-air balloons were sent up bearing the image of Saint Francis. It was lit not only with electric light, but also with hundreds of candles. A new organ installed in a proper choir played in easy competition with the leaky antique instrument that is hidden behind the altar of the old church. The Indians came, wandered around in their bare feet, touched everything – with their hands and their eyes. They slowly took inventory of the new church, and then all of them ran back to their Madonna.

More resourceful and persevering than Eneas, the padres, who had noted the Indians' attachment to the holy Virgin, sent to Quito for one of the brothers who was a sculptor. He brought his tools and retired into the woods around Baños, where he began to carve a Madonna out of a seasoned piece of hardwood.

One of the Indians, the one from whom he had obtained the wood, saw him and told the others, and when finally the Madonna was finished and set up in the new church, the Indians said, 'Oh, no,' and shook their heads; 'that is not the real Madonna; our Madonna is in the old church. She came riding one night on a black donkey.' Like children they remembered the story. Again they ran back to their church and asked the sacristan to tell it once more, and bought more candles than ever and decorated their Madonna with large bouquets of lilies and sang, 'Santa María, Santa María, ora pro nobis!'

But even then the Franciscans did not give up. They reasoned that if Saint Francis, the Madonna, and Heaven did not help, perhaps the Devil would.

There arrived from Quito a large painting of Purgatory. It is one of numberless similar canvases that can be seen hanging in almost every large South American church. Baños until then had been without one.

Painted on panels which, when put together, form a picture twenty feet wide and eighteen feet high, it baffles the onlooker for a while with the maze of its figures. It is as obvious as a circus poster and painted in the same hues. Framed in fumes and flames and in the upraised arms of penitents, it depicts the Devil's holiday. He stands fanning flames with green batwings attached to his shoulders; his sweating assistants have the faces of black pigs from whose fangs issue blue and yellow flames like those from a plumber's torch. The catalog of their amusements is a tiresome repetition of cooking people, sawing them in half, pinching and cutting up the rueful throng. Liars' lips are sewn together, thieves mutilated; and, to make it clear that this torture is not ended by death, one of the devils is shown driving spikes into a lecher's head, while the next one pulls them out again. In the center of the tableau is a most ingenious machine. The Devil himself is busy turning the crank. Attached with thorny twigs to a large, flaming wheel is a young, most carefully painted woman, altogether nude. She looks voluptuous and her sinful lips are half open; her flesh glares white in all the red, blue, and gaseous colors around her. The instrument to which she is tied is so built that as the Devil turns the crank, the girl's breasts and abdomen will sail into a crowded arrangement of spikes, hooks, small ploughshares, and knives, which will disembowel her. The last victim, from whose blood the knives are still wet, is now at the bottom – an old bearded man, with the word 'Adulterer' written across his body, roasting over an open fire.

Fortunately there is escape from all this. The sinners' eyes are hopefully lifted to a high, narrow bridge at the end of which stand two angels, one with a chalice in his hand, the other holding half open the door to Paradise. Beyond, half a mile inside Paradise, on a throne of silver clouds, sits the holy Virgin surrounded by Franciscan friars, with wings like angels, reading Masses for the poor souls below and advising the Madonna for which of the sinners she is to intercede.

Hand in hand with the painting came a week of bell-ringing, processions, and exorcism. The Indians were there, all of them, and children were trampled as they crowded close to the picture. The padres explained it to them in detail – they asked to have the devils pointed out to them, and they listened to the story. The women sometimes left the church in tears, thinking of departed relatives and of their husbands' and children's future.

The padres granted reductions in the cost of indulgences, and lowered the prices of Masses for the souls of the dead. It was possible to buy an amnesty of three hundred years in Purgatory for five realitos, and for a few days a thin stream of coins went into the treasury of the Franciscans.

All at once it stopped again, and the church was deserted. The sweet warm smell of the Indians, the revolting perfume of sweat and poverty, moved back to the Madonna. Soon afterward the new church closed. The doors and windows were bricked up, the old church inherited a bell and took a few of the pews. The great stone building stood forgotten; an avocado tree split its nave, and the fruits hang down over the altar. It echoes the cries of bats and of the small birds that are born in the electric light fixtures and in the tower.

The Franciscans left. Four donkeys, loaded with the eight panels of the picture of Purgatory, walked across the square and up toward Ambato.

Prison Visit

ATOP ONE of the foothills of Pichincha, high above the city of Quito, bathed in sunlight, stands a white building with a cupola. It is the Panóptico, and it has an evil name. Don Juan Palacios in Guayaquil had recited its horrors to me, and wherever I asked permission to visit the prison I was told with politeness and much regret that this one wish could not be granted. Diplomats in cautious conversation told me again that its cells were subterranean and wet, that the prisoners were chained to the walls, underfed, without proper clothing. Bony, feverish victims of political miscalculation, who died slowly, without consolation, and stank to high heaven. Lucky were they who were sent to exile in the Galápagos Islands or marched into the jungles of the Oriente; there death was quick and in the daylight.

The magnificent name of the prison and its story drew me up the hill, which I climbed in short stages of thirty paces at a time. For a while, when you return from the low lands, it is difficult to breathe in Quito, and you proceed by resting on a street corner, advancing thirty paces, leaning against a house and then a tree. Thus I arrived at the Panóptico.

Outside, propped against the building, were two sentries in khaki uniforms, with legs crossed, resting their hands on the barrels of their guns. They were talking and laughing; one turned, when the other pointed at me, and raised his eyebrows.

'I would like to see the Director of the prison.'

Ah, he said, but that was not so easy; there had to be arrangements made for this ahead of time, a letter, an introduction, a pass, or else one had to arrive in the company of an official of the Government, or at least of a policeman.

I told him that I knew all that, but that my visit was an exception, that I was a prison official myself, from the United States of North America, that I was the secretary of the warden of a prison.

The soldier's eyes grew respectful and obedient, he leaned away from the building, saluted, and dragging his gun behind him he almost ran up the portico to the door, where he told the story to the man who sat on guard there. The guard stood up and said: 'But certainly, come in, come in, the Director will be happy to see you.'

Door after door opened. By the time I arrived in the reception room of the Director's apartment I had shaken hands with several officials and rapidly answered questions.

What prison?

A prison in the State of New York.

Ahhh!

A man motioned to a red leather couch in the comfortably furnished room. There were white curtains, a few cages with birds singing in them, and under my feet a green carpet. Much light came in at a high window.

A small man entered. He wore a long, tightly-buttoned black coat. One of his hands was in a black glove; he held this hand behind him. He had a small white spade beard, a distinguished face. He stood away about ten feet from me, and bowed. I got up.

He said, 'Sing Sing?' I answered, 'Sing Sing.' The door opened again and a young man was shown in. The little old man turned to him and said with raised eyebrows: 'Warden Lawes, Sing Sing.'

The Director bowed deeply. He was followed by a retinue of secretaries and assistants and guards. As he sat down on the couch beside me and pumped my hand, he repeated 'Sing Sing' as if it were the name of his first love. He picked a stray hair off the collar of my coat, and then, standing up, I was introduced to the staff, and someone was quickly sent for something to drink. An order was given for luncheon, and then from a drawer of his desk the Director slipped a worn Colt .25 into his pocket and said: 'Permit me,' and went ahead.

'I will go ahead,' he said. 'You do not know the way.'

He was athletic, of good bearing; I think partly Indian. His clothes were simple; he used his chest and lips at times as Mussolini does, the body swaying with both hands at the hips, the lower lip rolled out as in pouting.

We passed two heavy gates, went through a long tunnel, turned to the right, and entered one of the cell blocks in the star-shaped building.

'Our population in this prison is five hundred and five men, and twenty-four women. Most of them are here for crimes of passion. The population of Ecuador is about three million.'

'Where does the music come from?'

'From the political prisoners. We have three of them. They are not forced to work, so they sing and play guitars; here they are.'

Without stopping their song the three young men nodded to the Warden. They were in a cell with flowers at the window and a small parrot in a cage; two sat on the bed, the third on a three-legged stool.

'Now we go to the shops.' We crossed a wide square and entered a house filled with the noises of hammering, sawing, the smell of wood and leather, and above that the smell of lilies from the prison yard. The prisoners sang here also; the windows were high and without bars. They stood up as the Warden came in; their faces remained at ease. Shoes were made here and some furniture, small trunks lined with paper on which flower designs were printed. In another part of the room men were carving small skulls out of ivory nuts, and one was arranging a miniature of the Crucifixion scene inside a small bottle. Some of the men smoked, some rested, all smiled as the Warden spoke to them. They all very proudly showed their work. The Warden told them all, 'Warden Lawes – Sing Sing,' and in a few words described my famous prison to them. He stopped and spoke to several men and told me what crimes they had committed. Some of the men asked him questions, and he answered with interest, thinking awhile before he spoke. He usually touched the men or held them by the arm; he bowed and smiled when he had finished with them, and he told his assistant to note several things the men requested.

From this room we climbed the stone steps up to the roof of the prison. Lilies were blooming in the gardens below; on the south side there was a swimming pool into which a stream of water poured from the mouth of a stone lion. A sentry lay on the roof. He got up and kicked the magazine under his pill-box and reached for the rifle which lay on the blanket on which he had been reading; he pulled down his coat and started pacing up and down, the gun over his shoulder.

'Does anyone ever escape from here?'

'Yes, sometimes,' said the Warden. 'Here, right here, is where they escape.' He pointed to the roof of the cell block that was nearest to the mountain. To clear a wall that is eighteen feet high a man had to run and then jump out and down a distance of some thirty-four feet; he landed in a thicket of candelabra cacti on the other side of the fence. I asked the Warden how they punished the men when they caught them. 'If he jumps well,' said the Warden, 'he's gone. It's not easy; he must want to be free very badly, and I would not like to risk it, would you? His friends will hide him and we have one less prisoner. If he jumps badly, he falls down into the yard here and is perhaps dead – at least he will break both his legs. He will never jump again; the pain, that is enough punishment. And you, Señor; in Sing Sing, what you do?'

'Oh, we lock them up in a dungeon, with bread and water and no light, for a week, two weeks, a month.'

'I do not believe in that,' he said with the Mussolini gesture. 'I do not believe in vengeance. Look here, down over the edge; this man is a bad fellow, I had to do something. I have put him alone by himself on half-rations. But I gave him the dog and cats and I come to see him and talk to him. I am troubled with his stupidity.'

I crept to the edge of the roof and looked down. In a court by himself sat a young, wild-haired fellow. His half-ration consisted of a big bowl of soup, a small pail half full of rice, and a loaf of black bread. The dogs and cats were sitting close to him waiting for the remnants of his meal.

'You know,' continued the Warden, 'he is my only problem prisoner; before, it was full of them. The military ran this institution; the military mind is stupid – boom, huuuump march, one, two, three, four, eyes right – shouting, marching is all they know. I am an advocate; I try to be humanitarian; not soft, please do not mistake me, I mean economic with life; that is my idea. I look at my prisoner when he comes in, I have studied the science of criminology, I have a knowledge of the system Bertillon. I am sorry when a man is brought in and I can see by his nose, his eyes, his jaw, and his skull, that he is a bad fellow for whom I can do nothing. That one I send away, to the Galápagos. It's not bad for them here; they can sleep and fish. Here he would do terrible damage.

'Here I keep the men and women who have perhaps even killed somebody, who have done something in one moment of their life that was wrong; they know it, I know it, we're both sorry; let us make the best of it. First of all I tell them to forget it and work. I know each man here. I hope they all like me as much as I like them.

'We have no death penalty here in Ecuador. The maximum sentence is for sixteen years; that is for cold murder.

'All prisoners receive wages, the current wages that would be paid if the man worked outside. The wages are divided in three parts. One-third goes to the prison, and by this the institution supports itself; one-third goes to the man for pocket money; and one-third is saved for him, with interest, for the day he is freed. If he has a family, the pocket money and the savings account are split according to the needs of his wife and children, but he must receive some money for himself and a small sun for his freedom; he may not want to go back to his family. Any of them can go out, if I say yes. A prisoner's wife can visit him; she can go out into the gardens with him, and bring his children. He can sometimes go home with her. And I like it when they paint. Here, look into this cell.'

We had come down from the roof. Almost every cell had pictures in watercolors or crayons – simple pictures of landscapes, saints, animals, in flat poster effects; some in brilliant colors, some uncertain and shaky. They were painted on the walls of the cells and sometimes along the corridors.

The Warden knew all the rare ones. He showed them to me with pride, and particular pride at the absence of pornographic ones.

'I would let them alone if there were any,' he said. 'A man's cell is his private room here. He can do what he wants. I am just glad I have never found any.

'Now let us go to the women.'

The twenty-four women live in a prison within the prison. Here there are more flowers, three tangerine trees, and clouds of linen hanging over them.

PRISON VISIT

These women have stabbed cheating lovers; one of them did away with her baby. They spend their days washing and ironing the drawers, undershirts, and socks of the cadets at the military academy. Their children are with them. Little boys and girls run and sing in the yard. They go out to school and come back to eat with Mama. The little houses, of one room each, are orderly, and all the women were smiling. One was nursing her baby.

'Born here,' said the Warden with pride, and pinched its cheeks.

We said our good-byes and walked back to the reception room. While we waited for luncheon he pouted again in the Mussolini manner, crossed his legs, and looked out of the window over Quito. He turned abruptly to pose a question which apparently had difficulty in forming itself into words.

'Señor Lawes,' he blurted, 'I have heard so much of you. I have read so much in magazines. Your stories are published in our Spanish journals very often. I have seen a moving picture that you have written. You are such an intelligent man and so – what is the word? – efficient, and also – what is it? – versatile. How do you do it? Here I have a little prison with five hundred people. I am busy all day and half the night and every Sunday – I have not had a vacation for a year. How can you do it? I think it's wonderful.'

The Dog of the World

THE FACT that one can go into a shop and buy a dog has always depressed me. The windows of pet shops, especially on holidays, when the animals are altogether abandoned, are among the saddest sights I know.

After losing a fine dog I promised myself never to own another, for if you really love dogs they change your life. You have to cross oceans on ships, for you can't conveniently take dogs on airplanes, and you must use particular ships, which don't require them to stay in the kennels. I often travel on freighters so that my dog will not be left alone. If you live in the city you feel guilty; if you let your dog off the leash in a park you get a ticket. Then the dog gets sick, the dog dies, and all those troubles are forgotten; all you know is that you miss him.

I was still grieving for a departed dog when my friend Armand said, 'The only way to get over it is to get another dog. I shall get one for you – the dog of the world – the greatest dog. I will get you the champion of all dogs, for I am president of the Club National du Bouvier des Flandres.'

'What is a Bouvier des Flandres?'

'*Alors*, the French have their poodles,' said Armand, 'the Germans the dachshund, the British the bulldog, the Swiss the St. Bernard, the Arabians the Afghan, and so on. But the Flemish – and you are half Flemish – have the Bouvier des Flandres.

'Hundreds of years ago, the counts of Flanders wanted a dog of their own, and they found that the only distinctively native dogs were working dogs – raw-boned, hard-working animals of no particular pedigree, accustomed to pulling carts and herding cattle in dirty weather. There was one great advantage to these dogs. They were simple, strong, intelligent, and healthy. There was nothing inbred or nervous about them. They usually lived in the huts of peasants as members of the family and were extremely pleasant companions as well as good protectors.'

We saw a Bouvier on the streets of Paris the next day. He was a fearful-looking creature with a rough coat and reddish eyes. He was black, gray, and sand-colored. There was nothing graceful about him. He looked like the hound of the Baskervilles.

'You have never owned a dog until you've had one of these,' said Armand, and a few days later he telephoned that he had found the one for me and that we would drive out to see him.

Armand's car is usually being repaired, for he drives with slow deliberation and other cars frequently run into him. The last crash had taken off a rear fender, and on the day this was replaced we drove out of Paris in the direction of Reims. After thirty-odd miles without mishap we came to a village and stopped at a small stone house. A very old man opened the garden gate. There was deep barking, and then I was presented to Madame, a son, a daughter, the grandchildren, and visiting relatives. The entire troupe followed us to the kennels, and there was my '*fils*.' In France people refer to your dog as your 'son.' He was six weeks old and blue-black; he had the shapeless-ness of a half-filled hot-water bottle; he had an immense head, large opaque eyes, and a long pedigree. We had immediate rapport with each other. He gave me the first of many sad looks as I patted him and left to go into the house, where a glass of wine was offered, and where I became officially the owner of Bosie. I wanted to take him along, but Armand said, 'He's only a baby. He must remain where he is.'

I returned to America, and every ten days or so I received a letter in the thinnest pen line. It gave me long reports about my *fils*, how *sage* he was, what a lucky dog he was because he would eventually go to America. On one of these letters appeared his footprint by way of signature. He took on shape, and I looked forward to seeing him again and to having him with me.

Back in France, some months later, Armand drove me out to see Bosie. I had told the people at the good old hotel I stay at whenever I am in Paris that I was getting my dog, and I can highly recommend it as a dog-owner's hotel. Everybody there was happy, and a special dish with water was in a corner of the bathroom. The maid had changed the fancy rose-colored eiderdown for a less costly coverlet.

'For,' she said, 'he will want to sleep on your bed, monsieur. Also, don't be worried about the carpet – this one is old and will be replaced anyway.' The tolerance for dogs at this hotel is due to the proprietress, who loves them dearly.

On the way Armand said, 'You can't have him yet. You don't want an average dog, a dog that pulls on the leash, that gets into fights, jumps up on you, and misbehaves. I promised you the greatest dog in the world, and that is what you shall have. I know an old clown who had the most famous dog act at the Cirque Medrano. He trains dogs with patience and love. He is retired now, and has agreed to keep the dog for a year and train him. After that you shall have a companion who does all but speak. He will be gay or serious; he will console you in your lowest moods. He will be perfectly behaved and never leave your side. He will entertain your friends. He will rescue a child from a burning building or, if ever you are in danger of drowning, pull you from the water. He will watch your car, protect you against attack, carry your packages or umbrella, and refuse food from strangers. I have arranged for it all.'

I enjoyed my 'son' only briefly; we took him from his former owner, proceeded to Chartres, and I received the second sad look from Bosie, when he was handed over to the clown. When I returned to the hotel, everybody was disappointed. I completed my European assignments and left for America.

The clown did not write, but the time passed and I came back again to France. At the hotel I was again given a room with an expendable carpet, and the eiderdown was changed for a blanket. Again Armand drove me out to Chartres, and the old clown asked us to hide so that Bosie would not be distracted. We watched from the window of a small garden house. The clown leaned a ladder against an open window a floor above the ground. Then he went indoors and reappeared with Bosie. The dog was now big, and reminded one of medieval missals illustrated with devils, gargoyles, and things that knock in the night. His eyes were red, his hair bristly. He wore a large collar and he was very mannerly, respecting flower beds, looking at the old clown, and sitting at attention when told to.

The clown addressed Bosie by the respectful *vous* instead of the familiar *tu*, giving him a series of commands which were carried out with precision and eagerness. Next the dog did some tricks, and finally the clown informed him that there was a fire in the house and a little girl was in a room upstairs.

'*Allez*,' he said to Bosie, 'be nice and rescue the little girl.'

Bosie went up the ladder, vanished into the room, and returned with a large doll in his mouth. He carried it carefully, coming backward down the ladder, and put it on the grass ever so gently. Then he looked at the clown, who patted his head but reproached him softly.

'Isn't there someone you have forgotten, Bosie?'

I could almost hear the dog say, 'Oh, yes,' as he turned and climbed once more into the 'burning' building. This time he returned with a large tiger cat in his fearful fangs. He held it the way cats carry kittens, and again he descended. The cat was put down, and it turned, sat up, and licked Bosie's large black nose.

'We have seen enough,' Armand shouted with enthusiasm and congratulated the clown.

There was wine again, this time in the little garden house, and then the clown brought out a statement on lined paper. He had written with a pencil the cost of training and boarding Bosie. It came to sixty thousand francs. I gave the money to the clown, who counted it. As he came to the last five-thousand-franc note his mouth got wobbly and his eyes filled with tears. He sat down on an upturned wooden washbasin. 'Bosie,' he said, 'come here for the last time.'

The dog sat down in front of him and looked into his face.

'I've been good to you, haven't I?' The clown could hardly speak. 'I've never had one like him before, so gentle, so courageous, so understanding.'

Both the clown and the dog turned their heads in my direction.

'You are tearing the heart out of me,' said the clown. 'You are taking my brother from me,' he cried, 'the only friend I have in this world!'

Close by was the tiger cat, and I have never seen a cat so close to tears. It was all so terribly sad and desolate. A steady stream of tears ran down the clown's face now, and his face, even without make-up, was the saddest clown's face I had ever seen. I cannot look at people in tears, and certainly not clowns. I was all for letting him have the dog. I started to walk away, but Armand, who understands his compatriots better than I, said, 'Just a moment.'

He turned to the clown. 'We shall leave him with you, but give us back the money for his board and tuition.'

'Ah?' said the clown. He dried his tears and pocketed the money. He got up and, in slow, bent motions, walked toward the door of his house, without turning. He said, 'Adieu, Bosie, go with your new master.' Bosie gave me the third sad look and silently followed me to the car.

Sawmill in Tirol

ABOVE SCHLIERSEE, on the side of a mountain, is an old tree, its trunk twisted by the wind that blows down from the mountain summit. A bench leans against it, and behind it stands a small whitewashed chapel. The sun shines on the wall of the chapel and the warm air comes under the shade of a the big tree. Below are fields of clover and wheat, a road, the lake, and the village, the smoke coming out of all its chimneys. All of it is framed by high mountains which hold up a small ceiling of sky, across which wander sun and moon and fields of stars. In this enclosed space lies the whole world, the beginning and the end of life, from the kindergarten next to the church and the play-yard attached to the school to the little walled cemetery with painted crosses and patches of peasant flowers.

In the early evening, music is played in a pavilion on a small strip of park along the lake. When it begins, heaven seems filled with fiddles and the forest becomes like the sides of a Gothic altar with wormholed angels whose worn gilded wooden curls hang over their simple devout profiles, and whose eyes look down on the thin long fingers that are folded flat together in prayer.

The men are all volunteer musicians, in their working hours masters of their trades. They arrive with shined but battered instruments of comfortable design, and their small sons run along carrying notes. They are perhaps twelve men, but on holidays, feast days, and Sundays there are twenty of them. Each one has a large, gray stone mug of beer beside his chair; the sons run to the inn to have them filled when they are empty. The beer is the musicians' only compensation.

It always takes a long while before they are ready. The conductor puts the clarinet to his pointed lips and takes it away several times before they are all seated comfortably. He waves up and down with it three times as a signal to begin and he keeps on waving the time with it. At important passages, to get more sound or very soft playing, he bends his knees apart as if taking exercises, widens his eyes, and sends his eyebrows up under the brim of his hat.

These men are afraid of nothing, that is nothing they love to play. They like Weber, Schubert, Strauss, many native composers, marches, folk music; they even play Wagner. They make music the way they work; they hammer and sew the notes together and take much enthusiastic liberty, most of all the flute. This musician, a tailor, will walk away from the music in a happy 'dulilululiu,' forget the score for a while, and come back to it when he is ready. Having done enough, he stops altogether, bends down for his beer, looks into the mug, and empties it. Another will see his child and stand up and shout a message for him to take home to his mother. The men with the brasses also stop at any time to turn their instruments upside down and shake spit out of them. Then they slowly get ready again, licking their lips when a favorite passage comes and passing the palm of a hand across the mouthpiece. Then, all together, they play such music as '*Connais-tu le pays?*' from *Mignon*. This they play at almost every concert, and also, though Bavaria is now a republic, the royal anthem. They are royalists, who deserve such a king as they once had, one who actually had to be pushed out of the city during the revolution, who could be seen sitting behind his little sausages and beer, on the same chairs as his people, and who would pull the sleeve of the man next to him and ask him to slide the mustard down and then say '*Dankeschön.*'

In a close circle around the music stand the children, their faces lifted up to the light and the instruments. Behind them are young people, their heads to one side, their young mouths and moist, warm lips loose and open, like those of young calves, entirely given up to the music. A few foreigners, not French or English people, but non-Bavarian Germans who come here for their vacations, go promenading up and down in loose-fitting coats. Out on the lake painted boats rest on the water, the oars dripping into them, paper lanterns hanging over them. The music goes out over the lake and echoes among the mountains; a crash of the cymbals comes back softly three and four times. At the end there is a trumpet solo, it tears out over the water like a brassy light without shade. Then the musicians pack up, turn out the lights, and wander to the inn for a little refreshment.

Over the mountains late at night rags of clouds collect, releasing their waters on the high summits, and in the early morning the peaks are powdered with fine snow which the sun melts into many brooks that turn into a foaming wild stream half-way between the level of the lake and the mountain top. The stream passes from house to house, turning the heavy wooden millwheels, and down into the lake and out of it on the south side, bearing the boats from which people fish.

The roosters start to crow while it is still dark; lights, at first two little flickers of it, spring up in the peasant houses; then a pale, flat orange color fills the little panes of their windows; the lamp is lit, and a shaft of its light swims out of an open door as a man goes over to his stable with the lantern. In the railroad yard below, the small engine is being fired; it is switching freight cars, but at seven-forty it will pull the train of six cars to Munich. The church bells ring, and little women in black come out of all the streets for early morning Mass.

On the mountainside, horses are being hitched to small-wheeled wagons that are to go up into the forest. In the clearings the branches are lopped off, cut in lengths, and piled in neat stacks of firewood, while the trunks are dragged down to the sawmill to be cut into boards and laid out in a shack to dry. Other horses will later take them to the carpenter in the village, who will make of them wagons, furniture, shingles, rafters, fence posts, doors, and window frames.

The people are in the fields; the cattle are being driven up to the high meadows covered with short, mossy, sweet-smelling grass and hardy little flowers. The children go to school, beds are put out in the sun, the women go to market. Work in gardens begins; the guests at the hotel open their windows, look out, and stretch themselves in their white nightshirts; Sophie, the waitress at the Seehaus, puts red-and-white-checked tablecloths out on the long tables on the terrace. Here is everything that one can find anywhere in the world: Father, Mother, and children, love and death, work and dancing, police and religion, and the four seasons.

There is a cold, cold winter, with the lake frozen over with thick green ice, snow over it, and the tracks of skates. The snow crunches as one walks through it. Icicles, some of them thick as stalactites, hang from the roofs all the way down to the ground. The little children who lick them have their ears wrapped up; they have red faces and mittens on a string, in each mitten an egg-shaped stone that has been warmed in the oven at home. They pull little handmade sleds with bells. Springtime here comes with trembling yellow-green leaves, wet fields, and crocuses; summer with tables outside in all the gardens under great chestnut trees; autumn with dark-brown burned leaves on all the roads, smelling and sounding warm as one walks through them ankle-deep.

From this branch under the bent old tree, in this godlike perspective, as if one hung in the sky, there is, in a brief yet eternal moment of time, clarity and understanding. It comes at the end of long stretches of thinking, sometimes distorted by my reading, and I have to put much that I like aside, along with my respect for the knowledge and brilliance of the minds that have written the books. I have to say loudly to myself that life is Mother and Father, house and garden, nurse and childhood, play, work, love, and children; that it is not what goes on in the Splendide.

I have to think of the poor man, the timekeeper of our hotel, in his furnished room near the Third Avenue Elevated, who woke me up every morning when his loud alarm clock went off. He would come to the window in the underwear he slept in, scratch his stomach and sides and the back of his neck, then rub his bald head. Later I would see him come out of the house below, in his only suit, and painfully walk up the street with his bad feet to a lunchroom called 'Joe's,' first buying a paper. He was a brutal, soulless poor old man with a little authority at the door where he could growl at people. He had nothing of his own but his awful room, and all his pleasure came from the outside, like the movies, where he saw for an hour and a half, without ever smiling, other people on yachts, in elegance, in a paradise forever beyond his reach.

From up here, before the whitewashed chapel, I can see a pretty performance every morning. The little policeman in his grass-green uniform lives in Neuhaus, and bicycles to work along the highway. When he comes to the lake path on which hangs the sign, 'It is strictly forbidden to bicycle on this lane,' he respectfully dismounts and obediently pushes his vehicle till he comes to the main road again. Under the sign on the other end of the path, he fishes with his foot for the pedal and swings himself across the saddle.

I walk down through the cool wet forest, its path covered with needles and bordered by small-leafed sour clover growing together with the ferns, and then out into the light green fields. I look at the flowers and think how benevolent God is, how even without the buttercup we would so lack it, how poor we would be without the shape, the motion, the smell of the horse. There is my dog; I throw a stick and he brings it back. If I throw two, he is confused and picks up neither. That and a few other things he can do, no more. So far goes the flower, it must stand there; so far goes the dog, he can run and bark and carry a stick; and so far we go – no further.

In our closet of gratitude we may hang many things: the flower, the dog, the horse, the performance of an actor, the morning in Schliersee, the little sausages in the restaurant next to the Church of Our Lady, the arrangement of vegetables in a market, words. I have found peace with myself for a while.

The one complete joy is the children, good and bad, clean and dirty. Their eyes are wide and light, they are barefooted and brown and play in the shallow parts of the lake. Little girls bend down to pick flowers while they watch a small brother in a carriage that has wheels like cotton spools. I think of how, after we are gone, they will love the mountains and the old houses as much as we do. They will feel all that we do, this scene, this music; they will walk the same paths, eat the same, and be the same. They all have the same hearts, lungs, eyes, feet, and hands that we have, and they will always have the same hopes and pleasures. They will be we, we shall be they; I can think of no better hereafter for us, a precise repetition of the earth here about me, with these same horses and flowers, with just such faces, such cooking, such beer and such music. Heaven is not beyond – it is being here again; in this little boy with brown legs hanging into the lake, there will grow another I, though I am not his father. For the same sun will rise tomorrow and the smoke will come out of the same houses, just as it did in my grandfather's time, and we shall always have to love some place and have a father and mother and children.

All this I thought on so many days, and it seemed so right and logical to me, that one morning I sat a long time at the lake, and I was certain that now, at the age of twenty-seven, I could arrange my life properly. I took the train to Tirol, for Schliersee seemed too worldly for what I had in mind. I went to the sawmill I loved so much up in the Dolomite Valley, where I had been happy as a boy. It was for sale and I bought it. The house and the inn, the mill and all the properties, were faultless. The old miller with the huntsman's beard and face had a wife who took care of the house and scrubbed it all day long. There were beautiful cattle, old worn wagons; the rooms, the furniture, the trees – everything was an answer to my desire for good design, for color, and for rightness. I wanted now to marry a simple woman, more simple even than my mother's idea of a wife, almost a peasant, with a healthy frame and an undisturbed mind, like a comfortable oven, who would cook and sing and be healthy and have children.

I wrote a long letter to Mother, telling her to pack up and come and bring with her old Frau Uhu, a family relic, an old servant she had from Grandfather's house, who answered when she was called 'Oohoo' and thus got her name. I wrote that from now on I would be complete joy and pride to her, live a simple life and walk around with my dog, have a wife and children. Mother packed and took a train, but when she arrived I was gone.

I had become almost ill on the third day. I walked around in the fields and touched the trees, and sat at the stone table where I had drunk my first wine as a boy. On my own face I could see that time had passed; I was the same, but I was now twenty-seven years old. I felt terribly old, and I felt guilty about not being happy here. Here all was perfect, but I could not walk around all day saying: 'How beautiful, how beautiful, how beautiful,' it was.

In the middle of the night I got up and looked for my passport; I was afraid I had mislaid it. I thought of New York, of the Battery, where the elevated trains come running down to the ferry slip, of the bridges. I thought of the trip I had taken to Montana, of Shoshone Canyon, and of living at the foot of Rising Wolf Mountain in Glacier Park. I thought of the wide prairie, of the smoky color of the mountains, of the weaving evening light on the sagebrush, like a sea of frozen ink with patches of yellow and copper playing over it, of an Indian riding along the horizon, alone on his horse.

But Tirol does not allow comparison with the American West. Suddenly this little sawmill in Tirol became a little painted music box, on which pretty uniform postmen, costumed peasants, English travelers and the nurses for their children turned about to the music of a zither. It was a travel poster, a mediocre stage set. I became so lonesome for America, for even the ugly gas tank that you first see when you come up the bay in Ambrose Channel, that I left the next morning, took a train from Salzburg, the express to Munich, Cologne, Herbesthal, Rotterdam.

The Elephant Cutlet

ONCE UPON a time there were two men in Vienna who wanted to open a restaurant. One was a Dentist who was tired of fixing teeth and always wanted to own a restaurant, and the other a famous cook by the name of Souphans.

The Dentist was however a little afraid. 'There are,' he says, 'already too many restaurants in Vienna, restaurants of every kind, Viennese, French, Italian, Chinese, American, American-Chinese, Portuguese, Armenian, Dietary, Vegetarian, Jewish, Wine and Beer Restaurants, in short all sorts of restaurants.'

But the Chef had an Idea. 'There is one kind of restaurant that Vienna has not,' he said.

'What kind?' said the Dentist.

'A restaurant such as has never existed before, a restaurant for cutlets from every animal in the world.'

The Dentist was afraid, but finally he agreed, and the famous Chef went out to buy a house, tables, and chairs, and engaged help, pots and pans and had a sign painted with big red letters ten feet high saying:

'Cutlets from Every Animal in the World.'

The first customer that entered the door was a distinguished lady, a Countess. She sat down and asked for an Elephant Cutlet.

'How would Madame like this Elephant Cutlet cooked?' said the waiter.

'Oh, Milanaise, sauté in butter, with a little spaghetti over it, on that a filet of anchovy, and an olive on top,' she said.

'That is very nice,' said the waiter and went out to order it.

'Jessas Maria und Joseph!' said the Dentist when he heard the order, and he turned to the Chef and cried: 'What did I tell you? Now what are we going to do?'

The Chef said nothing, he put on a clean apron and walked into the dining room to the table of the Lady. There he bowed, bent down to her and said: 'Madame has ordered an Elephant Cutlet?'

'Yes,' said the Countess.

'With spaghetti and a filet of anchovy and an olive?'

'Yes.'

'Madame is all alone?'

'Yes, yes.'

'Madame expects no one else?'

'No.'

'And Madame wants only one cutlet?'

'Yes,' said the Lady, 'but why all these questions?'

'Because,' said the Chef, 'because, Madame, I am very sorry, but for one Cutlet we cannot cut up our Elephant.'